TWENTIETH CENTURY BALLET

TWENTIETH CENTURY BALLET

A. H. FRANKS

GREENWOOD PRESS, PUBLISHERS
WESTPORT, CONNECTICUT

Originally published in 1954
by Pitman Publishing Corporation, New York,
Toronto, London

Reprinted with permission

First Greenwood Reprinting 1971

Library of Congress Catalogue Card Number 71-97382

ISBN 0-8371-3926-0

Printed in the United States of America

Dedicated with gratitude and affection to
Philip Richardson, a leading spirit in the
twentieth century dance scene.

CONTENTS

ILLUSTRATIONS

ILLUSTRATIONS (*continued*)

ACKNOWLEDGEMENTS

The Author and Publishers wish to thank the following for the use of photographs as indicated: Derek Allen, photograph facing p. 36; Lipnitzki, facing p. 37 (top), p. 100 (top), p. 197; Paul Wilson, facing p. 52, p. 69 (bottom), p. 85 (bottom), p. 149; Houston Rogers, facing p. 68, p. 84 (bottom); Frank Sharman, facing p. 69 (top), p. 196 (bottom); Baron, facing p. 84 (top), p. 164, p. 165; Denis de Marney, facing p. 85 (top), p. 133 (top); Roger Wood, facing p. 100 (bottom), p. 117, p. 132, p. 148 (top), p. 180 (bottom), p. 181 (bottom); Angus McBean, facing p. 101 (top); Roy Round, facing p. 101 (bottom); Sasha, facing p. 116; Kenny Parker, facing p. 133 (bottom); Edward Mandinian, facing p. 148 (bottom); The Photo Repro. Co., facing p. 180 (top); André Kertesz, facing p. 181 (top); and Maurice Seymour, facing p. 196 (top).

Introduction

THE HISTORY OF man is as much concerned with his ideas as with his material achievements. Since ballet is the most ephemeral of all the arts we cannot indeed make any detailed survey of his material achievements in this field. From the first presentation of *Giselle* in 1841 to the end of the nineteenth century, a mass of new works was composed, yet today we possess only a vague conception of their form and a smaller one of their actual dance content. *Giselle* itself, in continuous performance for well over a hundred years, has undergone so many choreographic changes that parts of the various current versions would probably be unrecognizable to the ballet's originators.

In the criticism of ballet, therefore, as distinct from the criticism of other art forms, we can refer only in the most general and inexact terms to the influence of choreographers of the past on the present generation. In certain rare cases we can trace the influence of their general principles, but usually we have to consider the method and style of contemporary creators more or less in isolation from their artistic progenitors.

As far as possible I have dealt only with those ballets which can be seen at the present time; although in some cases the discussion of defunct works has been necessary for the continuity and completeness of my theme. For example, I rate Nijinsky as a choreographer of major importance, yet only one of his ballets remains alive; and even that has through old age shed most of its pristine vigour and excitement. In consequence, in order to treat Nijinsky's style, method and approach in sufficient detail to support my belief, I have had to discuss other of his ballets at some length.

Mainly, then, starting with Fokine and proceeding largely by chronological stages, I have considered the extant works of this century's leading makers of ballet. In many cases I have also quoted from the writings of other critics whose opinions, even when in disagreement with them, I hold in high regard. Further, wherever possible I have outlined the theories and principles from which choreographers have forged their own particular style.

Those who seek no more than superficial entertainment from ballet frequently decry criticism which discovers more in a work than its creator consciously put into it. Was Shakespeare, then, fully conscious of all the qualities, both poetic and dramatic, which a long line of distinguished critics from his own time to the present day have discovered in his work? Of course not. Such critics are the intermediaries between artist and audience; they are the critics who develop understanding and discrimination.

One belief of mine which has been confirmed rather than undermined by time and experience is that all our knowledge in any particular field of art should through constant observation, followed by analysis and criticism, be collected, developed and co-ordinated to one end: the better perception, understanding and appreciation of the created product. I can think of no activity which offers a richer mental reward.

A.H.F.

CHAPTER ONE

Michel Fokine

CHOREOGRAPHERS RARELY EXPRESS themselves either with force or clarity on paper, especially when they seek to explain personal aims and ideals. Two illustrious exceptions to this literary disability, however, are Fokine and Noverre. Each in their vastly different styles, these two great figures wrote down a number of natural laws and theories for the benefit of their choreographic progeny. A comparison of their manifestos provides ample evidence of two kindred spirits; innovators linked closely across a hundred and fifty years, each seeking to free ballet from the superficiality, degeneration and mass of outmoded conventions under which it seems at times that all forms of expression must languish.

Fokine recorded his five principles in a letter to 'The Times': a wise choice of medium, for although no more then than now given to the wooing of balletomanes, this organ added the lustre of its own undeniable authority to Fokine's logical but impassioned statements.

Noverre, after the fashion of his time, expressed himself less tersely; in fact his 'Lettres sur le Danse et sur Les Ballets' exceeded Fokine's single letter in length by about forty times. His verbiage is in turn pompous, sententious, repetitive and gustily rhetorical, but his suggested reforms of the corrupt ballet of the eighteenth century raise themselves high above this luxuriant undergrowth.

Every one of Fokine's five principles is an instrument by which ballet is to be granted a dramatic and emotional expressiveness unknown during the Petipa epoch. Indeed, the word 'expression', or its equivalent, forms the keystone of each statement.

Similarly, Noverre had condemned the ballet of his time for its lack of dramatic development and expressive power. He exhorted the choreographer not to limit himself to 'arranging with grace, precision and facility steps to a given air', but to 'study the character and accent of the passions and transmute

them into his composition'. In this exhortation he even antici-
pated Fokine in revolutionizing the function of the *corps de
ballet*. 'Make the members of your *corps de ballet* dance,' he cried.
'But let them express with dancing something that will contribute to the picture: let them be mimes suddenly transformed in
appearance by the passions with which they are imbued.'

Noverre left several writings to posterity in addition to his
famous letters. Fokine, on the other hand, wrote but rarely,
and we are fortunate in possessing that one document which
expresses so clearly his complete artistic credo. Apart from this
I have come across only one other important piece of writing
by him: a translation of an article first published in a Russian
periodical, 'Argus', in 1916. The first of the eight sections into
which this article divides is entitled 'On Ballet Routine'. Here
Fokine condemns what we know as conventional mime,
quoting several amusing examples from the 'old ballet' to point
his argument. Gesture language is not the only outworn convention to collapse under the weight of his brief but pin-
pointed bombardment, for he also attacks what appears to
him as absurdities. Talking of Siegfried's mother, for instance,
(*Le Lac des Cygnes*), he says: 'When she appears on the scene,
she circles round the stage; but can any mother explain why
she does this?'

Section two, 'The Development of Signs', makes a plea for
the abandonment of fixed signs and the creation of others
based on the natural laws of expression. Here Fokine asserts
that a dance is the development and ideal of a sign. As illus-
tration of this theory he suggests a comparison of prints of
Cerrito, Grisi, Elssler and Taglioni with others of dancers of
the end of the nineteenth century. The former, says Fokine,
possess qualities of expression, whereas the latter provide nothing
but poses utterly devoid of feeling.

> There is a complete difference in principle. Taglioni
> raises herself *sur les pointes* in order to be as light as to seem
> hardly to touch the ground. The dancer of the period when
> ballet was in decline uses her *pointes* in order to astonish the
> audience with her strength and endurance.

In this particular argument, it seems to me, exhilarating
though it is to be able to make such a definite comparison,
Fokine has shed some of his customary logic. Between the two

periods of his comparison the camera had clicked its way into some prominence, not to say notoriety. Partly because of the relentless scrutiny with which this instrument examined its subject-matter, and partly because of a remarkable change in viewpoint among painters, the romantic, idealistic figures dreamt rather than drawn by lithographers of the first half of the nineteenth century had fallen from grace. For all their miraculous poses and apparent defiance of gravity they had been supplanted, if the camera did not lie, by creatures more liberally endowed with bone and muscle. Compare the illustrations on page 35 with those on page 42 of Beaumont's 'Ballet Design: Past and Present' (1946 edition). Lithographs in ballet's romantic period set out deliberately to exploit the ethereality of Taglioni and her contemporaries; whereas towards the decline of the century artists had returned to nature. The Degas dancers—remember that Degas had been influenced considerably by photography and was himself adept with the camera—are a good example of what I mean. In sketches and paintings by Degas, dancers are drawn as he saw them, complete with technical blemishes and imperfect physique.

Nevertheless, although Fokine seems to me to have erred in the development of his argument, his theory that dance derives its vocabulary from the cultivation and idealization of signs is not disproved, provided we regard these signs only as the expressive elements of the dance. My only issue with Fokine here is that Petipa generally created dance for less expressive and more spectacular purposes than did Filippo Taglioni or Jules Perrot, but that is not to admit that the dancers, and the dance itself, of that later period had shed the expressive power of that from which it had stemmed. On the contrary, I think Petipa, when he wished, could score more expressively than his predecessors, no matter how much of his later work is said by detractors to belong to his pupil and colleague, Lev Ivanov.

In his next section, 'The Old and the New in Ballet: The Creative Power in Ballet', Fokine pleads for the preservation of the beauty of the dance as Taglioni knew it. By which I think he means that the fantastic and supernatural themes of romantic ballet can be suitably expressed by classical dance only when that form of dance is used expressively and not as a sort of superior acrobatics. Despite his manifest enthusiasm for ballet of the romantic style, however, Fokine states emphatically that such a style should be employed only when it is applicable. 'Ballet steps executed *sur les pointes* cannot be used in a Greek Pyrrhic dance,' he says. 'On the other hand it would be unnatural to dance a Spanish dance in a Greek chiton.'

That may sound obvious. Style, atmosphere and period must be in harmony one with another, as well as contributing to the development of the plot or theme. But is it always obvious? Judgment has sometimes to be exercised on far less simple examples than those which Fokine has quoted. As far as the conventions and expressive powers of ballet allow, the first part of *Le Jeune Homme et La Mort* is realistic. Would Fokine then have disapproved of *pointes* in this ballet? If so, on what grounds? And would he have raised horrified hands at Bach's Passacaglia in C Minor accompanying such a work? I think perhaps he would. Yet today there are many patrons of ballet in possession of bountiful good taste and sensibility who claim that this particular work is one of the greatest to be produced since the war. There is no simple answer. The question of taste is difficult enough on its own, but when combined with the problems of compatibility of style and temperament between the various ingredients of ballet, then the problem is insoluble.

Section four sounds yet another cry against convention and tradition; and this time Fokine has chosen an easy target. Referring to what he frequently calls the 'old ballet' he scoffs at it for using 'Russian top boots and the French school of dancing in one ballet, the short ballet skirt and historically correct Egyptian costume in another'.

'Is not that confusion?' he says. 'The style of the dance is always inharmonious with that of the costumes, theme and period.' The hardened ballet-goer accepts such apparent absurdities and does not for a moment permit them to return him to the disenchantment of logic. Aurora's princes might have stepped out of the pictures in the National Gallery: one from a Gentile Bellini, one from a Botticelli, another from a Leonardo, one from any of a score of works in the Duveen room, and the last tagging sheepishly along behind, having issued from one of those small, esoteric galleries which show paintings of such artists as Oliver Messel. Amid all this extravagant design, varied colour and rich fabric, Fonteyn-Aurora weaves her spell; her perfection of *attitude*, miracle of balance *sur la pointe*, and personification of the ideal of classical dance, supremely displayed in the short tutu. Undoubtedly this scene offers an outstanding example of disunity of style, but in what way should alterations be made if, defying tradition, we now endeavoured to remodel the work in a spirit of fervent logic as laid down by this Fokine dictum?

Either we must transform Aurora into a stage princess or etiolate her suitors by putting them into the uniform of *danseurs nobles*. The first alternative needs no discussion; and the second would rob the scene of richness and colour.

As far as the 'old ballet' is concerned, then, Fokine's logic must not be allowed to intrude. He most probably did not intend to imply that it should, but in the effort to demonstrate his theories on the new ballet he inevitably ridiculed the old, for these theories were begotten of his revolt against the Petipa formula. Fokine undeniably achieved a logical thematic pattern in his works which had certainly not existed for about fifty years, and probably not even then. His conception found sympathy in the ethos of the age which gave it life, but that is not to deny the greatness of the style which preceded it. None will refute Ingres because of Cézanne, or Beethoven because of Bartok. The great work of any period lives for more cogent reasons than its antiquarian value.

In *Les Sylphides*, one of the first examples by which he introduced the 'new ballet' to Europe, Fokine dispensed with a plot and sought to organize a series of movements and patterns that would evoke a mood in the mind of the beholder—just as the organized sound which is music sets up an emotional response without relating itself to the material world. This attempt at a parallel, of course, is far from perfect, for although the sounds which issue from musical instruments—and even from the specially-trained human larynx—bear little resemblance to the sounds of everyday, the instrument of the choreographer is the human body. It may justly be claimed that the *pas* and postures of European classical dance are quite foreign to the movements of everyday, but the body of the dancer, despite partial concealment by conventional costume, is still of such a structure as to be approximately like yours and mine. The transcendental spirit of exaltation evoked by some passages of music is thus far more rarely to be gained by balletic means, for the genius of the choreographer is bound tightly to the narrow range of movement that lies within the scope of a trained dancer. Which perhaps explains why Disney at his best employed figures that make a farce of physical anatomy; and why Balanchine believes in the cinema as potentially the best medium for the exploitation of ballet.

Nevertheless it is possible for stage ballet to deal to some extent in abstractions; and *Les Sylphides* is the first such ballet to grace the twentieth century. The term 'abstract' as applied to ballet has been the cause of much controversy, for it is argued that a group of human beings is in no way an abstraction. Balanchine himself, our most noted specialist in this type of ballet, ridicules the term, but does not to my knowledge supply an alternative. I think it is both apt and expressive; and that the dissenters are indulging in a fastidious use of words. Glibly we employ the word 'classical' in connection with ballet; *The Sleeping Beauty*, for instance, with music by Tchaikovsky, sets and costumes by Oliver Messel, is called a classical ballet! In using such a term we refer only to the style of dancing, not to the other ingredients. Similarly, in using the term 'abstract ballet' we mean that the work is based on dance and pattern without a plot or theme. It must nevertheless be admitted that most of the ballets which can be classified as 'abstract' are partially concerned with human relationships. *Les Sylphides* certainly contains such elements, as do most of Balanchine's essays in this *genre*. Even *Symphonic Variations*, perhaps the most truly abstract of all ballets, is not entirely free from such references, but that does not in my opinion by any means invalidate the term.

In creating *Les Sylphides* Fokine demonstrated the nature of some of his reforms. Deploring the lack of coherent development, the diversions and the absurd conventional gesture in the Petipa ballets, he produced a work in which there is no disjunction between mime and dancing. Indeed, the ballet calls for no mimic action as such, the dancers portraying its

mood through subtle facial expression as well as through movement. But unfortunately dancers do not always feel the mood of
the ballet, and if they do they are not necessarily in sympathy
with it; thus, one is frequently treated to a spectacle in which a
well-built young lady of ten stone or more tries to offset her
solidity by wearing the expression of a sylph. The conception
of what this expression should be usually amounts to a blank
stare into the distance and a fixed suspicion of a smirk which
may or may not be intended to convey either wistfulness or
whimsy.

The Diaghilev production was composed in three rehearsals,
some of the groups being shown to the dancers on the stage just
before the curtain was due to rise. Yet since that day in 1909
the ballet has had wished upon it countless subtleties and
complexities; and worse, an ever swelling literature of sloppy
sentiment. The term *romantic reverie* by which the ballet is
frequently described is mild in comparison with several
fatuous programmatic exhalations. In one American programme, for instance, according to Grace Robert in her
'Borzoi Book of Ballets', it was imaginatively described as 'A
lovely old-fashioned nosegay, in which the central male blossom
is surrounded by the most fragile rosebuds of the *corps de ballet*
and the whole set in a *toot* of roseate lace-work of Chopin's
masterpiece.' As Miss Robert pithily adds: 'This is the sort of
thing that keeps strong-minded people away from Ballet'.

The reverent approach which young audiences of the post-
1939-45 war were exhorted to make to *Les Sylphides* has gradually been supplanted by boredom or at best indifference. This
change of outlook can partly be accounted for by the almost
unbelievable number of performances the ballet has received
since the war. At one time it appeared that *Les Sylphides* had
become the curtain raiser for every company to visit London
and its environs. We saw plump sylphides and emaciated
sylphides, wistful sylphides and blousy sylphides. We saw
backcloths contaminated by tombs in perspective and out of
perspective, and backcloths said to be based on a picture by
Corot. Certainly these so loftily inspired backcloths possessed
the crepuscular quality of the work of that well-known member
of the Barbazon group, but I could see no other resemblance.
One company, by strangely original lighting and a cycloramic

background, sought to introduce variety. As this same company had also found Fokine's choreography in need of renovation, we were quickly made aware that this actual performance was entitled *Les Sylphides* only by courtesy of the programme. The music was sometimes provided by orchestras whose conductors held wildly individualistic notions as to tempo and interpretations, sometimes by pianos on solitary duty, and sometimes by instruments the noise of which I was unable to identify. On rare occasions we were treated to first-class performances, but who could appreciate the bouquet of good brandy after a series of foul cocktails?

This precursor of twentieth-century abstract and symphonic ballet, then, depends far more upon form, structure, and integration between dance and music than upon a mood of 'lyrical tenderness', 'lovely old-fashioned nosegays', and 'toots of roseate lace-work'. By attempting to invest such a ballet with a literary sentimentalism we rob ourselves of the opportunity to see what is in fact before our eyes—and what is presented to our ears. It is hardly necessary to be acquainted with the story of Chopin's inspiration for the Mazurka, for example, in order to realize that certain pieces in the suite are anything but lyrical and 'ethereal'. Some extraordinary performances of this ballet are due in part, I am convinced, to an attempt to build into it a mood which was not intended in the original choreography.

The marked references to certain specific common human gestures—the opening, the attitude of the listening girl, for instance, and parts of the *pas de deux*—are probably relics left over from *Chopiniana*. At any rate they are quite out of place in a work free from all other literary pretence. To me they are like isolated and therefore meaningless words shoved into the score of a symphony.

But these are small blemishes. *Les Sylphides* is undoubtedly a great ballet, and it is all the greater in our knowledge of the condition of ballet at the time of its conception. Nevertheless, in the last resort its very delicacy and fragility expose the limitations of the human instrument to express fantasy, even in such an abstract and generalized form as it has here been essayed.

Whereas in *Les Sylphides* Fokine used very little more than the

elements of dance, not concerning himself with plot of characterization, in the making of *Le Carnaval* he added both these elements, as well as tying himself to the style, atmosphere and
conventional gesture derived from the *Commedia dell'Arte*. Here
it seems that he was determined to demonstrate the third of his
five principles, in which he stipulates that conventional gesture
shall be employed only when the style of the ballet requires it.

Although not perhaps to such an extent as with *Les Sylphides*,
a myth has gradually clouded our view of *Le Carnaval*, notwithstanding a few writers who have reminded adulators of Fokine
that he composed this ballet very quickly and for a specific
occasion: an entertainment at a ball which was to be called
'Carnaval'. The choice of Schumann's early piano suite of that
title can therefore hardly be considered strange, especially if we
remember Fokine's romantic predilections. A slight knowledge of
certain aspects of Schumann's life, however, furnished him with
part of his literary structure. Despite the fact that the work was
to be presented only during an interval of the ball, Fokine
entered into the idea with enthusiasm and even succeeded in
persuading Leon Bakst to design special costumes. Three days
were allowed for rehearsals, all of which took place in the ballroom. Thus it was composed to be seen from four sides, not
from an auditorium. As the guests at the ball were themselves
in fancy dress, the ballet seemed to emanate from the audience
itself; indeed Fokine enhanced this idea by having his dancers
make their entrances from among the audience. Yet apart from
a minimum of small adjustments necessary in the transference
of the ballet from the ballroom floor to the stage, *Le Carnaval*
in the repertoire of the Diaghilev company was essentially the
same as the original.

Having spoken of the rapidity with which the ballet was
composed, however, I must explain a few details about Fokine's
method of composition, or the very speed itself will be taken
as an implication of rush and lack of plan—and even of care-
lessness. Before starting rehearsals he had the entire ballet
worked out in his head. His method then was to teach each
soloist and each group their parts, bringing the whole together
for final rehearsals. Only on very rare occasions did he find
it necessary to make alterations during rehearsal. Small wonder
that dancers liked working under him so much, for all too often

choreographers used them much as Beethoven used his score during the pangs of composition, altering and adjusting innumerable times, and sometimes returning to his original concept before proceeding to the next passage. It has always seemed to me that the intelligent choreographer should work out his ballet in detail before it comes into rehearsal, for if dancers are to be used for preliminary notes it must be remembered that they are animated, sensitive creatures, and will insinuate their own personalities into the choreographer's mind, thus influencing him unduly in the making of his ballet. This is quite a different situation, of course, from that in which the choreographer creates with a specific dancer in mind.

In all likelihood, therefore, Fokine had a pretty clear mental picture of *Le Carnaval* before embarking on rehearsals. At that stage, especially as he was working with dancers who were well acquainted with his methods and teaching, the actual learning of the dances, groups and patterns simply entailed the arduous but straightforward and satisfying work of learning parts.

According to eye-witness accounts of the early productions of *Le Carnaval*, the subtlety of its characterization has disappeared, to be substituted by rumbustiousness and childlike horseplay. Maybe! But attempts at a comparison of revivals with their originals is an extremely unsatisfactory habit among certain critics, who quite wrongly assume that they are in the position of a delicate pair of scales and are thus capable of weighing the original against a revival. In fact it is obvious that they are by no means in such a position, for their own fulcrum is undergoing a process of constant adjustment. A young critic who saw the first production of *Le Carnaval*, or even Diaghilev's revival in 1918, must see contemporary productions with very different eyes. Not only has he been subjected to world-shaking events, but his own experience has gradually transformed his own taste.

The various characters in *Le Carnaval* flit across the stage in a series of mildly amorous pursuits. Perhaps in the past the melodramatic pathos of Pierrot wrung sympathy from those who had not yet succumbed to the realism of Shaw and Ibsen, but still lived in their own outmoded world. Chiarina and Papillon, too, delighted audiences of their time more than today, for we are no longer in tune with stage butterflies and flirtatious

minxes. Despite wild claims as to the complexity of characterization in the original, however, responsible critics of that time
were fully alive to its true nature, as the following extracts from
J. E. Crawford Flitch's 'Modern Dancing and Dancers'
published in 1912 will testify:

> Of course this foolish, fluttering world of philanderers we
> never for an instant really believe in. They are the graceful,
> graceless figures of a Conder fan come to life. They are as
> hollow as the porcelain amorists our grandmothers were
> wont to put upon their chimney-pieces. We laugh at their
> impatient ardours as well as at their harrowing griefs.
> Even Pierrot we refuse to take seriously. He himself does
> not expect it—else he would not pretend that Chiarinaa
> were a butterfly and attempt to catch her beneath his
> conical white hat, and then, lifting it cautiously half-an-
> inch from the ground, make a gesture of farcical despair at
> finding her escaped. The whole ballet has the effect of
> transporting us into an unreal world—not the fantastic
> and fairy world, but a half-familiar world, a Lilliputian
> world, in which all the serious traffic of our hearts is
> mocked and parodied. We laugh because we do not
> recognise the likeness of these parabolic puppets to our-
> selves, for if we did we should surely weep. If its intention
> were a shade more serious the ballet would become a
> sermon with *vanitas vanitatum* for its text; it carefully
> stops short, however, at that indefinite border-line where
> trifling passes into satire, but not before it has shown us
> that the ballet can be made the vehicle of ironic laughter.

What a pity that no post-war enthusiasts have been exhorted
by critics for whom we all hold great respect to look for 'an
undercurrent of subtle humour varied with moments of pathos'.
It must, however, be readily admitted that the ballet had
undergone inevitable corrosion since its debut. If audiences are
out of tune with such a mood and sentiment, the dancers are
equally out of sympathy with the roles they are called upon to
portray. The act of donning a crinoline or peg-top trousers
is not sufficient to recapture the essence of the Victorian
atmosphere—much less a vivid parody of that atmosphere.
Small wonder, then, that the ballet frequently turns—I refuse
to say degenerates—into a series of frolics.
With *Petrouchka* Fokine gave a practical demonstration of all

his principles not fully exemplified in *Les Sylphides* and *Le Carnaval*. Dancing and gesture, he said, must serve as an expression of dramatic action, and dancers must be expressive from head to foot. Now, therefore, he sought to achieve firmly dramatic ends rather than solely atmospheric or stylistic ones.

Petrouchka has been labelled the first dance-drama, but such a claim is hardly fair to Salvatore Vigano, who, about a hundred years before, had produced *Gli Strelizzi*, a work of which Rossini complained that it was composed of 'too much mime and not enough dancing'. Unfortunately we cannot know today even the approximate shape and style of the movement of which this and other Vigano ballets were formed, but reproductions of the scenery show strong naturalistic tendencies; and from contemporary writings it seems apparent that Vigano employed his dancers not so much as members of a *corps*, but each to give some individual interpretation of character. Further, he made a special point of fitting these movements to the mood and style of the music as well as to its rhythm, using pieces by a number of composers for some of his ballets, and even composing pieces himself if unable to find suitable melodies already composed.

Even if *Petrouchka* could not justifiably claim the distinction of being the first dance-drama, however, authoritative opinion is generally agreed that it gave the ballet theatre a new force and vigour comparable with those of the new art movements, some of which had just preceded it and others of which were contemporary. The influence of Kandinsky's expressionism in painting, for instance, is no more clearly traceable than in this new realism of Fokine in ballet. Indeed the influence of *Petrouchka* has been vividly marked in the work of a number of leading choreographers, culminating today in the inventions of Tudor and Helpmann. Schönberg's musical innovations, which have led him and many young followers towards a truly dramatic style, as well as towards simplicity and compactness, have in this ballet a more strongly marked counterpart, for Fokine too sought compactness and simplicity. If we leave atonality out of our survey this comparison between Fokine and Schönberg can be taken yet further, for both used smaller groups of executants than their predecessors, both were pioneers who made very few concessions to the bourgeois, and both stressed orchestral values following an epoch in which executive virtuosity had been allowed to corrupt the art itself. As had Noverre before them.

Originally the idea for *Petrouchka* came not from Fokine, but from Stravinsky and Diaghilev. Stravinsky had been working on a score of which the theme expressed a duel between a puppet and an orchestra. In the climax a terrifying discord from the orchestra was to put the puppet to death. When Diaghilev heard some passages from this score he immediately saw the possibilities of an exciting and dramatic ballet. A scenario was worked out according to the programme by Stravinsky and Benois, although there is little doubt that Diaghilev himself also played a considerable part in the making of a plot which is so ideal for interpretation in terms of ballet. In his 'Reminiscences of the Russian Ballet', Benois throws fascinating light on the way in which the story gradually developed. It appears that although Benois did hear various key sections of the score, the three collaborators worked quite separately, their only communication being by means of voluminous correspondence. Finally the scenario was fitted to the music. Yet in his sixteen-page chapter on *Petrouchka*, Benois mentions Fokine but once, and then only to state how he suffered from the heat during rehearsals and that 'even Fokine used at moments to have difficulty in mastering some of the rhythms (which were indeed unusual) and memorizing themes, now so well known and in those days so daringly original'. As Stravinsky dedicated his score to Benois it may be that they both considered Fokine's contribution of somewhat minor importance.

Writing much later, Serge Lifar, in his 'Ballet: Traditional to Modern', subscribes to this view in no uncertain terms. Of the influence of painting on ballet, he exclaims:

> The choreauthor's role in this ballet is almost negligible, to such an extent that its production could, strictly speaking, have been achieved without his taking part in it. The painter, particularly a painter endowed with M. Benois's culture, would have sufficed to dispose on the stage the various coloured masses of *danseurs* and *danseuses* dressed in picturesque costumes, while the painter again, or the musician, could have asked them to execute a Russian dance; a painter, an expert in dance matters, could likewise have devised a pantomime as primitive as

that in *Petrouchka*. *Petrouchka* is one of the most perfect creations of the 'Ballets Russes', but, taking it all in all, it is not a great dance revelation on the part of M. Fokine.

In fact any well-composed dance-drama must rob the choreographer of his paramount importance and allow him no more than partnership on equal terms with his two other collaborators. In an 'abstract' ballet there is obviously no obstacle to pure dance invention, whereas in a dance-drama plot, characterization and decor impose choreographic limitations. Audiences are thus swayed in relation to their reaction to those elements. In the same way, Hogarth the painter, as distinct from Hogarth the story-teller, has been passed almost unnoticed by endless generations of picture-gazers simply because of the drama he relates. If visitors to the Soane Museum could see beyond the sordid tale of the Rake and discern the subtle contrasts in colour and masterful composition, then Hogarth would receive more of the credit that is his due.

On the other hand Fokine receives more than due credit from the majority of ballet-goers, because it is customary today to consider the choreographer as the leading partner. In *Petrouchka* the idea is not his, nor the development of the plot, nor the setting, which is vital to the ballet and not merely a decoration. Nevertheless it seems to me that Fokine's contribution fully holds his own with those of Stravinsky and Benois, for he has given perfect visual animation to the story, and developed it skilfully without betraying the expressive power of stylized movement into a mere drama without words.

The dance style is completely free; out of it Fokine created a number of individual characters who fill but never crowd the stage. I do not think it is possible to create a fully three-dimensional personality by means of movement, but it is possible to produce a series of gestures for the expression of certain qualities. For instance, two street dancers go through their hackneyed routine, *sur les pointes*, with a vulgarity of their own, doing a job with thought only for its pecuniary reward. Similarly the ballerina, the only other character to dance *sur les pointes*, displays a complete lack of originality and absence of human feeling consistent with her sawdust nature.

The jostling revellers and all the vivid fairground scenes are beautifully produced; when in any performance the crowd players betray a lack of understanding of the ballet or time their movements badly in relation to the rest of the crowd then it is easily possible to realize the importance of Fokine's contribution. After many visits numerous little vignettes still remain unseen; the horseplay of the burly coachman with the dignified but less robust young cadets, for instance; or the antics of the mob in their efforts to get a good view of the side shows. These and innumerable other details continue to strike the eye as new interpolations. Every member of the dance crowd has been treated as an individual personality and given movement to express at least a tiny part of that personality. Just as in *Les Sylphides* Fokine abolished the *corps de ballet* by means of individual dance or dances for small groups, so in a very different way has he carried these principles into the more naturalistic form of dance-drama. *Petrouchka* is a remarkable achievement even when regarded in the light of modern developments; how much greater, then, when we remember that it is the first work of its kind—Vigano notwithstanding.

One of the works represented on the opening night of the first Diaghilev season in Paris, May 18th 1909, was the Polovtsian dances from *Prince Igor*. The impact on an audience accustomed to the stale *ballet blanc* formula of the Paris Opéra must have been considerable. At that time male dancing had been in almost complete disrepute for many years, masculine service being required only in the capacity of *porteur*. The *corps de ballet* remained no more than a placid background for the virtuosity of a few leading dancers; in fact ballet at the Opéra had become a period piece, with no prospects of inspiring a new school of thought or apparently of enraging the youth of that time into revolt against its fatuity.

Fokine's *Prince Igor* must have offended many members of that first-night audience as much as Picasso offends Sir Alfred Munnings; but at least the lusty dances could easily be understood by lay audiences. Intended to be an integral part of the opera, the dances yet retain great dramatic power and vitality when presented alone. Even today, when the exaggerated gesture and ridiculous situation of such a ballet have turned it into a museum piece, a vigorous performance still evokes strong reactions in a sympathetic audience.

The dances are supposed to be ordered by the Polovtsian

chief for the purpose of entertaining the captive Prince Igor, with whom he wishes to make a treaty. The chieftain himself leads his warriors in a series of wild dances, leaping into the centre with savage energy to stir them into a wilder frenzy when they show signs of flagging. By way of contrast the women of the camp also fling themselves into what would probably be considered abandoned dances at that time, although now they seem dated to eyes that have seen a more accurate if still only superficial picture of the way in which various peoples of the world dance. Some captive women are also brought in and forced to perform, which they do with a sham modesty and fear. At times the warriors lift these girls as though to carry them off to their dens but change their minds for no accountable reason.

Frankly I now find *Prince Igor* rather a dull ballet. Ballet-goers today are not in sympathy with the spirit in which such works came into being. Just as a modern actor is inclined to throw his lines away rather than risk an accusation of 'hamming', and just as most present-day solo instrumentalists reduce sentimentality to a minimum, so are we inclined in our ballets to approve of a different kind of realism. Compare the attempt at stylization in the murder scene from *Miracle in the Gorbals* with the equal stylization of the warriors in *Prince Igor* and it seems apparent that melodrama remains an important ingredient of ballet, but it is a melodramatic representation of some aspect of contemporary life, not the unlikely romance of a nomadic people in whose existence we no longer believe.

In style *Scheherezade* is in many respects similar to *Prince Igor*. It is built upon the foundation of a strong melodramatic plot, allowing ample opportunity for voluptuous female dances and posturing and desire. Fokine has also sought to evoke the spirit of the Arabian Nights as it existed in the imagination of the people at that time; just as in *Prince Igor* he sought to satisfy the popular conception of a wild nomadic tribe. Silent films on kindred themes made during the same period show an equally outmoded approach.

For *Scheherezade* an even more violently exotic setting was devised than for *Igor*. Leon Bakst designed scenery far removed from the drab, unrealistic sets which had been in vogue until the advent of Diaghilev, taking inspiration from Oriental art and producing an effect that was more oriental than the Orient itself.

The most significant of the contemporary strictures on *Scheherezade* concerned the choice of music, Rimsky-Korsakov's symphonic poem having been written on a theme which differed considerably from Fokine's visual orgy. The music accompanying the massacre of the negroes, for instance, was used by the composer to suggest Sinbad's shipwreck, a somewhat fantastic contrast. Fortunately these strictures had little or no basis in logic, however, and were as easily dismissed then as they would be today. The absurdity of attempting to attach a definite theme to such music was indeed well exposed by Fokine, for his dances suited its style and mood so well that the two might have been composed in the closest collaboration between choreographer and composer.

With *Le Spectre de la Rose* Fokine again broke completely away from existing forms of ballet construction, employing the classical technique for the expression of a romantic reverie. This had been done of course during the reign of romantic ballet a hundred years earlier, but Fokine sought the utmost possible simplicity, translating the delicate mood of Gautier's poem into visual terms by means of an inspired *pas de deux*. No synopsis is necessary apart from the lines of the poem:

> Je suis le spectre de la Rose
> Que tu portais hier au bal.

Normally I do not believe that ballet, especially ballet dealing with dreams or fantasy, can achieve an illusion of reality. Even in the second act of *Giselle*, with Fonteyn at the very height of her powers, I still see no more than a wonderful piece of effective dancing, with all the stresses, rhythms, pauses and flow by which a great choreographer gave life to the limited classical vocabulary. Certainly I do not see a Wili, despite the pathos Fonteyn brings to the role, who is lighter than air and seems likely to sink into the earth at her appointed hour. Contemporary audiences do not seek to be led into a dream world of literary nonsense, but to one of greater truth and greater reality than their own through the incomparable force of expressive human movement.

> For we have heard the Trumpets of Reality that drown the vain din of the Thing that Seems.

Nevertheless, largely through the simplicity of its theme, largely through its suitability for expression in terms of ballet, and largely through Fokine's inspired treatment, *Le Spectre de la Rose* comes nearer than any other fantastic ballet to taking me with it on its journey into a dream.

The choreography demonstrates perfectly Fokine's contention that the classical technique should be used only when completely suitable to the theme. By what better treatment could such a dream be translated into theatrical terms? The classical *pas de deux* is ideal for such a purpose. Fokine did not call upon mime, that obsolete recitative of ballet; neither did he attempt to exploit Nijinsky the virtuoso to the detriment of Nijinsky the artist. That extraordinary piece of virtuosity, the leap through the window, which has been the cause of so much controversy, was brought in with such good taste that the first audience privileged to see this work gaped more at the sudden appearance of the Spectre rather than at the amazing physical accomplishment entailed by that appearance.

It has been authoritatively claimed that Fokine created *Le Spectre de la Rose* for Nijinsky and Karsavina, yet Fokine in an interview with Arnold Haskell, published in 'Balletomania', denied this in the following emphatic terms:

'I never conceive works for particular artists, but the particular artist does lead me to make modifications.'

He then proceeds to adumbrate the extent of Nijinsky's influence on *Le Spectre de la Rose*:

'I did not create *Le Spectre de la Rose* for Nijinsky but because of his particular style it became less masculine, and quite different from what I myself made of it.'

There are many signs in the contemporary theatre that Fokine's ballets fail to hypnotize post-war audiences as effectively as they did a previous generation. Unless they can be preserved without suffering mummification in the process they will, I fear, gradually drop out of the repertory. Fortunately, however, Fokine has been revered so often in print that his name will probably live in glory side by side with that of his eighteenth-century predecessor.

Today choreographers seem to be expected to produce ballets in a variety of styles; Ashton followed a series of works based almost entirely on the *danse d'école* with *Daphnis and*

Chloe: Massine followed *Les Présages* with *Gaité Parisienne*: and even Balanchine steps down occasionally from his austere and classical tower to compose a ballet which has some direct contact with common and contemporary humanity. But before the advent of Fokine there was only one style for the serious ballet-maker to follow: the style of Petipa. To Fokine and to Fokine alone must we then pay tribute for freeing ballet from such a circumscribed field. None can deny that Massine has exploited stylized folk dance from a variety of sources far more successfully than Fokine ever did or attempted to do, but would he have done so had not Fokine blazed the trail? Balanchine and others have made many advances in their researches into the misty, some might say mystic, relationship between music and pure dance, but *Les Sylphides* was the first twentieth-century example. Helpmann and Tudor have forged important links between ballet and contemporary human problems with their great studies in dance-drama, but *Petrouchka* still lights the way for dramatically disposed choreographers.

Nevertheless, if we free ourselves from cloying sentiment we must agree that the reforms and principles laid down by this great innovator will be of infinitely greater value to posterity than the spasmodic performance of a few of his works in doubtful choreographic authenticity—just as Noverre's letters have been a treasury to all who followed him.

Vive Noverre! *Vive* Fokine! Praise be that we have been bequeathed no dry, museum-piece ballets from the eighteenth-century letter-writer. Now let us hope that posterity will be equally charitable and beneficent to the first innovator of the twentieth century.

CHAPTER TWO

The Nijinskys

THE MYTH SURROUNDING Nijinsky the dancer has quite overclouded Nijinsky the choreographer. Today it is so easy to minimize his few choreographic efforts, for where are his ballets to be seen? And when they are to be seen how far have they strayed from their original pattern?

The current fashion is to dismiss the Nijinsky ballets as the work of a schizophrenic: as though that were sufficient to damn them. If it were, then the work of all great artists would surely remain suspect until proof of their mental stability were formally established. The fact that Nijinsky the choreographer composed in a style that was a complete antithesis of the great classical tradition of which Nijinsky the dancer was the greatest exponent, has made it that much easier to dismiss them. Add the various apocryphal anecdotes as to how the ballets were composed and who was really responsible, then the absence of appreciation is easily understood.

Even so, the strange and intangible power of *L'Après-Midi d'un Faune* still captivates many audiences, despite indifferent performances and the reactions against Nijinsky's choreography to which we have been subjected.

This was his first creative work. Before starting on it he had avowed his disapproval of the stultifying restrictions imposed upon expression by the classical technique. Unlike many, he put precept into practice and used a movement style based on angularity, tenseness and virility. In place of the lightness and defiance of gravity for which audiences had applauded him, he substituted heaviness, confining both the faun and the nymphs to earth.

Authorship of the theme of *L'Après-Midi d'un Faune* is sometimes attributed to a collaboration between Bakst and Diaghilev, and sometimes to Nijinsky. As Romola Nijinsky is the strongest advocate of Nijinsky's authorship, however, her evidence is frequently regarded as suffering from undue bias and accordingly discounted. Stravinsky puts the claim for Diaghilev and

Tamara Karsavina as the Ballerina in *Petrouchka*, a role in which this great artist was the first to appear. MICHEL FOKINE

The choreographer and Robert Cohan in a scene from *Letter to the World*, based on the personality of Emily Dickinson.

MARTHA GRAHAM

Bakst, and it must be admitted that he was working so closely within the Ballet Russe organization at the time that on the face of things he must seem a reliable witness. On the other hand we must remember that Stravinsky had apparently very little belief in Nijinsky's creative ability. He has stated that Nijinsky did not possess even rudimentary ideas on music, and has described at length the painful labour of working with Nijinsky on his choreographic tasks. But, as Lincoln Kirstein pointed out in his admirable assessment of Nijinsky in 'Dance', it is only natural that in comparison with the greatest musician of his day even the greatest dancer might seem ignorant from a musician's point of view.

Kirstein holds a different view. He says:

> . . . the present writer after some study of availing remains, after discussions not only with his detractors but with people who knew and loved him, firmly believes that great as he was in the province of the performing dancer, he was far greater as a practising choreographer, in which function he either demonstrated or implied theories as profound as have ever been articulated about the classic theatrical dance. Not only was he a provocative philosopher of the dance but he was also an immediate source of a kind of gesture, which for twenty years, disguised under dubious and numerous aspects, is increasingly known as 'modern' or 'concert' dancing.

Although Kirstein has made a profound study of Nijinsky's life and works, I feel that in an attempt to counter-balance the harsh criticism to which the ballets have been subjected he has fallen into the trap of jumping too far over the other side of the fence. Be that as it may, Nijinsky certainly created in a style which has had considerable influence on the work of many subsequent choreographers. Today it is perhaps of no more than antiquarian interest whether Nijinsky created this new style or whether Bakst, as has been claimed in responsible sources, indicated 'even the slightest gesture'. Doubtless Bakst knew far more about Ancient Greece than did Nijinsky, but Bakst could hardly have tried to think and conceive in what amounted to virtually a new medium; although his outlook towards Greek art might well to a very large extent have influenced Nijinsky.

Nijinsky's revolt against the classical idiom as testified in

L'Après-Midi d'un Faune caused him not merely to ignore its vocabulary but to employ a style which is the antithesis of classicism. In place of the unfolding, expanding gestures of the *danse d'école* he substituted turned-in movements and gestures, and a flat plane. The idea was presumably to animate the Greek vase friezes, but Nijinsky took his treatment a great deal further than necessary for the accomplishment of his illusion. Throughout the ballet the faun makes his movements across the stage from side to side, his feet pointing in the direction of his progression, torso turned obliquely towards the audience. The hands too are held so that they are perpetually at a flat plane. The nymphs also retain this two-dimensional pattern, so that they traverse from side to side in a series of short but regular impulses.

Within the extreme limitations set by this framework Nijinsky created a ballet of great mystical power. The opening pose of the faun on a promontory establishes him immediately as half human, half monster. His desire to fraternize with the nymphs, their curiosity and fear, and the temporary courage of their leader, are shown with the economy of an early Impressionist painter. The music serves as an atmospheric and emotional background—and no more. Those who use the relationship between music and movement shown here to illustrate Nijinsky's lack of musical sensibility are themselves lacking in sensibility of a different kind.

For *Jeux* and *Sacre du Printemps* he went to extreme poles for his themes, yet used a similar choreographic style: a style which showed a formal if not an emotional advance on his first ballet.

Jeux, not now to be seen in any repertory, took its inspiration from one particular aspect of the second decade of the twentieth century: the craze for sport which was so important in developing and symbolizing the growing emancipation of women. It was frequently referred to as a 'tennis ballet', an unfortunate subtitle, for lovers of sport scornfully ridiculed it as a futile attempt to satirize the game of tennis. This it was not, for Nijinsky employed the extremely superficial tennis motive merely as a convenient theme by which to introduce a girl and two boys in a witty generalization of what he apparently considered to be the attitude of adolescents towards sport, love and life. Perhaps I endow the ballet with more profundity than it actually possessed. But now, so many years later, we must remember that in this work Nijinsky was the first to treat a contemporary theme through the medium of ballet. Perhaps his style and invention were too far ahead of his time. We shall never know. Today nobody can possibly remember even the main design of the ballet, much less the detailed pattern of its figures. Further, even if there did exist anyone possessed of such a phenomenal memory, he would still not remember the ballet as it really was.

That is why we should always avoid seriously trying to compare in detail a work of the past with that of the present. The fulcrum of our beliefs is constantly changing. We dislike today what we most admired yesterday for the simple reason that with the growth of experience our own powers of perception and therefore our unconscious selection of what to observe and what to remember varies from season to season.

Le Sacre du Printemps must be dismissed with equal brevity, for that too suffered oblivion after only very few performances. One is now left with a brilliant consideration of the work by André Levinson, unreliable eulogies by Romola Nijinsky and crude dismissals by others who were obviously unable to classify the work in any of their various pigeon holes.

The movement style was again an antithesis of the *danse d'école*, this time organized on a more elaborate scale than in *L'Après-Midi d'un Faune* and *Jeux*. Angular, primitive and barbaric movements marked for long periods each of the accented notes of Stravinksy's complex score. Incidentally, no ballet had ever before been composed to a score of this nature. Later in the Diaghilev era the *avant-garde* of musicians held sway, but Nijinsky undoubtedly made the first balletic experiment of this kind, even if it can be said that the choice was not his own.

Frequently in considering the contributions of choreographers to the general stream of ballet, the name of Nijinsky is excluded from our lists. On the strength of one extant ballet, which has been scarred by unsympathetic performances, added to the fact that we are bewildered by the stupendous myth that is Nijinsky the dancer, we are wise not to attempt assessment. In any case, in the absence of both *Jeux* and *Sacre du Printemps* our

efforts would be as futile as an attempt to evaluate the influence
of Piero della Francesca on painting merely by reading Vasari's
description of the Arezzo frescoes.

During the first world war Nijinsky was interned in Hungary.
By all accounts his experience in confinement led to his mental
breakdown. In 1916, after several high officials had interceded
on his behalf, he found himself in America. Here he soon put
himself to work and produced *Tyl Eulenspiegel* to the Richard
Strauss tone poem. Again one is compelled to rely on verbal
description, for the ballet was never performed outside the
U.S.A. and only a few times there. Some of these writings are
vivid, eloquent and full of enthusiasm, yet they still remain
pitifully inadequate.

From these descriptions it is however possible to affirm that
Nijinsky extended his style to produce what has been called a
mime drama. More important still, it seems to me, is that he
showed a keen sense of humour and, still defying convention, he
used the Tyl Eulenspiegel legend to exploit his own ridicule of
stale custom and barren intellect.

The authentic ending of the legend Nijinsky adapted to his
own purposes. Instead of having the queer fellow die in his bed,
Nijinsky caused him to be hunted and then to appear in
ghostly but jovial form. Perhaps it was this adjustment of the
end which led Fokine to assert that Nijinsky had filched much
of his choreographic style from *Petrouchka*. Undoubtedly, to a
very large extent, this accusation was true; but after all,
Shakespeare was influenced by Marlowe, Rubens by Titian,
Beethoven by Haydn and Fokine by Petipa. From descriptions
and discussions of *Tyl Eulenspiegel* it appears extremely unlikely
that Nijinsky had resorted to any kind of actual plagiarism.

Nijinsky, then, created but four ballets. It is widely believed
that he was entirely dependent upon Diaghilev for what little
creative ability he is supposed to have possessed; that he was
unmusical and fumbling in composition. The fact that he
needed so much preparation for his work, and that *Sacre du
Printemps* went into 126 rehearsals, is frequently used to detract
from his artistic capacity. Undoubtedly Diaghilev's influence
upon him was tremendous, as it was upon every artist with
whom the impresario came into contact, but Nijinsky created
Tyl when he was no longer working with Diaghilev. As for the

length of time he required for preparation, nobody who has read a biography of Beethoven will believe for a moment that endless second thoughts and alterations in any way denote creative inferiority.

Nevertheless Nijinsky, like all other choreographers of the first half of the twentieth century, will be remembered for his influence rather than for his actual work. So it is with Cimabue and Giotto; but that does not make their work less significant.

Bronislava, Vaslav's sister, made her first serious choreographic attempts when Diaghilev called upon her to assist in the 1921 revival of *The Sleeping Beauty*. Among other numbers she created the dance of the Three Ivans, which took the place of the variation originated for Prince Desirée. This virile, boisterous number, which employs some of the steps of the style of the Russian Gopak, is retained in the Sadler's Wells Ballet production. Without doubt it is much to be preferred to the Desirée variation, for the music seems to have been made especially for it. Further, after several *divertissements* of a gentle, child's fairy-tale nature, this one served in admirable contrast.

Of the other works she created for Diaghilev, only *Les Biches* has been seen since the war. This first saw the light of a theatre in 1924 and was for a time included in the repertory of the de Cuevas company.

In musical and choreographic structure *Les Biches* comprises a series of dances in contrasting measures, interspersed with *pas d'action* of a strictly 1920 temperament. Thus Madame Nijinska satirized a house party of that epoch. Handsome athletic young men cavort among a crowd of flirtatious and attractive young women. One of these young women outshines the rest and she came down to the post-1939-45 audience as another of the myths of the past glories of ballet. I refer of course to the Girl in Blue: pictures of Nemtchinova in the role appear in several books and when the ballet was presented at Covent Garden in 1948 even the younger members of the audience felt that they possessed a personal standard of reference on which to judge Marjorie Tallchief, who now took Nemtchinova's place. The *adagietta* of the Girl in Blue is undoubtedly the most easily remembered feature of the ballet. Founded in classicism and danced mostly on *pointes*, symbolizing in broad terms a Noël Coward *cum* Michael Arlen heroine, this fragment seems to me to be the only part of *Les Biches* which now makes any commentary on that mad period. For the rest the ballet held little interest above a few amusing gestural commentaries on typed characters.

The only other ballet by Nijinska which has been seen in post-war England is *Brahms' Variations*. This ballet certainly contained some richly inventive passages, but only occasionally did one forget that dancing, unlike music, is shackled by the limitations of human anatomy.

Nijinska has created various other ballets since the war, among which the *Chopin Concerto*, set to the Piano Concerto in E Minor, is probably the most important. It has never been seen in England, but several distinguished New York critics have been lavish in its praises. George Amberg, in his brilliant work 'Ballet: the Emergence of an American Art', says:

> The most striking impression of the composition is one of an impeccable style, with both the nobility of tradition and a contemporary feeling. The purity of its dancing, the transparency of its structure, the cleanness of its movement pattern, created an effect of truly classic perfection.

Of *Les Noces*, a major work made for Diaghilev, all is now silence. Would we, I wonder, endorse the enthusiastic views of the critics of that time if the ballet were revived today? I doubt it. Nijinska's influence on Ashton, according to his own statement, must have been considerable, and through him acted both directly and indirectly upon other choreographers. Her ability to indicate character suggestive of period atmosphere solely through distorted classics dance interlarded with gesture movement as distinct from mime undoubtedly inspired Ashton in his own stylistic experimentation. But Nijinska can yet find fresh impetus for her own inventive gifts. A new work from her might well add to the repertory of some fortunate company; a work brilliant in structure and content and at the same time right outside the many streams along which choreography today seems to flow.

CHAPTER THREE

Leonide Massine

'**M**ASSINE', SAID DIAGHILEV, 'is the only dancer who ranks as my intellectual equal.' This admission, or boast, according to the way you look at it, was probably true, but it is equally true that Massine owed the development of his intellect almost entirely to the influence of Diaghilev. With Diaghilev he sought the culture of Europe, from the salvaged glories of the past in the temperate atmosphere of art galleries to the more passionate present in the caverns and taverns of Flamenco Spain. Massine himself has proclaimed with typical bluntness that any choreographer who does not frequent museums is a fool. His ballets provide abundant evidence both of his research in galleries and in obscure Iberian villages, although the influence of the latter may be more apparent through its obvious effect on the *pas* themselves, whereas his study of the greater painters has guided him in ways less obvious—in plastic and general design as well as in the indirect subtleties of balanced composition.

In practically all his works Massine exploits the classical technique, enriching his expressive vocabulary by liberal use of stylized folk material and naturalistic gesture. Adept in the organization of large groups, whether for pure dance or decorative effect, he frequently deploys his invention to such an extent as to have two or three focal points of interest occurring simultaneously. Occasionally one of these focal points dominates the stage, with various contrapuntal features of secondary interest in different corners. At other times he develops a minor role either in character or idiosyncrasy until that role in the hands of a well-schooled and well-cast dancer often generates a magnetism more powerful than that of the main characters, with exciting if sometimes exasperating results. In *Mam'selle Angot* for instance, the *pas de deux* between the caricaturist and Mlle. Angot has to compete for attention with an all-male *pas de quatre* led by the frustrated barber; and in *La Boutique Fantasque* numerous fragmentary suggestions of individual character appear in the children, particularly in the precocious American girl, in such a way that little glints of fun and excitement in these roles compete strongly for the focal point during the enactment of the major passages.

Despite his extensive travels, despite detailed study of a variety of native customs in several parts of the world, despite the fact that he has created ballets based on Spanish dancing, Scottish dancing and American history, Massine appears personally to have assimilated none of the characteristics of any of these countries. More than any other member of the Diaghilev company he has brought the spirit and science of the Diaghilev style and atmosphere to the contemporary scene.

In America he undeniably accomplished work of great value in the development of that country's present technical standard, but he endowed native choreography with no nucleus of a native style. His ballets remained projections of his own temperament, which owes its vitality to his Slav blood, and its approach to life and art solely to the Diaghilev influence. In England too he has enriched our repertory without at any time betraying in his work the faintest tinge of an English influence, or even making the slightest concession to the English character. Flitting between one country and another, today in London, tomorrow in Milan, the day after in New York, he shakes off the tell-tale dust of each country almost before it has had time to settle, and lives in his own self-sufficient and self-supporting Olympus, whose boundaries no customs officer can maintain and whose inhabitants are the dream creations of the supreme cosmopolite.

Naturally the young Massine, fluttering his wings in the violent breezes of revolutionary new movements in art, embraced cubism, constructivism and surrealism in turn. Picasso and the *avant-garde* surrounded Diaghilev; their enthusiasms and theories infused the choreographer and he soon began to compose in contemporary terms. For the first time since the romantic period ballet broke through its shell of isolation and came to grips with the new art movements, then so much more concerned with problems of expression than with what to express. The tremendous impact of Impressionism, with its discovery of an entirely fresh and exciting visual world, although it had been strong enough to broaden what was, at that time, the restricted outlook of British painters, had left ballet unaffected. The Nijinsky ballets were undoubtedly responsible for Massine's first dim realization that an Atlantis was rising before his eyes; no more than the environment of the Diaghilev ballet, together with his own eager responses to this artistic revolution, was needed for the creation of choreographic works in an idiom, groping and experimental perhaps, that was in close sympathy with post-1914-18 war artistic thought.

Parade is superficially the most obvious of these works. Passed into limbo now, it is regarded by those who saw it chiefly as an unsuccessful work which was hampered by some cubistic customs that did not come off. Subsequently, through the vehicle of the *Ballets Suèdois*, Jean Borlin employed sets by Fernand Leger and other abstractionists, as well as 'Modern' music, but despite the storms of indignation with which they were received both by revolutionaries and conservatives, today the works themselves are forgotten.

Although *Les Femmes de Bonne Humeur*, seen since the war, according to those who were present at early performances, only in emaciated form, apparently employed less revolutionary methods, there is still undeniable evidence of a new and completely contemporary approach to thematic and choreographic problems. While the trappings and methods of other forms are cast off, the new vision and spirit of experimentation remains. The new impetus to art, whether of painting, poetry or music, succeeded in stressing the personal element to a greater extent than had been dreamt of during the long period of the Renaissance. Neither painter nor poet concerned himself any longer with the public he was supposed to be addressing, but used allusions, images and metaphors that frequently had associations only in his mind. Clarity of expression was no more to be regarded as an essential feature of art forms; on the contrary, the obscure and the esoteric reference was frequently and deliberately sought after.

In *Les Femmes de Bonne Humeur*, Massine remained lucid enough in the working out of this themes, but expressed himself in contemporary terms by endowing his characters with a greater individual personality than had previously been achieved in ballet. Although Nijinska had hinted at this quality before him, her creatures remained symbols and abstractions of common human characteristics.

Apart from his symphonic ballets Massine has invariably sought the aid of a strong but not unduly assertive plot. During his first period with Diaghilev these plots were worked out choreographically with scrupulous consideration for their clarity. On his return to the company after an absence from 1920 to 1924, however, Massine apparently no longer thought it worthwhile or even desirable to make such naive concessions to the public. Beaumont has aptly described the ballets Massine produced during the last years of the Diaghilev oligarchy as cerebral. Artists of all kinds, many of them artists who should have known better, at this time seemed to believe that a necessary ingredient of art was obscurity. It is true that in certain rare cases an artist reaches his most lofty pinnacle of expressive clarity only by remaining obscure to all but the esoteric few. In ninety-nine cases out of a hundred, however, obscurity is synonymous with mediocrity.

Nevertheless, in spite of a cruel lack of concern for the peace of mind of his audience during this period, Massine yet produced some striking choreographic passages; although this claim is difficult to support, by virtue of the fact that not one of the Massine works of this last few years has come down to a curious, if highly critical, posterity.

Before reaching his next phase—which dates from his collaboration with de Basil in 1933 to 1939—Massine worked hard and for long periods for the variety stage. For a few years he composed the dance routines and spectacles for the stages shows at the huge Roxy cinema, New York, as well as personally appearing in these shows.

He made scenes for C. B. Cochran reviews; brilliant dances and groupings far surpassing anything of a similar nature previously produced for the commercial theatre. This experience supplied his creative personality with aspects that at times seem to be mutually exclusive; Massine the entertainer and Massine the symphonist.

Between *Les Présages* and *Choreartium*, both made in 1933, came the *Le Beau Danube*. Massine has stated that he began work on the Strauss ballet immediately after completing *Les*

Présages in order to give himself change and recreation before setting to work on Brahms' Fourth Symphony.

In his methods of composition, as in his personal context, Massine is aloof and uncommunicative. The fact that he very rarely permits visitors into his rehearsal room has contributed to the grossly exaggerated reports as to the autocracy and secretiveness which surround his choreography. Stravinsky does not compose amid guests, however amiable, nor does Christopher Fry write his plays in the theatre. Yet the choreographer, whose task is in a way more difficult than either of these, in that it has to be imposed upon human instruments, is expected to be impervious to the prying eye and the thoughtless comment. Very few choreographers enjoy it, but fewer still are prepared to take the strong line of isolation that is likely to give them a reputation for unapproachability.

At work Massine follows no particular method; neither as a rule is a role composed deliberately for any particular person. When collaborating with a composer with whose music he is unfamiliar he prefers to have the score in his hands before beginning to transfer his ideas to the limbs of his dancers. If thoroughly familiar with the dancers' work he prefers to discuss the general plan of the ballet first and then compose without the score. Throughout the throes of creation he maintains the closest possible co-ordination with his collaborators. However, as will be seen from a list of the sixty-odd ballets he has created, he admits to a preference for contemporary composers, but sometimes works with one of the past.

Normally he does not work out the actual dances before rehearsals (a fact which is alone sufficient to explain why he abhors rehearsal audiences) but merely visualizes them in hazy outline. Regarding the dancers solely as instruments for the expression of his ideas, he seldom takes them into his confidence as to his purpose. This may perhaps appear unwise as well as unnecessarily secretive, but it seems to me that in this way Massine aims at the avoidance of gratuitous co-operation in the actual composition of his work. If the dancer knows too much about the ballet individual interpretations will vary to a greater extent than Massine is prepared to accept. Perhaps that accounts for the way in which Massine's ballets suffer more than most by constant performances, when the lynx-eyed surveillance of the originator has been removed.

A further aspect of Massine's method is sometimes regarded as an idiosyncrasy. He starts with any scene, it may be the last, the first or one in the middle, and then pieces them together like the editor of a film. Largely he works out the various details during rehearsals, working separately with the principals and *corps de ballet*. Although refusing to submit to the domination of music, he has compared his solo dances as melodies for a single trumpet and his groups as orchestral *tutti*. He does not always depend upon music for his inspiration, just as frequently finding stimulus in theme or period. In his version of *Le Sacre du Printemps*, for instance, he was motivated by both music and theme, whereas in *Les Femmes de Bonne Humeur* he manifestly sought to express a particular atmosphere. Sometimes, too, he tries to evoke a mood redolent of a particular country, as in *Le Tricorne*, employing native dance and theme for his purpose. Whichever element supplies him with his strongest motivation, that is the element by which he allows himself to be influenced. According to his own statement, in all his works he aims at achieving the highest possible power of expression, a felicitous balance between movement and technique and, in his larger ballets, a counterpoint of mass movement contrasted against individual dance.

The fact that none of his second period ballets (1925-8) has either lived or been revived is not necessarily an implication of the inferiority of these ballets. Bizet died in 1875, yet his Symphony in C, now well known to ballet-lovers, did not receive its first public performance until 1938. A choreographer stands no chance of such deferred posthumous performance. A new ballet, if the world is sufficiently hostile to drive it out of performance, stands very little chance of revival. In 1928, for instance, *Ode* did not exactly win eulogy from the critics; neither did it perceptibly push up box office returns. Yet today we might, I repeat, might, like this ballet very much indeed. Nobody knows, for we remember it in relation to our attitude of the time, not in the light of our mental and intellectual state today.

Les Femmes de Bonne Humeur, first performed in 1917, has been described by Beaumont as follows:

> a masterpiece and one of the best examples of Massine's ability to make dancing mimetic.

Summarized in the programme as a choreographic comedy in one act, this work is often claimed to recreate the atmosphere of eighteenth-century Venice. True, Leon Bakst did design the scenery and costumes, which are reminiscent of those in which Guardi and Canaletto took so much delight. The theme too has a lighthearted, musical comedy nature, likely to convey something of the superficial frivolousness of a certain type of society in a city which had become decadent and corrupt after a long period of prominence as head of an empire. But the atmosphere of the true Venice—no! To do him justice one cannot attribute such an aim to the choreographer. The merit of the ballet is in no way affected by its degree of authenticity, any more than 'The Merchant of Venice' is the poorer for its absurd treatment of that city's wonderful system of law.

The ballet, even taking into consideration the probability that the post-war revival was no longer performed as well as the original, and that the choreography had lost much of its subtlety, was by no means great when weighed in the balance of contemporary taste. Bounded by passages of dance and long stretches of mimeo-melodrama, nowhere did it touch the pulse of a people grown up amid current theatrical trends. In this work Massine developed his various points in a more leisurely mode than ever before or since. In the plot an odd climax of wit or satire appeared as a result of an almost tedious scene. Twists and surprises were contrived with a noisy clanging of machinery; a slap-stick element got the whole confection nowhere, even in the few strands of dance which were not too cluttered up with the turgid literary context.

In 1919 Massine produced two ballets which immediately established themselves in the Diaghilev repertoire: *La Boutique Fantasque* and *Le Tricorne*. These two ballets were among the first to be mounted by the de Basil Company, and were revived by the Sadler's Wells Ballet as soon as possible after its occupation of Covent Garden.

La Boutique Fantasque depends for its success on a commonplace story about fairy dolls, a suite of charmingly melodious and not too well-known Rossini melodies, and a dance style which, following the Massine formula, is developed by compounding stylized folk dance with classicism. From its opening, with the shopkeeper and his assistant opening the shop and establishing themselves as individual personalities, the ballet builds up to a spectacle which constantly grows in size, sound and variety. The dolls produce their wittily contrasted dances against a background of ever-increasing excitement from the rest. The others, far from remaining background characters, however, establish themselves as individuals. The Can-Can dancers are finally separated and the scene closes on a note as calm as the opening, with an equally appealing atmosphere of expectancy. Then again the movement grows from nothing into a great apotheosis, after the dolls have shed the restrictions of clockwork and wooden joints to perform in all their human freedom. Next comes a shorter lull, when the dolls return to their shelves before the shop opens the following morning, after which, with an irresistible surge of movement, the dolls drive the customers from the shop to bring the ballet to a close.

From beginning to end each figure on the stage is given a vivid and well-planned life of its own, yet no matter how crowded the scene becomes there is not the slightest trace of confusion. The humans mime and resort to a form of dance which is little more—but how much more—than exaggerated natural movement; whereas the dolls give rein to a wide variety of dance styles, in which the *danse d'école* merges with numerous other styles. The Can-Can in particular is an outstanding example of invention; here is all the style, movement and vivacity of the notorious Parisian *danse de scandale*, given new charm and appeal through its exaltation to the sphere of *pointes* and turn-outs.

Massine and Tudor are diverse in method and purpose; but the shopkeeper's assistant in *La Boutique Fantasque*, the first character in contemporary ballet to possess an individual idiosyncratic gesture—admittedly of a vulgar nature and employed as a laugh-raiser rather than an effort to disclose human personality through movement—is a dim beginning of a search for a choreographic style to express an individual in place of a generalized human characteristic.

In that same year Massine created another great ballet to which the Sadler's Wells Ballet also paid tribute in 1947 by promoting it to the Covent Garden repertoire: *Le Tricorne*.

The structure of this ballet denotes very clearly the influence of Fokine, for the fusion of *soli*, *pas de deux* and *ensembles* derives directly from *Petrouchka*. The plots, too, have their similarities, not in climax and situation of course, but in the extent of their detail and their development. Fokine, in several works, sought a variety of folk terms, but advanced only a short distance beyond Petipa in his actual research into movement and rhythm native to certain countries. Massine, aided tremendously by de Falla, went so much further that it might almost be claimed that during the pilgrimage of himself, de Falla and Diaghilev, research was carried out to such an extent as to enable the authentic native forms to be absorbed into and thus to enlarge the vocabulary of expressive theatrical dance.

While de Falla studied and recreated folk melodies, Massine closely observed the rhythms and gestures of the Andalusian people as they went about their normal life. From all this mass of material he recorded a great deal by a ciné-camera and then set about assimilating it before making the first ballet ever to be based purely on a native idiom—a ballet which was at the same time to be performed by dancers alien, if not unsympathetic, to its form and style.

The value of such careful assimilation becomes evident in the opening moment of the ballet. The miller seeks to evoke music from the bird, but in order to do so he stands in the attitude of the matador as he waits, poised, to aim his urgent *banderilla* into the soft skin of the bull's neck. It is an opening as brilliant, in its way, as the first scene of 'Hamlet'. In the opening of the play one is not conscious as to whether the players are speaking in prose or verse: and in the opening of *Le Tricorne* one is hardly conscious of watching either dance or stylized gesture, for the image is completely expressive and thus carries conviction without the lowering of artistic temperature that would attend a reliance upon a vague naturalism. At the same time the atmosphere of the ballet is set: the gay but tempestuous mood of the Miller, who plays so boyishly with the canary, but who stamps in anger when he fails to extract a sound; the coquettishness of the Miller's Wife; the erotic veneer of some of the dances, and the enactment of the literary element in a fusion of dance, gesture and mime. By the time the Dandy appears on the bridge, the style, tempo and form of expression have all been firmly established.

A Spanish ballet too frequently materializes into a thinly

connected series of Spanish dances and remains an expression of those dances rather than an integrated theatrical work. Massine at times has barely avoided this pitfall in *Le Tricorne*; but when unable to mould the form of the dance he has either married it to a development of the theme, as with the Kodalin at the opening in which the Miller and his wife play their game of flirtation; or he has used it, as in the Farucca, to build up an appropriate action in which to show the dance itself as an expression of the Miller's prowess.

In 1933, now with de Basil, Massine began his 'symphonic' experiments, that year producing both *Les Présages* and *Choreartium*. In 1936 came *Symphonie Fantastique*, in 1938 *The Seventh Symphony*, in 1939 *Rouge et Noir* (Shostakovitch's First) and in 1941 *Labyrinth* (Schubert's Ninth). None of these works is to be seen today, although post-war audiences did have the dubious pleasure for a time of witnessing emaciated versions of *Les Présages*, and *Symphonie Fantastique*. All we can profitably talk about today, therefore, is the general question of symphonic ballet. From 1933 until 1939 music critics of the calibre of Edwin Evans and Ernest Newman entered the lists in defence of the *genre* against a multitude of self-styled purists who professed to recoil in horror at the mere thought of such desecration of Brahms' Fourth Symphony. The balletic treatment of Tchaikovsky's Fifth had received a certain amount of condemnation, but after all, Tchaikovsky was a ballet composer and had even expressed delight when a critic whose opinion he respected beyond all others had attempted to condemn his Fourth Symphony by a statement to the effect that the work was too danceable.

A number of dance-lovers as well as music-lovers have gone so far as to claim that some music is danceable and some is not. What they mean of course is that certain melodies and rhythms seem appropriate to them to be set to dances, whereas others seem inappropriate. Any work generally recognized as great they put outside the scope of ballet; and claim, furthermore, that to set dances to such music is to display a lack of feeling for music and to damage the effective power of the music itself by giving it arbitrary and unfair aural associations.

In *Choreartium*, Massine, according to his own statement, sought to follow choreographically the contrapuntal structure

Mary Munro and Alexander Bennett in *Death and the Maiden*.
ANDRÉE HOWARD

A scene from the 1954 Paris Opéra production of *Firebird*, with Ni
Vyroubova, seen background centre, in the leading role. MICHEL FOKI

A scene from *Carte Blanche*, which is in the repertory of the
Sadler's Wells Theatre Ballet. WALTER GORE

and form of the symphony and at the same time to match visually its musical patterns and moods. Two great difficulties beset such an aim: the instruments which make music do not obtrude themselves before the audience, whereas ballet is inseparably tied for its expression to the human body; therefore dance itself can never rise to the absolute abstraction of music; further, the laws which govern the structure of music to a very large extent facilitate composition, the full-length work rising inexorably from the germinal idea; whereas dance composition receives neither the benefit nor the hindrance of a fully coherent set of laws. Thus the maintenance of rich choreographic invention through a long symphony becomes indeed a stupendous task.

Even so, I hope sincerely that choreographers will continue to follow Massine's great lead in an effort to develop closer relationships between dance and music. In such a relationship the dance creator is freed from the necessity of fighting a losing battle to produce convincing dramatic images and can instead give full rein to the expression in movement of purely formal and emotional reactions. The material of music is organized sound, the material of dance is organized movement; each has a common basis in rhythm and by a true unity each can reinforce the power of the other.

Sandwiched in time between the 1933 symphonic essays came *Le Beau Danube*. It is generally believed that Massine resorted to this lighter form by way of relaxation after the sustained effort of *Les Présages* before tackling the even more formidable *Choreartium*. Perhaps if Massine were prone to introspection he would regard as ironic the fact that the symphonic works have disappeared, while the lighter work still lives, having been included in the repertories of several companies.

In truth, however, *Le Beau Danube* is one of Massine's most successful works from every point of view. The weight of the subject-matter of any work of art is, or should be, relatively unimportant in a consideration of the work itself. No plot or theme is inherently unsuitable for expression in terms of ballet, for the great choreographer can knead what is apparently intractable material to his own ends. Frequently in all art forms the subject-matter intervenes between the artist and his

audience, diverting attention from his personal vision and
treatment to the subject itself. As a theatrical art ballet depends
much more upon its subject than the plastic arts, but success
must still hang upon the translation of the subject and not on
the subject itself. An inferior choreographer can for a short time
conceal his lack of vision and originality by a weak choreographic translation of a powerful plot, but discerning sections
of the audience very soon detect such a weakness. On the other
hand, only a really great choreographer can employ a strong
plot to make a successful ballet, for none but a Tudor or a
Helpmann can interpret such a plot in terms of movement
sufficiently expressive to make words superfluous.

A programme note to *Le Beau Danube* is superfluous, for in
thirty minutes of action, dancing—dancing as distinguished
from mere swollen natural movement—makes every detail
of the nonsensical plot abundantly clear. As is to be expected in a Massine work most of the characters are endowed
with certain outstanding qualities, without any attempt at
a detailed development. The modest demeanour and innocence
of the young girl is contrasted directly with the coarse abandon
of the street dancer, the military bearing and aristocracy of the
Hussar with the mincing *hauteur* of the dandy.

When well danced the ballet yet retains for me all its charm
and gaiety, warming the heart with its simple philosophy,
distilled through continuous and exciting, if not particularly
original, dances. Today there are many who assume that without Danilova as the Street Dancer, Riabouchinska as the young
girl and Baronova as the First Hand, the ballet has become no
more than a pleasant and pointless romp. They talk about the
way in which Danilova fluttered her skirts, Riabouchinska's
gay innocence and Baronova's fascinating beauty. Undoubtedly these early interpreters did set the ballet off with a swing;
and undoubtedly Massine was unsurpassable as the Hussar,
but since 1945 we have seen several first-rate interpretations of
all these roles by dancers who, rather than slavishly copying
their predecessors, have sought within the very definite
limitations laid down by the choreography to base their nuances
of expression on a more contemporary approach.

In 1934 Massine, already by that time probably the most
widely travelled and the most restless of all choreographers,

made an attempt to create a truly American ballet, *Union Pacific*. He faced no mean problem. In Spain he had found a rich native dance idiom, but in the young and polyglot U.S.A. he found only pioneering spirit and no wealth of expression peculiar either to the continent or any part of it. Since then American choreographers have solved the apparently insoluble by employing native gesture, tempo and rhythm to produce works which could certainly have sprung only from indigenous sources. Massine imposed his own Diaghilev-Russian temperament and method on a well-known phase of American history, so that the ballet itself does not possess a vestige of American movement. Later he made two more works based on American themes, *The New Yorker* and *Saratoga*, with equal absence of real American influence. None of these works remains in performance.

In 1938, for René Blum's Ballets Russes de Monte Carlo, Massine created *Gaité Parisienne*. Recently this ballet was danced by the late 'International' Company and was permanently recorded in colour film by Warner Bros, in Hollywood in 1941. Recorded is not the right term, for the film version was modified and conditioned especially for the medium.

Gaité Parisienne is built on yet another of those plots which provide Massine with ample and logical reasons for various kinds of dance. Once again he has shaped to his own ends a native form—although this time it is more a colloquialism than an idiom. I refer of course to the Can-Can, that boisterous, vulgar excuse for a leg show of the Paris music halls of the late nineteenth century. In *La Boutique Fantasque* he went to the same source, but spiced the movement with such a leavening of *pointes* and turn-out so as to endow it with charm and magical romance. Now he sought, and I think successfully, to exploit rather than conceal its true qualities.

Here once again are the contrasting characters: the dainty, sweetly simple flower girl and the pert, sophisticated glove seller; the naive, enthusiastic Peruvian and the aristocratic, haughty soldier; the elegant creatures who visit the lively café on the arms of their consorts and the abandoned Can-Can dancers.

The film version of this ballet encountered some adverse criticism when it made its first appearance, but since then it has hardly ever been off the screen. Used as a 'filler' sandwiched between two feature films, or as a coloured relief from cartoons and nature study in the News Cinemas, this and its fellow, *Capriccio Espagnol*, have become hardy perennials throughout this country. In 1941 the entire de Basil outfit invaded Hollywood, causing a sensation even in that extraordinary city. Famous film stars apparently sought admittance into the closely guarded studios to scrutinize the exotic dancers just as they themselves were normally the subject of scrutiny. The films were produced quickly but courageously. No attempt was made to maintain the illusion of a stage, the cameras weaving their way right into the heart of the actual dancing. This was undoubtedly the reason why large groups of ballet-goers, who behave more as guardians of a sacred temple than mere puritanical aesthetes, abominate what they term cheap Hollywood corruptions of Massine's masterworks.

I have discussed the film version of both these works at length elsewhere, but I must repeat that despite certain obvious blemishes in what were pioneering efforts in the development of a firm relationship between film and ballet, they remain for me more exciting than the stage productions. The ability of the cameras to become the hub of the movement is in itself a quality which can enhance these particular works, especially *Gaité Parisienne*. The only major drawback in my opinion is the melodramatic commentary in an American accent which accompanies both works—the one concession to a moronic mass appeal—together with the fact that tinned music, no matter how excellent the apparatus of reproduction, falls far short of the real thing.

Capriccio Espagnol is based, like *Le Tricorne*, on Spanish dancing, but differs from the earlier works in every other respect. Rimsky-Korsakov's music supplies both a rhythmic and atmospheric background wholly in keeping with the stylized movement. This music is divided into five sections, each of which becomes in the ballet a *divertissement* well varied from the others. Yet again the successful formula came into operation. Contrasting suites of dance follow one another: the dance of the gypsies, the dance of the hidalgos, group dances and solo dances.

From 1939 to 1941 Massine, still working with the Ballet Russe, produced three pieces of pretentious nonsense in the form of so-called paranoic ballets. The themes and décor for these were provided by Salvador Dali, a fact which alone suggests surrealistic and nightmarish notions. The first of these works, none of which is to be seen today, although *Mad Tristan* did for some extraordinary reason win temporary resurrection at the hands of the de Cuevas company, was *Bacchanale*. Based on Wagner's Bacchanalia from 'Tannhäuser', the symbolism of this work was so obvious, according to enlightened Americans, for England never trembled under the impact of a performance, that, apart from a brilliantly drawn backcloth, had very little except mad obscenity to offer. This was succeeded by *Labyrinth*, which had its literary foundation in the myth of Theseus and Ariadne, and depended musically on nothing less than Schubert's Symphony in C Major. According to the reports, the fourth tableau of this concoction contained a classically inspired *pas de deux* of great beauty, but it seems that none of the rest were memorable except perhaps in nightmares of the very worst kind.

Mad Tristan, as will possibly be recalled by those who had the interesting but not edifying experience of attending one of the few performances of this ballet at Covent Garden, was choreographically barren, being merely a vehicle for a number of sensual, Daliesque tricks that evoked embarrassment and ridicule.

During the early war years Massine, still in America, mounted certain new works for Ballet Theatre. Of these *Mam'selle Angot* is known now better in England than America, for in 1948 the Sadler's Wells Ballet presented this work after it had been revived and revised by Massine for their benefit.

Perhaps the authorities at Covent Garden considered it advisable to provide an immediate contrast—not to say antidote—for the rigorous solemnity of *Checkmate* (revived in 1947) with the determined frivolity of *Mam'selle Angot*. If so it would surely have been more fitting in the national company to produce a work with an Anglo-Saxon brand of humour and frivolity. As it is, *Mam'selle Angot* at times glows with a typical continental humour and saucy gaiety; at other times the glow dies down to a dull flame in which all becomes a monotone of boredom.

The ballet lasts nearly forty-five minutes: far, far too long, especially as the tuneful but spineless melodies of Lecocq possess insufficient variety and form to interest the regular ballet-goer. Massine likes to people his stage with a certain amount of prodigality; often in several of his works various things are going on at the same time in different parts of the stage; but as a rule these various incidents remain within the angle of one's vision. As I have already mentioned, a particular instance of this nature occurs during the *pas de deux* between the caricaturist and Angot, and the *pas de quatre* by the barber and his friends. Both dances are in their way delightful and each complements and spotlights the other.

Following *Mam'selle Angot* Massine next created a work especially for Sadler's Wells, this compliment taking the form of *The Clock Symphony* which began its brief spell of life in June 1948. With the exception of *Mad Tristan* it was probably the least inventive Massine ballet ever to be shown to North Atlantic audiences. Christian Bérard and Massine vied with each other in restoring as many of their past clichés as possible, the whole being supported by the dainty but unsubstantial Clock Symphony of Haydn. The only part of this work I can now remember is a pair of legs playing the role of pendulum to a clock. That was quite charming, but all else is forgotten.

In 1951 Massine worked long and arduously on yet another ballet commissioned especially by Sadler's Wells, this time producing something of a very different nature—*Donald of the Burthens*. Here he sought to employ Scottish dancing as he had employed Spanish dancing in *Le Tricorne*. Studying under Scottish dancing teachers for several months before tackling this choreographic problem, he apparently mastered at least the steps and form of a number of well-known Scottish dances, all of which he has utilized in his movement patterns.

In the early phases of this ballet he has succeeded in integrating the Scottish steps into expressive choreography, but the long scene of jubilation after the King's recovery is little more than a suite of not very well executed Highland dances. It is certainly true that the trained ballet dancers include various figures of a kind beyond the ability of many Highland dancers, but the mere interpolation of a double *tour en l'air* and a few *entrechats-six* is not sufficient in itself to transmute a national form into expressive ballet.

The one character who is given movement worthy of Massine at his best is that of Death which, ironically enough, has not been endowed with the slightest suspicion of a Scottish dialect. Various soloists have appeared in this role; although one, Beryl Grey, is perhaps better than the others, the choreography is so strong that the power of the character remains undiminished notwithstanding considerable contrast in individual interpretations. The writhing, rhythmic movements of Death carry with them a strange compulsion so that the character becomes rather a force than a being. The continuous chain of movement, full of originality, taken from no obvious source, seems to me to represent a strongly personal and perhaps only dimly felt belief in the mockery of death as well as in its inevitability.

There are several notable and even memorable instants both in the theme and in the choreography. The turning of the sick King's bed in order to remove Death from his head, for instance, is doubtless a sound theatrical idea; but unfortunately it is exploited in such a matter-of-fact way as to lose most of its force. Such an idea, far from being left to exploit itself, needs equally rich choreographic expression. On the other hand a mass dance, accompanied only by a rapid Scottish song, remains a passage of remarkable persuasion.

The fact must however be faced that since 1938 Massine has produced no really great ballet. Is he a spent force? Is he now producing works merely for the benefit of what must already be a singularly impressive bank balance, or is his genius only in temporary eclipse? Some of his detractors urge that he is no longer really interested in ballet but is continuing to regard the life for which Diaghilev so richly prepared him as a career rather than a vocation.

Nobody, probably not even Massine himself, knows whether that accusation is true or false. Neither shall we know unless he produces another masterpiece or alternatively fades quietly out of the serious choreographic scene.

CHAPTER FOUR

George Balanchine

O F ALL CHOREOGRAPHERS, Balanchine offers the widest scope for general discussion and the least scope for critical analysis of his separate ballets. In common with many of his contemporaries he has created works in a number of styles, sometimes depending upon a plot or theme but most frequently taking his inspiration from music to evolve abstract ballets—a term, as I have already said, to which Balanchine himself makes strong objection.

'I try to reflect the flow and concentrated variety of the music through the interlaced bodies of the dancers rooted to a central spot on the stage,' he says. On the other hand, despite his reliance on music, he believes that dancing is an important independent art. Choreographic movement he regards as an artistic end in itself; if such movement is free from the need to develop a plot or to present a dramatic situation, the movement, he holds, is thereby given an opportunity to fulfil itself in its own special way. 'The visual aspect, not the story, is the essential element,' he declares, but realizes at the same time that it is not possible continually to create ballets solely founded in music. 'If there must be a story, let it be so legible and simple that all can understand it and follow its development.' He strongly opposes the belief that everything can be conveyed in terms of ballet, and believes that the audience should be able to enjoy the movement and spectacle without regard to the story.

In music the repetition and modulation of a particular phrase provides listeners with great enjoyment. The more perceptive the auditor, the more subtle are the modulations he is able to apprehend and appreciate. A pleasant melody, after its first announcement, seems to give more pleasure with each repetition, provided, of course, that such repetition is not overdone. The human ear takes more readily to that which is familiar, especially if while retaining its fundamental shape and form the melody undergoes slight and titillating modifications.

Movement, according to Balanchine, when it is organized in a similar fashion to the music to which it is a visual parallel, is capable of gaining an equally powerful audience response. A phrase of brilliantly inventive solo dances may be repeated by a group, reflected by another dancer and modulated in such a variety of ways that only the most perceptive members of the audience are able to detect the source. The point always at issue with such ballets, and it seems to me to be a point for which there are as many answers as there are members of the audience, concerns the validity of employing the same method of construction for a visual composition as for an aural one.

Obviously there are several precedents in support of the Balanchine method, perhaps the most forceful lying in the fact that repetition is an important element in the composition of painting as well as in music. Yet the two cases are not quite the same, for the painter seeks as a rule to repeat or echo only a particular pattern or shape, without normally repeating the subject-matter itself, whereas the composer often repeats an actual passage, offsetting too obvious a repetition by employing different keys, different sets of instruments or perhaps by making slight changes to the phrase itself.

Modulated repetition undeniably plays an important part in much great art. Whether its effect is as moving in a Balanchine ballet as in a Bach fugue, or whether it is as potentially moving, must remain a purely personal matter between Balanchine and each member of the audience.

At work—or at least at that particular part of his work which is visible—following preliminary study of the music and the mental conception of certain fundamental movement shapes, Balanchine is quiet and patient. Without seeming either cold or impersonal to the dancers, he uses them more as instruments than as human beings. At the outset he allows them no inkling of the nature of their various roles, for that would condition their portrayal of these roles; but notwithstanding his mild demeanour, he is the dictator. Although he never invents any of the actual dances until he comes face to face with the dancers, he then works with speed and facility. After rehearsing principals and *corps* separately he next jig-saws the various pieces together, and very little more rehearsal is necessary for the completion of his work.

Balanchine's constant seeking after new relationships and new ways of expressing old relationships between music and dance is so strong a feature of his choreographic output that even when he is apparently founding a ballet upon a strong plot the score often remains the primary influence in its construction. Of all composers he prefers Stravinsky, a fact which is hardly surprising in view of the attitude which each of the two Russo-Americans has towards his work, and in view of the interest Stravinsky has always shown in composing for ballet. Balanchine says:

> Speaking for myself I can only say that Stravinsky's music altogether satisfies me. I am moved to try to make it visible, not only the rhythm, melody and harmony, but even the timbres of the instruments.

This assertion appears to me to be one of those inexplicable Balanchinisms which puzzle all who try to find logic in every aphorism. Is he setting himself up as another Dalcroze, arbitrarily inventing sets of visual patterns to represent the sounds of the orchestra? If so, 'it were a grievous fault', for Dalcroze aspired not to produce an art form, but to provide movements as an aid to the analysis of musical construction. Balanchine on the other hand is trying to marry one expressive form with another. The repetition of movement accompanying the repetition of melody might alone, and sometimes most certainly does, evoke a response from an audience. On the other hand the modulation in key, or repetition of a phrase by a different set of instruments, can hardly be matched by visual images. I mean, for example, that a musical phrase first announced by violins and then repeated by 'cellos must evoke quite a different response from visual images in which the violins are paralleled by female dance and the 'cellos by masculine dance.

Balanchine himself is obviously aware of this indisputable fact. Surely in his invention of movement pattern he does not expect his audience necessarily to apprehend the relationship he has imposed on sound on the one hand and movement on the other. The methods whereby he seeks to obtain suitable variety in design and rhythm are purely his own affair. If a particular movement seems to him to match the timbre of any one set of instruments it does not mean that he has failed or that his audience is lacking in perception if they are unaware of such a relationship. All members of the audience will react differently in accordance with their own experience. In other words, in his own private world of the imagination Balanchine has used certain highly personal reactions to the music to facilitate his invention. The success of this invention must be judged only by the intensity and quality of our reactions to it, not by the accuracy of our guesses as to how he has achieved a particular effect.

Many choreographers feel that the invention of movement and its synchronization to the music is the essential feature of their task. Balanchine believes in a far closer relationship between music and movement. He says:

> I can always invent movement and sometimes it can be fitted into the right place, but that is not choreography. The music dictates the whole shape of the work.

Indeed, Balanchine's reverence for music is so great that he objects to the borrowing of its terms by writers on ballet. Counterpoint is one which has come in for his especial attention:

> There is a lot of talk about counterpoint in dancing. It is generally believed that counterpoint is based on contrast. Actually counterpoint is an accompaniment to a main theme which it serves to enhance, but from so uniting it must not detract. The only kinds of counterpoint that I can see in dancing are the movements of arms, head and feet which are contrapuntal to the static or vertical position of the body. For instance, in the *croisé* position the body is vertical, but one arm is raised, the other horizontal, one foot points forward while the other supports the body and the head is inclined towards one of the shoulders. All this is an accompaniment to the main theme, which is the vertical position of the body. In dancing one should not strive to achieve counterpoint by contrasting the movement of two dancers or two groups of dancers on the stage. This results not in counterpoint, but in disunity. There is no need to apply musical terms to the dance, but if it is done their meaning must be clearly understood.
> The eye can focus perfectly only on objects which are in the centre of its field of vision. Those objects which are not head on are seen clearly only because the observer knows and imagines that they are, while he focusses on the

centre object. If some new or secondary form is placed in the secondary part of a composition, the eye instinctively changes its focus and convinces itself of the identity of each individual form. And as vision is the channel through which the art of choreography reaches its audience, this inevitably results in confusion and a loss of attention to the main theme. But the eye can follow the movements of a large group of dancers if these form a harmonious pattern within its central field of vision.

In his explanation of counterpoint in dancing Balanchine fails to achieve a verbal logic to match the logic of his choreography. After supplying a personal definition and refusing to believe in any other, he goes on to discuss and condemn a quite different kind of counterpoint and incidentally the kind I always mean when I employ the term. Balanchine is obviously right in stating that the eye can focus only on the objects which are in the centre of its field of vision, but that is surely no reason why a choreographer should rob himself of the contrapuntal possibilities inherent in setting off a solo dance by movement in counterpoint in the background. This device prevents the audience from having an uninterrupted view either of the soloist or the group, but provided it has been employed with skill and discretion a striking effect is often obtainable. In most of Massine's ballets the device is used quite frequently, perhaps at times too frequently. Ashton also employs it sparingly but to rich purpose.

There seems to me to be a further flaw in the argument, although not perhaps a surprising flaw when one remembers that Balanchine is a skilled musician. Very few music-lovers are able to identify all the strands of sound in a symphony orchestra, but that inability does not prevent them from enjoying the combined effect of that sound just as much as the next man. Similarly, although the eye can focus to its best effect only on a certain small area, the content of that area, when transmitted by the optic nerve to the mental and emotional processes, is strongly conditioned by what lies just beyond its fringes.

In his employment of the limited vocabulary of classical dance Balanchine achieves variety by extensions and even distortions of the *pas* to such an extent that Petipa, and sometimes even Fokine, would certainly fail to recognize the original of many a Balanchinesque pose or figure. In this way he has not only obtained variety but, infinitely more important, has played a major part in keeping classical ballet in close touch with contemporary life and with the character of the great nation he has adopted as his own. In this achievement he is foremost among all choreographers in employing the pause, the silence of the dance, and immobility, as well as the richly inventive *enchaînements* of classical *pas* which form the recognized stamp of practically all his work.

A ballet which deals with a highly topical theme may be as out of touch with contemporary life as *Giselle* or *The Sleeping Beauty*, for the treatment of the theme is what counts in ballet, not the theme itself. Balanchine can take a theme from a classical model to produce a work in perfect harmony with twentieth-century style, impetus and rhythm. He rarely uses idiosyncratic gesture, but could anything more clearly typify one aspect of contemporary America than the opening movement of *Bourrée Fantasque*? The slick, humorous, sophisticated tension between girl and boy epitomizes a particular aspect of the American character as surely as a short story by O. Henry.

In only one ballet has Balanchine used native subject-matter, *Alma Mater*, a ballet with which, judging by the reports, he was not in sympathy himself, yet much of his work is a skilfully-dressed window for the display of American youth at its best. Interested in the dancer as an instrument for the expression of his own ideas, he yet glorifies the human body in general; at the same time, by creating especially for the particular qualities of certain dancers he is able to express individual style and character without depending upon any conscious predisposition of the executant in the achievement of characterization. That is why it so often happens that a Balanchine ballet performed by new soloists completely loses its point.

In a self-sufficient and purely arbitrary reconstruction of the music into his own visual terms, Balanchine frequently stresses formal pattern to the exclusion of expression. Indeed, he himself has stated, although it must not be held against him too strongly, for it was in answer to a question following a lecture and made to give point to a particular remark, that he does not know what people mean by emotion in dancing. In certain

works the activity on the stage becomes more like a demonstration of eurhythmics than a ballet. Frequently, too, the movements of the dancers appear to be quite inappropriate to the
music. In some of his work, set to the flowing, tranquil music
of eighteenth-century composers, the dancers, making a step
to accompany every note, at times limp around the stage in a
manner quite alien to the smooth persuasion and rippling line
of the score. Despite his acknowledgment of the value of the
pause he often forces his dancers to continue a restless wave of
movement which, like a Henry James sentence, goes on and on,
to be stopped by nothing but shortage of breath.

The ballet which most clearly marks Balanchine's first
period, although he had already composed some successful
works beforehand, is *Apollo*. This first saw light in 1928, when
it was known as *Apollon Musagète*, a title it retained for some
years. Nijinsky, Nijinska and Massine, the choreographers who
preceded Balanchine in the Diaghilev company, had diluted
and even at times rejected the classical technique. In doing so
they undoubtedly enriched the scope of ballet both as to its
thematic material and its expressive power. On the other hand
an art must die unless its fundamental laws are from time to
time restated in a new way. This re-statement came at the
psychological moment from Balanchine in *Apollo*, which in my
opinion yet remains the most outstanding example of all his
creations, as well as the first in which he made a new claim for
the *danse d'école* phrased in twentieth-century idiom. In this
ballet he revived classical dance in all its purity, yet with a
difference which identifies it from the Petipa *enchaînements*
as clearly as a modern automobile stands out against an Old
Crock. The difference is difficult to explain only because we
are concerned in *Apollo* with a flow of steps, many of which are
almost identical in shape and pattern, for this was before
Balanchine began his wholesale modification of classical *pas*. But
whereas Petipa built up his dances, joining appropriate
figures together, skilfully allowing ample contrast, with plenty
of rests in the form of arabesques, Balanchine concerned himself, and at his best still does concern himself, with the
impetus of the dance itself, allowing the figures more or less to
dictate themselves by necessity out of the momentum of his
dancers in their response to his own reaction to the music. In

addition to this, Balanchine provides an occasional surprise in his choreography by changing the impetus of the dance and starting off a flow of images in a different direction. Like Petipa he invents new figures in keeping with the classical vocabulary; also like him he interpolates such figures partly for the purpose of providing the dance with a new impulse, and partly to suggest some particular character or quality to further a slender plot.

In *Apollo*, for instance, the intertwining of the charioteers with the Three Muses evokes an intense feeling of expansive movement in limitless space. In this work Balanchine had to employ a certain amount of mime, but obviously sought to dispense with it as soon as his slender literary theme had been made as clear as necessary for the development of his true theme —the dynamic growth of dancing into a series of climaxes fully satisfying in their own right. After he had conducted the first performance, Stravinsky said: 'Balanchine has arranged the dances exactly as I had wished, in accordance with the classical school.' It was the first attempt to revive academic dancing in a work actually composed for the purpose.

In Delos the nymph Leto gives birth to Apollo. He is given a lyre and Three Muses appear, each presumably to endow the young god with her especial quality. Apollo presents one with a scroll of verse, the second with a theatre mask and the third with a lyre, after which he leads them into a flowing *pas de quatre*. This completed, he singles out his favourite Muse, Terpsichore, for a special *pas de deux* and then all four leave for Parnassus. This last scene is presented in the form of a charioteer holding the reins of his three horses, who cavort through space in what was, to me, the most thrilling *pas de quatre* of my experience. In it, apart from the unceasing flow of striking movement and wonderful poses, the hands of the dancers, symbolizing the reins, remain joined in an early, and perhaps the best, example of the well-known Balanchine *penchant*, evident in so many of his ballets, for hand and arm convolutions.

The birth scene is handled with perfect taste and skill. At the rise of the curtain Leto is seen on a rug in highly stylized birth pangs, which Edwin Denby has aptly described as 'Tossing grandly to and fro in the labour of a goddess'. In a flash Apollo appears in swaddling clothes, from which, with two nymphs holding the end, he frees himself by means of multiple *pirouettes*.

With his lyre he plays his early uncertain melodies and the three Muses are attracted to him. Their first efforts are stilted and halting, but inspired by the young Apollo's gifts, each soon unfolds her latent powers. The first girl abounds in lightness and ethereality, the second in imperious spirit and control, and the third, Terpsichore, in a magnificent epitome of the very soul of the goddess of dance. Her solo is matched and contrasted by *Apollo* in a purely masculine *enchaînement* which is itself brought to a perfect conclusion by an Apollo-Terpsichorean *pas de deux* of a delicate amorousness punctuated by arabesques. Then all three Muses and Apollo gradually build up the climax into the wonderful chariot drive of which I have already spoken, reaching Parnassus in what is perhaps a slight anticlimax, for surely such a momentum of dance should itself bring down the curtain, not the comparatively earth-bound movements that do actually form the conclusion.

The powerful yet subtle contrasts in the various dances, the driving force of the full pattern of purely classic figures, the ever-changing rhythms, so finely in tune in their visual and aural relationships, and the flowing inventiveness of the imagery were, in 1928, far in advance of their time. As a consequence the ballet was badly treated by audience and critics alike. But later, both in North America and in England, post-war audiences perceived something of its wonder. On this side of the Atlantic we had a few glimpses of it in 1946, when Ballet Theatre filled a memorable season at Covent Garden. I have not seen it since, but still hold it in higher esteem than most other Balanchine productions.

Long residence in the U.S.A. has naturally exerted a strong influence on Balanchine's style without blunting the choreographer's own neo-classical approach. Indeed, this approach has recently become more marked than ever, for the rapid tempo of American life, together with its frantic adulation of streamlined and athletic young womanhood, has naturally affected his work. The flowing patterns and irresistible impetus of his compositions remain as powerful as ever, but the emotional stress, such as there is, is essentially a product of the New World.

The ballets are mostly original in their arrangement of steps and in their groupings and poses. But this originality is

In her own ballet *Les Algues*. JANINE CHARRAT

Gemze de Lappe and James Mitchell in *Gold Rush*, one of the
works in the repertory of the Agnes de Mille Dance Theatre.
This particular ballet is from the musical play *Paint Your Wagon*.

AGNES DE MILLE

of such a nature as only the most ardent ballet-goer can detect, much less appreciate. For the rest the variety is determined by the music. Whether composing to Tchaikovsky's Serenade for Strings or Bizet's Symphony in C, Balanchine appears to have sought no other end but a visual counterpoint to the score, and the rhythm is therefore determined by the score.

As is to be expected in works of this kind, actual choreographic humour is scarce. But that is not to accuse them of an overwhelming seriousness, for quite often the tremendous and joyous agility of the dancers stimulates an audience into a joyous response. In fact, even in his most grave passages Balanchine can rarely be accused of heaviness or portentous solemnity.

When he does break into humour he usually discovers a delightful little choreographic joke. I will content myself with one example; the opening movement of *Bourrée Fantasque*, in which the soloist (Tanaquil Leclerq during the 1950 performance of the ballet in England) steps prettily over her partner's foot and accompanies him in what I can describe only as a short series of chuckling fragments.

Happier in *allegro* than *adagio*, Balanchine excels, with the occasional lapse I have already mentioned, when composing to the rapid and flowing passages such as occur frequently in the seventeenth and early eighteenth century composers. In *Symphonie Concertante* (Mozart), for instance, the cadenzas of the violin and viola were brilliantly put into visual terms, whereas the solo movement in the same score betrays an unfelicitous lack of response.

Of Balanchine's two works in the English repertory, *Ballet Imperial* and *Trumpet Concerto*, the former is as important as the latter is trivial. *Ballet Imperial* had first been mounted on an American company, but it is hard to imagine such a work being performed as well anywhere outside England. In keeping with its title the work possesses an imperial flavour, the dances and gestures demanding a regality and courtly grace which stem from the traditions and ceremonies of a monarchy. The opening, wherein two lines of dancers, male and female, acknowledge each other by bow and courtesy, establishes the atmosphere. What follows is a geometrical pattern of dance, involuting, convoluting, circling and entwining. When boredom threatens, a fragment of solo dance or a little quirk of striking movement appears, and we are once again ready for the geometry of a group in flowing classical dance. Highlights are the dances of the two ballerinas; each has a solo and a *pas de deux*, and each has a distinctive style, the one smooth and romantic, the other abrupt and with liberal distortion of the classical ideal. In the English production of this ballet insufficient stress has been put on the contrast between these two dances. Tchaikovsky's Piano Concerto, on which the ballet is constructed, bountifully plays its part in urging and supporting the flow and rhythm of the dance pattern. Very clearly does the ballet demonstrate the difference between the approach to the ally of music by an advanced twentieth-century choreographer and that of Petipa. At no time so far as we are now able to detect did Petipa concern himself with the orchestral fabric of the score, nor even as a rule with its rhythm, but only with its beat and melody. Balanchine on the other hand goes to the heart of the music and seeks a parallel to its architectural form.

When he made *Trumpet Concerto* Balanchine must have lacked inspiration. Haydn's score is certainly a surprise choice for a ballet; having chosen it the choreographer ought to have respected its special flavour instead of imposing upon it a mock drill-square hotchpotch comprised of girls in pill-box hats and typical music hall conceptions of military habiliment for chorus girls. Well though they performed their unaccustomed and dreary task of going through routines more suitable for the 'Television Toppers', the outdoor music, the banal costumes and unimaginative dance arrangements quite defeated the young dancers. My most acute recollection of the fiasco is that of Beriosova, pill-box askew, wasting her unique style upon a variation that was so hackneyed as to be embarrassing.

But at the beginning of 1954 Balanchine had made over eighty ballets; some of them had naturally fallen below the high standard he has set for himself. Even so it did seem a pity that such a dismal failure should be inflicted upon the young Sadler's Wells Theatre Ballet. The Balanchinian brand of neo-classicism, with its stress on the flowing, vital energy of youth, would, I thought, have been especially suited to them.

One of Balanchine's greatest works is *Concerto Barocco*, which is performed to Bach's Double Violin Concerto. From the brisk opening, through the *adagio*, right to the *allegro* the style is consistent within brilliant contrasts of dance pattern and remarkable transmutations in pulse and impetus. The usual small but non-stop chorus keeps pace with Bach throughout, and provides a series of formal patterns in which great emphasis is made on striking arm movements as well as the frequent 'broken' line so typical of the neo-classical school. The supported dance of the ballerina features those lifts in *arabesque* in which her partner transports her slowly across the stage in ascending and descending arcs. These aerial figures have a breathtaking quality that takes one soaring with the music into space. In such a composition as this there is more exciting dance, more brilliant exploitation of the classical technique to harness the animal energy of brilliant young American dancers, than in any other single ballet to come to England from across the Atlantic.

In all his abstractions Balanchine employs the same means to obtain subtle differences. Sometimes these differences are so slight that large sections of each audience find no difference at all, and accuse him of wholesale plagiarism of his own work. Sometimes, as in *Serenade*, he adds a flavour of personal romance to his dance content, in keeping with the Tchaikovsky score; and at other times, as in *Symphony in C*, he stresses nothing but the glittering brilliance, the fluent power, the godlike rather than human qualities of the classical technique.

At intervals Balanchine comes down from the turrets of his classical castle and indulges in his own special kind of dance-drama. Then there is no limit to the extent to which he will temporarily renounce classicism. In such works as *The Prodigal Son* and *Orpheus*, for example, he employs a compound of semi-naturalistic movement and highly stylized gesture. *Orpheus* slowly builds up its ritualistic atmosphere, its great drama in which earthbound boys and girls convince us that they are creatures from some Olympus of the mind, by means of a combined onslaught from Stravinsky, Balanchine and Noguchi. Incredulity and disbelief are swept aside in a series of slow majestic movements and symbols which make dreams more real than reality.

Yet another and equally rare diversion for the leader of the neo-classicists is to devise a work based on a fairly strong theme out of a number of dance styles. Perhaps the most readily

remembered example is *Night Shadow*. The most percipient
criticism of this ballet I have read came from Annabel Farjeon
in 'The New Statesman and Nation'. This criticism is not of the
original production, but of a performance by the same company
(de Cuevas) in 1954 with Marjorie Tallchief now in the role
created by Ethery Pagava:

> . . . the choreography is, saving one *pas de deux*, wonderfully
> dull. This dullness comes partly from taking a collection of
> now stock figures and situations, which have become almost
> traditional in contemporary romantic ballets. There are
> for basis the ballroom dancers. . . .
> . . . there is the frustrated poet in love with someone else's
> soulful wife or fiancée, and in the background are those
> deadly old ruins that veer from Doric pillars to the
> Victorian Gothic. In the case of Balanchine's ballet these
> romantic props serve as equipment for a sort of academic
> exercise on the theme, and it is not until the soulful girl
> appears in her nightgown, sleep-walking, that there is
> suddenly an individual kind of inspiration.

This is a perfect summing up, although I myself feel it
necessary to enlarge on that 'individual kind of inspiration'.
The sleepwalker enters on points and sustains the longest passage in the whole repertory of ballet of *pas de bourrées sur les
pointes*. With a candle in her hand, fixed facial expression, and
body that sways gently into the direction of her movement, she
wafts to and fro around the stage as though urged by gentle
eddies of air. Her lover, fearful lest he might wake her, stands
in her way. She changes direction without apparent effort. He
lies down and puts out an arm. She steps over it. He gently
turns her round; she continues into a delicate series of pirouettes.
It all sounds so simple in construction, yet it is a dance that
moves and excites, building up a sense of pathos and even
tragedy. Perhaps Balanchine was content to employ his conventional props and background as a frame for this remarkable
dance. Had he sought a more imaginative background *Night
Shadow* would perhaps have been a great ballet instead of
remaining memorable only for this one passage.

Not all of Balanchine's enormous choreographic output has
been concerned with high theatrical art. Like most American
choreographers he has found expression in films and in musical

plays—and on one occasion he is said to have made a circus ballet for sixty elephants in pink panties. Occasionally for the cinema he has produced a ballet of great and lasting quality, as in the *Romeo and Juliet* and *Water Lily* items in 'Goldwyn Follies of 1938'. In fact in 1937 he said:

> It is mainly because of its purely imaginative—I would even say artificial—quality that ballet is important for motion pictures. It introduces a completely imaginative world whose form is of an imaginative life. This for me is the realm of complete fantasy. It has its own laws, its own meaning, and cannot be explained by the usual criteria of logic. On the other hand, the possibilities opened by motion pictures for the classic ballet are of even greater importance and interest.

Those few words, I think, epitomize a whole philosophy towards both ballet itself and towards the relationship between ballet and the cinema.

Another aspect of Balanchine's work which I always find rather surprising is his occasional revision of old works. *Firebird, Swan Lake* (Act II), and more recently *Casse-Noisette* have all been subjected to his renovation. His efforts with *Swan Lake* aroused no small controversy, but it was a controversy over nothing, for the purists were as usual absurd in their insistence that the work should be left in its pristine form. As though it ever had been! What Balanchine had done with this revision was to invest the dance content with his own special brand of vitality and to give the newly arranged dances themselves a twentieth-century impetus. If the second act of *Swan Lake* is justified in isolation from the other acts—and I think it is—his is certainly the most interesting version.

Like the unceasing flow of his own *enchaînements* Balanchine's work continues. The question now is, will he be blessed with new inspiration or will he degenerate into a constant reiteration of a mere formula? Already at times it has seemed that he was inventing rather than creating, that we had seen all that he was now presenting so many times before. But then he has given us something fresh, still firmly established in his own style, with an entirely new if subtle change in its dance content. There is no reason why he should not surprise and delight us, and bore us and delight us again, for many long years.

CHAPTER FIVE

Serge Lifar

THE GUIDING PRINCIPLES on which Balanchine and Lifar have founded their theories are in direct opposition to each other. 'The choreographer cannot invent rhythms, he only reflects them in movement,' says Balanchine. Whereas Lifar urges with equal certainty, 'Musical rhythm is born of dancing rhythm.' By a little painstaking comparison between the stated theories of the two choreographers one can place side by side two long lists of such diametrically opposed statements. The reason is not far to seek: Lifar has rebelled against the classical tradition, whereas Balanchine has sought only to follow and enlarge it.

Lifar has expressed himself on paper at length and with clarity. In common with the work of other creative artists in various media his practical examples sometimes contradict his theories, but that by no means invalidates the theories themselves. Most widely known and most often misinterpreted is his alleged assertion that ballet should not be accompanied by music. In fact what he did assert, in writing, after a fruitless and inconclusive argument to show that rhythm was born of dance, was: 'The true accompaniment of Dancing is not music, but its rhythmic pattern'.

As an apt example Lifar quotes the effect of a strongly marked march or valse of indifferent quality upon the majority of men in comparison with the effect of similar rhythm in symphonic form. Everyone who has marched behind a military band will concede Lifar his first point. On the assumption that the richer the musical quality of a score the weaker its rhythmic power on the human body, he assails the Balanchine palisade more vigorously by concluding that there can never be an exact relationship between danced movement and music. It is possible to dance to the accompaniment of music, but it is not possible to dance music itself.

From these premises Lifar develops his theory that the choreographer (a poor word for which he substitutes the more correct 'choreauthor'), if he seeks to be truly creative and not bound by other men's children, must compose his own rhythms. The imposition of his own rhythms by the musical composer upon the creator of the dance he regards as despotic bondage. In complete contrast to Balanchine he urges that the composer of dance must create the rhythms of his dance images, otherwise they are not his own original images at all. In his support it is well to remember that Stravinsky has admitted to the discovery of certain rhythms by a close observation of human movements. Perhaps by quoting such a composer one puts up too rude a finger at Balanchine, and it is therefore only fair to add that Stravinsky in no way implied that he had taken any sustained rhythmic inspiration from human movement. Nevertheless Lifar's firm belief that the choreographer must be free to invent, unrestricted by a musical framework, will win the sympathy of all creative artists who know what it is to be shackled by restrictions set up by human agency.

Unlike many professional apostles of the dance, who make wildly extravagant claims to the effect that theirs is an art which by far excels all others, Lifar states with the utmost rationalism: 'It would be foolish to say that one art is more beautiful than another, one can only like it more or less.' He then develops an argument against any attempt through dance to tell a story, convey ideas or to express various shades of emotion. The greater the power of any form of expression to interpret everything, the greater the weakness of that form to express the strongest reactions. 'Human speech can interpret everything, but how restricted it becomes when it has to express emotion.' On the other hand dance can express far more vividly the simplest and strongest emotions.

Lifar is on safe ground here, for his argument is easy to demonstrate. Although he does not quote it, the best example can surely be given from a child who, after all, has not yet been conditioned, and therefore repressed, by a multitude of social conventions. When the child wishes to express a really overbearing emotion of joy or anger it jumps or stamps, thus expressing its feelings in rudimentary dance form with far greater force than if it tried to interpret these reactions by means of words. Without necessarily agreeing with him one can easily understand Lifar's belief that poetry is a dying art, by virtue of the fact that it can interpret so much but is yet unable to express adequately the strongest emotions. Here, as others including myself have done, he quotes one of the finest of the Noverre axioms:

> A step, a gesture, a movement and an attitude express what no words can say: the more violent the sentiments it is required to depict, the less able is one to find words to express them. Exclamations, which are the apex to which the language of the passions can reach, become insufficient and have to be replaced by gesture.

Quite clearly and unambiguously Lifar makes his case for the justification of a ballet—the new ballet—free from musical accompaniment, adding that whether it be musical or non-musical it must be born of its own sources and not of music.

In this connection he urges that if music is to be employed the composer must construct his score in accordance with the rhythms and dance plans laid down by the choreographer. In his 'Manifeste du Choregraphe' Lifar perhaps puts his case so strongly as to invite misinterpretation, but since then he has reaffirmed time and time again that he is fighting tooth and nail not against the presence of musicians in the pit of the ballet theatre, but against the domination of the composer over the true creator of the ballet. He holds that a dance, whether of short or long duration, should be built up on definite rhythmic patterns, which recur from time to time.

Lifar first attempted to free his creative processes from the bonds of music in 1935, when his *Icare* made its bow before an astonished audience. The actual choreographic structure of this work is founded in the classical technique, although already Lifar had begun to condition the idiom with the angular, staccato movements and postures which now feature in most of his work. *Icare* is another of those essays in choreography which have faded from the memory, so that critical discussion on it is no longer possible. But undoubtedly in *Icare* Lifar did demonstrate some of his theories. That the composer of the musical score should necessarily impose the rhythm of the actual dance steps upon the choreographer is clearly invidious; obviously a dance movement is inseparable from its rhythm and the choreographer must therefore be responsible for the creation of that rhythm. If this responsibility were reapportioned the already thin ranks of choreographers would surely be reduced yet further, for today, still under the influence of the dance conditions provided for ballet in the seventeenth, eighteenth and nineteenth centuries and leading to its logical conclusion in the Petipa-Tchaikovsky era, there remains an overwhelming tendency to depend completely upon music for this structural function.

But *Icare* by no means represented an attempt to divorce ballet from music. The ideal, it seems to Lifar, is for the composer of the music to work to rhythms and rhythmic patterns supplied to him by the choreographer in the form of created movement. The one weakness of this theory, as I see it, is that the whole must always be greater than the sum of the parts and that the addition of the music to the choreographer's composition will transform, for better or for worse, the actual choreographic creation—or at least the effective power of that creation. Further, the musical accompaniment must surely condition the actual interpretation of the executants. Perhaps, as Lifar hints, the only complete answer is for the choreographer to serve as his own composer; but that is a solution which is at present as unpractical as it is, in one way, idealistic, despite the fact that in earlier but less highly specialized days the two elements were frequently produced by one brain. In the absence of such a state of affairs, the most serious obstacle is to persuade the composer of the musical score to construct his work upon a given rhythmic plan. Even if he is prepared to renounce the primacy of music in its relationship with dancing, a further obstacle remains against the perfect fusion of the two elements: how is the choreographer to explain to his collaborator the subtleties of atmosphere and nuances of expression which each particular phrase is intended to convey? Tchaikovsky accepted almost without question the dictatorship of Petipa, but in that great period of classical ballet the sentimental appeal of a Valse, the gaiety of a Mazurka and the various other rhythms and *tempi* laid down were adequate for the uninhibited but superficial appeal to the emotions of these ballets. Today both the choreographic and the musical approach are vastly different; whatever the method of composition a far closer understanding between choreographer and composer is required.

Incidentally, although balletomanes speak glibly of Noverre

it does not seem to be generally known that he adopted an even more dictatorial attitude towards the great Gluck than Petipa did towards Tchaikovsky. Noverre first worked out in suitable detail the plot and scheme to provide for dramatic development and an appropriate interpolation of set dances. Then he stated the movement and gestures by which he could best interpret the various characters. Not until he had completed these stages did he commission the music. In consultation with Gluck he then outlined the steps, gestures, movements and attitudes of his characters.

Laying down a set of general principles for the collaboration between choreographer and composer, Noverre, in his 'Lettres sur la Danse et sur le Ballet', wrote:

> Owing to the intimate affinity between music and dancing, there can be no doubt, sir, that a *maître de ballet* will derive marked advantage from a practical knowledge of this art. He will be able to communicate his thoughts to the composer and, if he join a bent for music, he will write the music himself or supply the composer with the principal qualities which should characterise his work; this being expressive and varied, the dance cannot fail to be so in its turn.

Lifar holds, however, without any fear of serious contradiction, that in common with music, 'Dancing cannot be narrative'. It can be a 'fragment independent of every other art, it can be a dance poem and it can be part of a spectacular production'.

The author of 'Manifeste du Choregraphe' tends at times to express his theories in unnecessarily complicated terms and to draw red herrings across his trail in the form of inappropriate comparisons. His exposition of the expressive scope of ballet, as I interpret it, however, seems quite clearly to be that dancing cannot be ultimately used to illustrate another art, and that it remains fundamentally opposed to any kind of programme. The original motive force behind any act of collusion, according to Lifar, is the reaction the artist experiences when in contact with 'an object, a phenomenon of life or art'. Following that initial impetus he creates a dance which bears a relationship to the original source of inspiration only by having an emotional equivalence with it. '. . . I know for certain that I illustrate nothing.' He states that without the programme of one of his ballets the spectator would consider the work purely aṣ a piece of effective dance and would never know the nature of the original source. *A propos* this vexed question of the programme note Lifar believes that it need consist of one word only—the title. Here he appears to be in rare agreement with Balanchine.

That the foregoing statement should be made by the creator of such works as *Chola Roustavelli* and *Salomé* is somewhat extraordinary, but choreographers are not the only artists to say one thing and do another. It is also as well to remember that Lifar is not always so unfaithful to his own dicta. He admirably sums up his own notions as to suitable themes in the following sentence:

> Dancing can be an unfettered, pure, self-sufficient work (in the same way that music can be written without programme; for instance, trios, quartets, sonatas and so on) but it can also be a single action, a drama, a ballet.

His next point is one with which surely everyone will be in agreement, but which nobody—nobody at least on this side of the Iron Curtain—appears to have done very much about: the training and education of the choreographer. Lifar benefited from the teaching of Cecchetti and Diaghilev; the former taught him to dance and the latter steeped him in a general artistic environment. Lifar holds that just as there are classes in harmony, counterpoint and orchestration, so should there be properly organized instruction in every aspect of choreography. Ballet masters and writers on ballet throughout history have urged the founding of an Academy of Choreography. Now Lifar adds his plea. Yet what has been done? In England it seems that only a few pioneers, and they mostly advocates and disciples of expressionistic dance, have attempted to form a curriculum and actually lay down any fundamental principles. In the U.S.A. more has been done. The results are evident in the work of such choreographers as Michael Kidd, Jerome Robbins and John Taras, who have benefited from the choreographic teachings of Balanchine.

On mime, Lifar subscribes to what is today a generally accepted theory. He does not admit mime or pantomime as legitimate elements of ballet except in so far as they are an actual and integral part of the dance itself. With Fokine and others he agrees that the whole body must dance, the face included, and that the contribution made by the various parts of the body must be in harmony one with the other. For his own purposes Lifar divides gestures into three kinds: those unconscious gestures which we make when we attempt to describe a feeling or something beyond the accurate descriptive power of speech; those which are conscious and mechanical, such as the gestures of craftsmen, and finally the conventional and allegorical gestures which can by tradition express various things but yet have no true link with what they express. Lifar considers the first of these kinds of gestures richest in choreographic possibilities, but warns choreographers that such gestures can heighten only the emotional quality of their work and cannot be employed for descriptive purposes. The second category of gestures Lifar permits should theoretically be given restricted play; obviously they have their uses, but are too lacking in creative and affective power to possess much value. The third category Lifar dismisses out of hand. He asserts, and I think his argument in this case is incontrovertible, that the audience need only to understand the symbol always to conjure up the same image—in the same way presumably that one would use a deaf and dumb alphabet. Dealing with this sign language at some length Lifar demands its expulsion from ballet of the twentieth century.

Up to this stage Lifar has made use of Noverre quotations to support and even advance his own theories. Now, however, he joins issue with his eighteenth-century predecessor. He says: 'I turn with genuine sorrow the pages where he relegates dancing to second place and refers to our technique with contempt.' He then quotes from the letter in which Noverre has called upon the Child of Terpsichore to renounce *cabrioles*, *entrechats*, and over-complicated steps. Lifar reacts here as any twentieth-century choreographer would react upon being threatened with the serious impoverishment of his vocabulary. He says:

> Dancing, embellished with feeling and acted by talent, will at last receive that praise and applause which all Europe accords to poetry and painting and the glorious rewards with which they are honoured.

Lifar attempts a twentieth-century solution to the problem of the interaction of mime with dance either by providing an element of dance in the recitative or by giving dramatic expression to the dance itself.

> Without any doubt or regret I exclude pantomime so far as it is an independent part, or a *narrative*, part of the art of dancing. I leave to it its sole means of sculptural and plastic expression, of miming with the whole body—with the eyes, features, hands, arms, as well as the legs. But from this moment pantomime becomes an integral part of dancing and sheds its importance and its own existence . . . everything that I can express I express in dancing, rejecting all means which are not the appanage of my art. 'In the beginning was dancing'—such is the Alpha and Omega of my dance creed.

In practice, as I have already said, Lifar has not always followed his theories. Some of his ballets which we saw through the vehicle of the New Monte Carlo Ballet in 1946 provided only a mixture of middle-period Diaghilev with a large element of the more athletic figures of the classical technique, and frequent distortions of that technique.

During that season Lifar also produced a long work—it lasted three hours—entitled *Chota Roustavelli*. This was based on a twelfth-century epic from Georgia in which Chota Roustavelli transforms himself into Taniel, the hero of one of his own poems, in order to play out his own imagined adventures for the lady by whom he is inspired. This ballet was undoubtedly far too long: although containing passages of choreographic ingenuity and imaginative power, it depended structurally far too much on repetition and tasteless virtuosity. Throughout Lifar appeared to be denying several of his own vehemently declared principles, for time and time again it became necessary for him to try in balletic terms to describe concrete ideas, despite a programme note of inordinate length.

The music was interesting even if ballet-lovers did find large chunks of it cacophonous. Lifar selected extracts from Honegger, Tcherepnine and Hansanyi and then imposed his own rhythms on them, marking these rhythms very clearly, chiefly by percussive effects. Unfortunately, although the score did achieve occasional heights of vitality and passion, all too frequently it suffered by the obvious superimposition of extraneous rhythms. One of the most effective fragments of the ballet, indeed, was a brief *pas de deux* danced by Serge Lifar himself and Olga Adabashe, accompanied only by the spoken words of the poem.

Accepting the classical repertory, Lifar uses it as a basis on which to develop his own series of original movements. Approaching the subject of choreography from such different angles, Lifar and Balanchine have this in common: each employs the classical technique and distorts it to his own ends. Lifar, however, normally produces a more angular and emphatic pattern of movement, whereas Balanchine seeks extreme fluency. Partly this difference can be explained by the fact that Balanchine depends upon the flow of the music for his structure and Lifar usually composes his own rhythms before devising a series of steps on those rhythms. But over and above this, the contrast in the character of the two men is responsible for the fundamental antagonism between their principles. Lifar has never known a certain and settled life; his early experience with Diaghilev, awakening him artistically, by no means conduced to his emotional stability. Then, in the war years, under German occupation, he must have known even greater instability. His works, like those in every other medium by artists who were personally affected by the war, express the age of anxiety in which we live. Balanchine, on the other hand, has not been so directly affected and his work, growing ever more and more American in concept, remains largely escapist in its aim. And why not? Ballet would be far less rich in theatrical value if all choreographers aimed consistently at achieving that catharsis to which the classical tragic playwright aspired; Lifar would be greater if he occasionally gave way to a less intense approach to his art and acquired a sense of humour.

Unfortunately very few of his original creations have been seen in England. Since his brief adventure with the New Monte Carlo Ballet he has remained with the Paris Opéra. It can hardly be denied that he has failed to fulfil his early promise; I strongly believe that Diaghilev would have brought him to complete artistic maturity and Diaghilev's death undoubtedly aggravated the impressionable young man's feeling of insecurity. Of his more recent works at the Opéra there has been such a wide difference of opinion and much acrimonious abuse by persons who are influenced by political and alleged patriotic considerations at least as much as by questions of artistic quality, that judgment is difficult. *Snow White and the Seven Dwarfs*, produced in 1951, although too long and breaking several of Lifar's own laid-down principles, possesses great charm and appealing movement as well as a suggestion of whimsical characterization.

I believe I am almost alone, at any rate among those who have committed themselves to print on the subject, in an admiration for Lifar's *Romeo and Juliet*. When first seen in London in 1946 this ballet was harshly condemned because the dancers failed to keep time with the beat of the music. Yet it seemed to me that Lifar successfully worked out his own rhythms and therefore his own movements, in sympathy with the strongly pronounced moods of the score. Had he continually bent himself to the existing rhythms of Tchaikovsky the choreographer would surely have weakened his own contribution. During long passages there was no departure of the dance rhythms from the musical rhythms, but at certain points the choreographer threw off the shackles in order to assert his own rhythms.

Whatever else may be said of it, *Romeo and Juliet* does demonstrate several Lifar theories; Tchaikovsky has built up his score on the various climaxes, both dramatic and emotional, of the play; Lifar has followed the same procedure, with the result that the ballet expresses certain fundamental emotions in choreographic terms created out of rhythms dictated not by the composer but by the choreographer himself.

Lifar the choreographer has not very much accomplishment behind him. But Lifar the pioneer has left a manifesto which will be studied by endless future students of choreography. Perhaps it would not be wise for every choreographer to attempt to shake himself free of music, but until some followers of Lifar can provide outstanding examples of the creation of their own rhythms, then choreography must remain a junior partner to music instead of its equal. Already one example is in being, created by David Lichine.

CHAPTER SIX

David Lichine

ALL THE CHOREOGRAPHERS we have discussed so far came under the direct influence of Diaghilev. They are the pioneers of twentieth-century choreography. They have based their work with varying degrees of vitality and dependence on the style of Petipa; they have developed ballet through a number of new and fascinating experiments; they have produced a few master works of some longevity and a vast quantity of ephemera of priceless value to the ultimate achievement of choreographic maturity.

Lichine is the first of the Russians to develop outside the direct influence of Diaghilev. His dance training did not begin until 1926, his first ballet, *Nocturne*, being presented in 1933. As he joined de Basil even before the actual birth of the Original Ballet Russe and stayed with that company throughout its career, however, he was strongly influenced by both Massine and Balanchine. Massine in particular played an important part in his formative years, for he played in several key roles of a diverse nature in the Massine series created for the de Basil company. This probably accounts in large measure for Lichine's eclecticism, for his rapid switches from intellectualism and occasional obscurity to gay and infectious humour. It also accounts for certain stylistic and constructional similarities between the work of Massine and Lichine, but never has Lichine been dominated by anyone to such an extent as to shed even a vestige of his own marked and strongly individual creative ability.

He has been anything but loquacious on paper, but from a few brief jottings of his which were published in the September 1947 issue of 'Ballet' it is evident that he suffers even more than his contemporaries from a feeling of artistic insecurity; by which I mean that he sees choreography as the most ephemeral of all arts. Others, not only choreographers, have long recognized that simple and obvious fact, but Lichine appears to me to be one of the few to be seriously affected by such a bitter

Margot Fonteyn as Queen of the Air in *Homage to the Queen*.
FREDERICK ASHTON

A scene from *Checkmate*.

Ninette de Valo

A scene from the television production of *The Dreamers*.

Kenneth Macmillan

thought. 'Choreography is like moisture in the mouth of an orator,' he proclaims. Surely such an image could spring only from one who suffers from morbid reflections on the subject. This desperate impotence to reach forward into posterity must react on his work, especially on his more serious work. Instead of the flowing statement of pure movement which less inhibited, but not in my opinion more creative, choreographers produce, Lichine in several of his serious ballets has resorted to long passages of histrionics and statuesque groups of a rather banal character; as though seeking permanence in a more easily remembered form than the flashing but evanescent stream of limpid dance which at times he produces in exciting variety. Fortunately some of his later works have remained free of such histrionics. Nevertheless most critics remain unimpressed by his work, except perhaps *Graduation Ball*, so beware when I say that I consider him one of the most important figures in post-1945 choreography. It is a considerable source of regret to me that not one of his works has been brought into the repertory of an English company.

The most popular of his ballets is undoubtedly *Graduation Ball*, created for the Original Ballet Russe during that company's long stay in Australia in 1940. This work is developed on one of those heaven-sent themes which absorb the conventions of ballet to such an extent that the audience is hardly aware of them.

The scene is a girls' school on the day of its Graduation Ball; the inmates are preparing to receive the young cadets from a neighbouring military academy. From the outset a delightful atmosphere of romance and humour is built up so that, with the young ladies, we await the arrival of the young male visitors —an arrival which is carried out with full military magnificence. One junior pupil, with a terrified daring, steps forward to gain a closer view of the glamorous uniforms, whereupon as a body the cadets throw up a perfect parade ground salute. At this she collapses and is escorted back to her seat by a cadet who is then persuaded by his colleagues to open the ball. After a shy and tremulous beginning he and his partner swirl into a gay, fast-moving waltz, the others rapidly following suit.

At the end of the dance a series of delightful *divertissements* is presented. A drummer jumps and cavorts with brilliant effect, the little girl performs a piquant impromptu, a 'Giselle and Scotsman' delicately recall the romantic period and there is a dance competition in which two girls in *tutus* vie with each other in *pirouettes* and *fouettés*, the while exhorted to yet greater efforts by their supporters.

Light relief is given full measure by a flirtation between the cadets' commanding officer and the headmistress, with a hilarious mazurka as a highlight, and the curtain is brought down when one of the cadets, having crept back to bid a less communal adieu to his girl, is interrupted by the prowling old beldame.

I have related the scenario only to show how perfectly suitable it is for ballet. Here is one of the few ballets of which no one can well claim that it can be done as successfully in any other medium. The potential charm of ballet is here released to the full. On the other hand, despite the dismissal of the work by various critics on both sides of the Atlantic as a 'delightful trifle' the work is full of subtlety and keen observation. Hints of character appear in almost every part—hints conveyed by the highest possible degree of choreographic skill and originality.

Denmark proved to be more perceptive in connection with this ballet than England, for in 1952 Lichine was commissioned to mount the work for the Royal Danish Ballet. This remarkable company has treated it to an entirely new interpretation without blunting any of the edges of Lichine's perfect form, with the result that they have infused each character with a fresh spirit, thus mingling their essentially Danish conception with the Russo-cosmopolitan original.

Helen of Troy, first presented by Ballet Theatre in 1943, was planned by Fokine as a companion piece to *Bluebeard*, but was eventually composed by Lichine when Fokine became too ill to work on it. In England during the 1946 season of Ballet Theatre at Covent Garden the large majority of English audiences, and the critics, enjoyed *Helen* far more than *Bluebeard*, a fact which provides yet further evidence of the wide differences between English and American humour. Grace Robert, a sound and perceptive critic, refers in 'The Borzoi Book of Ballets' to '. . . low comedy and even burlesque clichés', and concludes her commentary with '. . . elimination of the more obvious low-comedy clichés and line routines would do wonders for it, the basic idea being not without merit'.

Presumably the basic idea was conceived by Fokine, thus leaving Lichine with very little credit. Be that as it may, English audiences displayed a very definite preference for *Helen of Troy* over *Bluebeard*. Certainly the whole work in all its aspects of dance, music, décor and scenario bears a strongly musical comedy flavour, but as in *Graduation Ball* Lichine has found a way to mould material that may well have produced nothing but superficiality into a series of situations well founded in humorous dance. Unfortunately the same people who condemn ballets which attempt to make profound statements, or express sordid subjects, also frequently condemn those which appear at first glance to be more suitable for the light than the ballet stage.

The character of Hermes does, it is true, lean rather heavily towards slapstick and the parody on *L'Après-Midi d'un Faune* is hilarious nonsense that might put a haze round the brilliant choreographic invention which comprises so much of the work. The parts of Paris and Hermes were apparently conceived with Eglevsky and Robbins in mind, for Eglevsky is given a series of solo *pirouettes* and flowing movements with little call for subtle interpretation, while Robbins has been allotted a highly appropriate kind of whimsical humour.

In 1939, employing the same book, music and décor as that upon which Balanchine had worked ten years earlier, Lichine did the *Prodigal Son* for the Original Ballet Russe. It is generally believed that Lichine had not seen the Balanchine version and that he worked upon a quite different choreographic conception. The plot of the ballet benefits by its clarity and Lichine has worked in simple movement and mimetic, rarely delaying the action for the interpolation of any kind of dance. There is, of course, some expressive as well as some exciting dance—no Lichine ballet I have seen is entirely without it—but mostly the situations are rammed home by obvious histrionics. Nevertheless the ballet deserves the popularity it has gained if for no other reason than its freedom from clichés, the startling ingenuity of the Inn episode and the sensational groups which punctuate the scenes.

In 1948 Lichine, now working with Les Ballets des Champs Elysées, departed completely from his previous formula and found sensation without seeking it by presenting a ballet more completely free of music than any so far created by Lifar. *La Création* is performed in utter silence but for the soft scrape of the dancers' slippers on the floor. The stage is bare, with the back wall standing out in an electrically exposed nakedness; inert bodies lie strewn about the floor, clay in the hands of the creator, the choreographer. As he adjusts them, at first with tentative, uncertain fingers, then with growing confidence, they come to life. Gradually their inchoate movement finds form, individual form first, then a co-ordination with others, until they imitate and express the choreographer's ideas. The silence stresses the tensity of the physical rhythms, which are the more sharply defined for being plastic rather than aural in form.

All the movements are based on the classical technique but are mostly stretched and moulded into that acrobatic style in which the young French dancers appear to take delight. This movement develops in individuals, merges into groups and works up in an irresistible legato tempo to complete coherence.

The leading dancers are referred to in the programme as His Uncertainty, His Temptation, His Dual, His Idea, and The Choreographer. Long poles resembling the *barres* used in the ballet classroom are the sole props, and the dancers wear only practice costume. I left the theatre firmly of the opinion that I had witnessed a major choreographic advance. Few of my colleagues were equally enthusiastic, but the 'News Chronicle' stated, 'The work was completely absorbing. The absence of music was a positive relief. It says much for Lichine's technique that this most abstract of ballets should hold a large audience spellbound.'

Beryl de Zoete, writing in 'The New Statesman and Nation', reflected my own reaction: '. . . a silent ballet of such profound and moving beauty as *La Création* has certainly not been seen before.'

Still working with Les Ballets des Champs Elysées, in 1949 Lichine created *La Rencontre*, or *Oedipus and The Sphynx*. This ballet deals imaginatively with the encounter between Oedipus and the Sphynx before the gates of Thebes. It opens with the Sphynx lying on a table, not unlike those employed by stage acrobats, and receiving massage treatment from some attendants. During the famous question time she climbs to another table, raised several feet above the stage, by means of a rope ladder. From that safe height she mouths her riddles to Oedipus who writhes below in an agony of endeavour. Finally a skilfully stylized but sensational struggle takes place between them which concludes with Oedipus hanging dead on the ladder.

Sauget's music and Bérard's décor (his last) add much to the enchantment which this work possesses. Much of Lichine's movement is effective and mysterious, but why does such a talented choreographer resort to the absurdities of naturalistic mime? The sight of the Sphynx melodramatically mouthing her riddles robbed the work for me of much of its excitement.

What Lichine now needs, surely, is that sense of stability which only a well established company can endow. Owing to the scarcity of such companies he, like others, wanders from company to company, producing where he can, always with different dancers and always in stultifying uncertainty as to whether the work will be given a really fair chance of success and survival. He, more than any other among his contemporaries, is in need of a studio, canvas and paints with no fear of being thrown out for at least five years. In that time I am confident that he would produce other works of the calibre of *Graduation Ball* and *La Création*, thus establishing himself with the handful of major choreographers of this century.

CHAPTER SEVEN

Ninette de Valois

D AME NINETTE DE VALOIS has long been one of those figures upon whom the press relies for its less| sensational and more meritorious success stories, as well as for intimate if at times apocryphal anecdotes of the master mind at work. To be chosen as a subject both for a 'New Yorker' and an 'Observer' Profile represents an indisputable accolade of fame.

Yet although de Valois has more than once betrayed her extreme sensitivity to criticism, she has taken these and many other tributes in her stride. Now, in the Crush Bar of the Royal Opera House, she receives both quizzical and adulatory stares with the same equanimity with which she used to receive indifference.

Her tremendous organizing and administrative ability, her enviable and indefatigable Irish pertinacity, her drive and energy are held by all sincere ballet-lovers in the highest possible admiration. Yet many of us, in any assessment of her achievements as a choreographer, have frequently arraigned those very qualities against her. For sometimes, and in certain situations, it does seem that her power to organize and to keep the machinery of creation in motion while the spirit of creation lies dormant, gives much of her work shape and form without emotional significance.To which de Valois' reply, if she bothered to reply at all, would possibly be that genius after all is one per cent inspiration and ninety-nine per cent perspiration. On those grounds she can well lay claim to greatness in each and every one of her endeavours.

De Valois was the first important British choreographer of the twentieth century. Although she never worked under Fokine when he was making a ballet, she did appear in several of his major works as a solo dancer with the Diaghilev company; and with that same company she came directly under the influence of Massine, Nijinska and Balanchine. Her own choreographic development, for she believes strongly in tradition, was therefore established on the classically founded but eclectic style by means of which Diaghilev had given ballet in Europe a new life.

In the flow and impetus of her all too rare dance passages can be traced the influence of Petipa as well as of Fokine and Balanchine. In such passages she focusses attention rigidly and without interruption on the solo dance, just as did those two acknowledged masters of the classical solo, but unlike Balanchine, she never isolates the dance from the dramatic development of the ballet.

In view of the extreme reliance of so many of her works upon a firm literary basis, the expressed opinion of de Valois that music is the foundation of ballet must at first glance appear a trifle strange. It is true that this opinion appeared in her book 'Invitation to the Ballet', published in 1937, and that since then she has publicly renounced certain unspecified theories which she held at the time of writing it. The exercise of great discretion is therefore necessary when summarizing her theories from this book; before doing so one must weigh them against her more recent work to ensure that they have not been supplanted by new and perhaps diametrically opposed theories. But even that method is by no means infallible, for every choreographer of this century—and probably of the past— who expresses his theories on paper seems at some time or other to have run counter to them.

In stating that de Valois still holds the view that music is the choreographer's libretto and that the scenario serves merely as extra or secondary matter for the foundation of her ballets, therefore, I think I am on ground fairly well cleared of mines and booby-traps. Despite their foundation in a strong scenario, her ballets without exception are constructed more firmly on the rhythmic and emotional content of the score than upon dramatic situation.

> As long as the music must precede, guide and act as the inspiration for the choreography, the ballet is not in a position to state that all and everything is at its command.

Here de Valois is apparently in complete agreement with Balanchine, but from this point her approach veers sharply away from his, for whereas Balanchine believes in the construction of a visual parallel to the form of the music, de Valois sees no artistic potentiality whatever in such a parallel. In her argument, to which she brings up heavy artillery reinforcements in the shape of brilliantly written and authoritative statements from Constant Lambert's 'Music Ho!', she admits of no inherent expressive power in the synchronizing of choreographic form with musical form: the establishing of a dancer or group with a particular section of the music and the return of the appropriate visual image whenever that section is repeated does not necessarily imply a real musical interpretation by the choreographer.

The pertinent quotation from Lambert on this point is included in de Valois' attack on abstraction:

> The repetitions of a certain underlying curve in an abstract or representational picture have no dramatic content because they occur in the same moment of time— one's eye can choose which it looks at first, or take in the various statements of the same form simultaneously. But the return of the first subject after development in a symphonic movement has an unavoidable touch of the dramatic simply through the passage of time that has elapsed since its first statement.

Yet this very kind of repetition forms a vital element in the work of such masters of composition as Botticelli and Piero della Francesca. Look, for instance, at the 'Nativity' of Botticelli in the National Gallery; harmonious repetitions of curves, groupings, colour and pattern occur time and time again throughout the picture, just as they do in Piero della Francesca's 'Ascension', which is described by Sir Kenneth Clark as possibly the world's greatest painting.

However, although the repetitions in a picture are perceived at the same moment of time, the repetitions of movements and patterns in a ballet are subject to the same element of time as that which governs music. But whether in painting, music or ballet, this obedience to certain fundamental laws of composition is not in itself sufficient to beget greatness in a work. Even I am capable of composing an *enchaînement*, but I am certainly not capable of infusing that *enchaînement* with all the exciting qualities of a flowing and dynamic pattern of evocative dance. There must be hundreds of students of music who possess a theoretic knowledge of the laws governing harmony and counterpoint, but how many of them ever succeed in writing one single piece of real music? De Valois herself, while relying upon music to dictate the form, style and structure of her dance, then calls upon a well-constructed scenario to assist her in the development of dramatic interest. She says:

> The theatre demands that every art employed in its presentation of the whole should be complete in itself as a harmonic complement to the other parts also engaged in making the whole. This perfection of balance it is the duty of the theatre's artistic director to see, attend and hold, and for each creative artist in his separate sphere technically to grasp and understand.

There are many who maintain that Balanchine has made a virtue out of necessity and that the comparative freedom from décor of his works in the New York City Ballet stresses the dance element and thus raises it to its rightful supremacy. On the other hand, when de Valois, as artistic director rather than choreographer now of course, adds a new work to the Sadler's Wells repertory, she makes sure—at least she has up to now—that it is a fusion of music, dance and décor. She has developed the tradition of British ballet towards this fusion of the various elements and in doing so has in my opinion contributed a great deal towards the improvement of significant art in general.

In her book de Valois gets home with a shrewd blow when she states that the young choreographer frequently loses his head when confronted with the necessity for discipline and adjustment in order to contribute to that perfection of plan between all the elements of a theatrical production. In some forthright comments she states that he is often unable to differentiate 'between the function of the medium and the exploitation of his own ego'.

Nevertheless we must not allow ourselves to grow confused between the ridiculous objection of the inferior artist to work within the accepted conditions of his chosen medium and the rebellion of the genuine creator. Further, the difference between the exploitation, or showing off, of the ego and the sincere expression of the ego which many believe to be the driving force behind all great art, is often divided by a dangerously narrow margin. Leonardo and other renaissance artists maintained that when we draw a man we are really drawing ourselves. De Valois herself has said that the choreographer who has personal experience but little stage work depends too much upon visual stimulation instead of mental and physical application. Yet surely choreography begotten of mental and physical application does actually represent an expression of the physical and mental self: the ego.

The first de Valois ballet, *Les Petits Riens*, was presented to a not unduly impressed public in 1928. From then until 1951 she was responsible for about thirty ballets, as well as for a variety of dance and movement arrangements for stage productions. For the Camargo Society in 1931 she mounted *Création du Monde*. I can remember very little of it except that it contained some highly dramatic movement, that there was a lot of writhing on the floor, that some of the dancers were rather lightly clad, and that one lady, who evidently possessed definite ideas both as to propriety and as to what ballet should be, proclaimed to her companion: 'How extraordinary, and she is such a nice little woman, too!'

In that same year came *Job*, a work in which the de Valois method of composition became both clarified and firmly established. In this ballet—or masque for dancing, as Vaughan Williams called it in his determination to avoid the connotation of 'toe-dancing' which stigmatized ballet at that time—her mimetic style allied to dance based firmly in the classical idiom is clearly demonstrated; as is her dramatic purpose in contrasting the weak with the strong and in presenting an imposing subject. De Valois can I think best be described as having done for ballet what Christopher Marlowe did for drama. Marlowe, by infusing life and passion into the verse that was uttered from the learned stage, became the first great English playwright. De Valois, by welding a few English dancers into a group capable of performing a complex ballet, by moulding classical dance to her own dramatic and creative purpose, became the first English choreographer. The parallel can be taken further. In each of his plays Marlowe took one powerful human passion, greed, ambition, revenge, and embodied it in his protagonist, so that the character was not a living, complex character such as Shakespeare developed, but rather a single personified quality. An examination of certain de Valois ballets, *Job*, *The Rake's*

Progress, Don Quixote, brings to light a similar underlying idea.
In Marlowe, again in contrast to Shakespeare, the conflict in
character was external; there was no turbulence of the spirit;
neither did he possess Shakespeare's 'lightening influence of
humour'. De Valois has, too, been concerned only with the
external conflict; neither has she often demonstrated any
marked sense of humour.

In spite of the fact that Vaughan Williams had proscribed
'toe-dancing' when permitting de Valois to set her work to his
music, the choreographer yet based the dance content firmly in
the idiom of classicism. Nobody interested in the ballet will
need to be told of the sharply changing moods of the music, nor
of its several passages of searching power; but to the heavy
demands of the score de Valois added very definite literary and
even pictorial elements, as though to make doubly sure of
avoiding the dreadful pitfall of the 'exploitation of her own
ego'.

The origin of *Job* lies in Blake's drawings, based on the Book
of Job—or rather in Geoffrey Keynes' long and inspired study
of those drawings. The fact that they have been reproduced in a
special edition of the book is misleading, for they by no means
serve as a mere series of pictures to illustrate incidents in the
story. In the Bible Job becomes embittered under the stress of
what he considers an unjust affliction, whereas the drawings
stress the evil of materialism and complacency. Blake's God
is simply a materialization of blessed humanity, Satan represents false values, and the setting sun symbolizes the darkness of
Job's life. Read what Geoffrey Keynes himself had to say out of
his enthusiasm for the project of a ballet based on the drawings.
I quote from his contribution to 'Job and The Rake's Progress'
in the excellent series of Sadler's Wells Ballet Books edited by
Arnold L. Haskell:

> Yet, long familiarity with the designs convinced me that
> the inner thread of Blake's drama possessed a fundamental
> simplicity—and that if this could be successfully extracted
> it would provide the theme for a ballet of a kind which would
> be new to the English stage. Blake had, moreover, uncon-
> sciously provided in his pictures several settings which could
> be easily adapted for stage scenes, and innumerable
> suggestions in his figures for attitudes and groupings which

cried out for their conversion by a choreographer into actuality and movement.

Thus de Valois had to work with a score which laid down a very definite plan of mood and emotion; she was prohibited from using *pointes*, which to a choreographer trained by Cecchetti must have been almost like compelling Bernard Shaw to write in basic English; the dramatic plan was laid down with little scope for deviation by the drawings; and obviously she must unconsciously, if not consciously, call upon her own reactions to the book itself. Was ever a choreographer before confronted with a task at once so simple because of such a strong foundation and well constructed, detailed framework, and yet so difficult because of the stringent conditions under which her own contribution must flower?

Throughout the work, exemplifying her own *credo* that the music must always be the guiding element, she allows the score to dictate the mood. The placid opening is well matched on the stage by a pastoral dance; the drama of Satan's usurpation of the throne is left entirely to the violent chords and to the situation itself, with a more or less static, if striking spectacle. In the scene with the Comforters de Valois experiences some difficulty, for Vaughan Williams, in employing saxophones, struck a bigger contrast in mood than the choreography seems able to match. As a result the aural cynicism is paralleled by a group of three gnome-like creatures who posture with some resemblance to their originals as conceived by Blake, but who become ludicrous rather than a personification of betrayal and indifference to the world's misfortune.

The episode in which Elihu says to Job, 'You are old and I am very young', is marked on the stage by a series of *arabesques* by Elihu as he makes his exit. Although there is of course nothing to illustrate the words, the contrast is very striking and the scene evokes a heavenly serenity which is one of the finest things in the whole work.

The final expulsion of Satan from Heaven by the Sons of the Morning, on the other hand, suffers from a banality which could have been overcome only by the most vivid and original imagination, for how is it possible on the stage to match in physical terms a scene that the words conjure up in one's mind?

Although nobody, to my knowledge, has questioned the basis

of the classical dance on which *Job* is founded, there are some who claim that the work has been influenced by what was then known as the Central European style. I can see no valid grounds for such a claim. De Valois' choreography always depends largely on naturalistic movement and in this work perhaps the very nature of the movement demanded gives it a superficial resemblance to the style of Mary Wigman, which was at that time the cause of so much controversy. De Valois herself has been particularly scathing about Modern Dance, for although she sees the necessity for occasional outbursts of expression by individual artists with a certain kind of personality, she could on the other hand see no future in 1938 in the undisciplined movement which this style developed, born as it was in the mind of each character and not dependent upon a school for its scientific growth and development.

The next of the de Valois ballets to survive to the present day is *The Haunted Ballroom*, first performed in 1934. Once again she set to work with a strong theme, although of a less literary nature, planned for her by Geoffrey Toye, who also composed the music. The first scene of *The Haunted Ballroom* demands a gay country house-party atmosphere, behind which lurks a sense of foreboding; and the second act an eerie supernatural atmosphere in which the final tragedy must not appear too melodramatic. The dance style in *The Haunted Ballroom* is an amalgam of classical dance and stylized every-day movement; further, the costumes are founded very obviously on the fashion of a definite period, so that the characters must behave to a large extent as normal human beings if the work is to gain and hold our credulity.

At the outset Geoffrey Toye's music certainly suggests both the supernatural and the gaiety of a ball; and the opening scene of a deserted and cobwebbed room and old-fashioned chandeliers is a credible blend of naturalism as well as a suitable environment for the breeding of ghosts.

The populating of this scene, too, is well contrived by the unfailing de Valois method of mime and purely stylized movement. The growing anxiousness of the young Tregennis is, however, carried out purely by histrionics and the few tours and twirls of the ladies are soon immobilized into mime and gesture when the master enters and explains the legend. As the master is provided with no dance whatever, this scene deteriorates into a trifling mimeodrama which really serves as little more than a programmatic introduction to the second scene.

This scene, with its metamorphosis of the room into a ghostly playground, is excellent in so far as the décor is concerned, but the costumes, with their long trailing sleeves and wispy bits of swirling material, are a ridiculous parody. Always seeking harmony between the various elements of her ballet, de Valois forms her ghosts into groups which deliberately employ these sleeves as part of the design, but such a device makes only a superficial impact and by no means advances its primary purpose of developing the sinister atmosphere. The final climax, however, unashamed melodrama though it may be, is effective in a way which seems to be in the compass, in England, only of de Valois and Helpmann.

One of Manet's last pictures, 'Un Bar aux Folies-Bergère', radiates pleasure in the actual appearance and texture of a variety of objects such as the champagne and other bottles and the rich tints in the barmaid's skin. It is also an attempt, a paradoxical attempt if you like, to infuse monumentality into impressionism. From a compositional point of view it is not to be compared with the Hogarth series from which de Valois was to draw her next inspiration, for it lacks balance and the figure of the girl is too central. The 'double vision' is an interesting development of the impressionists and is here exploited by Manet to add interest. The girl is painted from the front, yet her reflection is seen as though the artist had moved some distance to the right.

Such features as this, and several others, were of course quite beyond the scope of the de Valois ballet inspired by this picture. Nevertheless the subject-matter undoubtedly makes a fascinating starting point for the ballet, and that opening scene, the three-dimensional reconstruction of the picture, is a memorable one.

After the opening tableau has made its impact de Valois peoples the space in front of the bar with characters of her own choice, among whom the most important, both in reputation and for the purpose of the ballet, is La Goulue. Some girls next dance a bowdlerized version of the Can-Can, and there is much amusing and flirtatious by-play carried out by well worked out mime. At the end the dancers and patrons gradually desert the bar, a cleaner wakes two drunks who struggle off, leaving the girl at the bar, gin in hands, gazing vacantly into space.

I have always found this ballet thoroughly entertaining. The girl at the bar, even when played by one of the several inter- preters to follow Diana Gould, never fails to arouse my sym- pathy. Manet, unlike Hogarth, was not by any means a social reformer, but painted what he saw, choosing his subject-matter for its own interest. Even so, his keen observation, perhaps un- known to himself, has expressed something in the girl's face which indicates resignation, boredom and a completely disillusioned air which, in one so young and bitter, immediately evokes deep sympathy.

After using one picture as a starting point for her own imaginative purpose, de Valois now once again had recourse to a series: 'The Rake's Progress'. When I saw them last in the Soane Museum they were hanging in a none too favourable light, but even that could not dim Hogarth's wonderful sense of colour harmony. Quite unlike Manet he was a master of composition; further, he was deeply interested in the theatre and many of his pictures are composed as though he saw all life as a theatrical production. He himself said:

> I have endeavoured to treat my subjects as a dramatic play: my picture is my stage and men and women my players, who by means of certain actions and gestures exhibit a dumb show.

The idea of presenting a facet of contemporary life through a set of pictures was by no means new in the 1740's, but Hogarth's social outlook was certainly new.

For the purpose of her ballet de Valois combined the first two pictures and omitted the fifth, in which the Rake marries for wealth, thus simplifying the literary aspect and enabling her to compress the work into six deftly contrasted scenes. The first develops a few adumbrations of character: the Rake preening himself after the acquisition of his wealth, the sycophancy of those who have gathered round him, the pathetic, perhaps too pathetic girl, whom he is supposed to have dishonoured. In this scene de Valois has found a felicitous blend of mime, natural

movement and dance, so that she is able to develop some
feeling that the stage is peopled with living characters; the fact
that so few of these interesting personalities are permitted
to develop with the ballet is in no way the fault of the choreographer.

The Orgy depends perhaps more upon Hogarth than any of
the other scenes, for care has been taken to follow the grouping,
even to the *déshabille* of some of the women, although even the
great freedom which the ballet theatre appears to claim as its
right in these matters would not permit of too slavish an imitation of at least one of the Hogarthian sluts. The way in which
de Valois modifies the group from time to time without throwing
the composition itself out of balance is masterly; as is the way in
which movement, never mind if it is of an amorous and even
lascivious nature, maintains interest and excitement. Subtleties
are provided by suggestions of dance and scurrying across the
stage, while the pallid singers' passage represents de Valois at
her best. The rhythmical swing of the musicians and the
woman's grotesque mimicry of song are perfectly matched to
music and setting, and strike right for once into the heart
of choreographic humour.

The straight scene in which the girl saves the Rake from his
creditors is on the other hand played out in the dullest of banal
terms; and in the next scene but one the Girl's needlework
dance, presumably intended to show the wistfulness with which
she is always thinking of her worthless betrayer, succeeds
only in presenting an elementary form of casually observed
work movements. The gaming house scene, the intense rhythm
of which is set by Gavin Gordon, achieves its purpose in an
adroit amalgamation of mime, movement and dramatic action.
The impatience with which the gamblers await the arrival of
the Rake is expressed entirely through movement and the game
itself mounts in awful excitement as the Rake's frenzy becomes
more and more marked by a form of histrionics exaggerated to
such an extent as is permissible only in the ballet theatre.

The Madhouse scene is far too long. Each of the madmen is
given a part to perform his 'party-piece', whereas each of them
should be used only to contribute to the evocation of pity at
such a savagely pitiable scene. Hogarth himself possessed an
uncanny power to exaggerate without the slightest suspicion

oletta Elvin as Lykanion, Michael Somes as Daphnis and Margot Fonteyn
Chloe in *Daphnis and Chloe*.   FREDERICK ASHTON

oletta Elvin as Queen of the Water; a scene from *Homage to the Queen*.
                                                                FREDERICK ASHTON

The 'Lady' declares her love for the 'Fool' to the disgust of the wealthy suitors and other guests at the ball in *The Lady and the Fool*. Patricia Miller as La Capricciosa and Kenneth Macmillan as Moon Dog are in the centre.

JOHN CRANKO

Marjorie Tallchief as Tchernichenka and two Caucasian Warriors in a scene from *Prisoner in the Caucasus*.

GEORGE SKIBINE

of caricature or burlesque, whereas the choreographic expression of the destiny to which dissolution has brought Tom Rakewell relies upon a few convulsive movements and has to be bolstered up with lewd histrionics consisting chiefly of grotesque facial distortions.

When I hear some of the shorter pieces of Handel I lament the fact that so few ballets have been inspired by this great eighteenth-century melodist. His music has a soaring exultant quality which is in itself a boon to the choreographer who composes in terms of elevation and *pointe* work rather than *terre-à-terre* and monumentality. Further and possibly most important, the tunes themselves are mostly written in true and accepted dance rhythms.

The Gods Go A-Begging is one of the very few ballets conceived by de Valois in terms of dance not unduly trammelled by dramatic or mimetic ends. Ten separate numbers each contribute to the development and apotheosis. *Allegro*, in which preparations are made for a *fête champêtre* by a serving-maid, her friend and six black lackeys; a *Minuet* in which the neighbours and their ladies arrive, as well as a Shepherd, whom they entice into a dance; a *Hornpipe* in which the Shepherd dances to the amusement of the aristocrats; a *Musette* in which the Chief Serving Maid dances, but is frightened by the amorous advances of two noblemen; an Ensemble in which the aristocrats dance; *Larghetto*, in which the Shepherd and the Chief Serving Maid, after the company has wandered off into the woods, dance together in mutual and tender affection; *Tamborene*, in which the lackeys afford light relief with a droll and agile number; Gavotte in which the Shepherd and the Serving Maid resume their dance, the love between them becoming ever more clearly indicated, until the company return and, indignant at the fact that two such lowly servants could enjoy such emotions, peremptorily order them to leave; *Dramatico*, in which the woods darken and a messenger arrives from the gods, the Serving Maid and the Shepherd being revealed as two members of the godly kingdom; a *Bourrée-Finale* in which the two divinities, mounted on pedestals in the manner of Watteauesque statuary, receive homage from the assembly.

Given a theme of this kind, which necessitates an accent on dance as distinct from pseudo-naturalistic dramatic develop-

ment, the de Valois dance invention is varied, charming and
supremely appropriate to the subject-matter. The changing
groups and poses emphasize the elegance and something of the
decadence of the court at that time. The dance of the disguised
deities is a fluent arrangement based on a deliberately limited
classical vocabulary and, unlike so many *pas de deux* by the same
choreographer, achieves its expressive ends through flowing
dance passages allied to delicate mime without heavy rhetoric.

Any attempt to consider the thematic development of a
ballet as distinct from the development of the dance content
must in many cases lead to ridiculously illogical criticism. Yet
Checkmate has been the victim of a flood of such criticism, both
in the chattering hubbub in the Crush Bar at Covent Garden
and in what should be the more considered verdict expressed
in cold print. I have frequently been faced with the following
questions: 'Why are the Red Pawns not matched by an equal
number of Black Pawns?' 'How is it that although so few pieces
have been taken the Red King is left defenceless?' Then there is
the more subtle class of question, put usually with a superior
air by the would-be profound analysts of ballet: 'Why make the
Red King so weak at the very beginning of the ballet, before he
has been put to the test of war?' 'And why are the Red Bishops
endowed with such weak movement when in fact on the board
they are capable of rapid and penetrating thrusts?' And so on.
The only suggestion I can make to such critics is that they
plead with de Valois to present a vast game of chess worked out
by two experts by means of human pieces. The idea has already
been exploited, but mercifully nobody to my knowledge has
tried to include it under the genus ballet.

Once again the theme is perfect for ballet and the choreographer has been able to bring to her support brilliant contributions by McKnight Kauffer and Arthur Bliss. The opening
dance of the Pawns has been stigmatized as 'musical comedy'
if that term does imply stigma. I think it is a delightfully
arranged dance which typifies the lightness and at the same time
the particular significance of these little pieces. The movements
of the complete set of Red Pawns are suggestive of the actual
limitations of the pieces on the board, but apart from that their
dance adds a piquant and lively character, as though to say
that no matter what portents, world-shattering forces of good

and evil, love and hate, strength and weakness are to be epito-
mized, this is after all a game. The only other dances of any
length are the Red Knight's solo after he has succumbed to the
Black Queen's charms and his duel with her. It is unfortunate
that the solo is danced to a Mazurka, for neither the rhythm
nor the orchestral effects of the music is appropriate to any
theme associated with love or tenderness; as the Red Knight's
figures are also to a certain extent conditioned by the forward
and sideways movement of the chess piece he represents, the
task of presenting an effective dance has proved too much for de
Valois' powers.

Apart from that, the ballet consists of mime and dramatic
movement, punctuated by snatches of dance. The way in which
the Red Queen leads her piteous old husband to his throne
does arouse a little pathos; the duel itself, too, protracted and
repetitive though it is, possesses a sinister strength and dramatic
climax; as does the merciless throwing by the Black Queen of
her Red counterpart to her henchmen. All these episodes
contain flashes of illuminating movement as distinct from those
which are required to enact the theme, but mostly the subject-
matter proves too strong for the treatment it receives. The grim
procession in honour of the Red Knight after his treacherous
death at the hands of the Black Queen provides an excuse for
the triumphal re-entry of the symbolic figure of Death; and the
final episode, in which the Black Queen torments her wretched
victim before his dispatch, is as clumsy an attempt at choreography as I ever hope to see from a major choreographer. The
torture and death suffered by the old man is conveyed only by
exaggerated facial expression and unoriginal naturalistic
gesture. Here was a choreographic problem worthy of a brilliant
resolution: how to endow such a character with an expression
of abject fear? He is too senile to convey such a statement by
means of agile dance, yet to reduce him to such limited facial
grimace, even with a Helpmann as the interpreter, is to renounce
the very essence of ballet. But de Valois, by permitting her
themes to dictate the nature of the visual image instead of
imposing her own imaginative choreography for the expression
rather than the representation of a theme, has once again
produced a pedestrian mime drama, varied by a minimum of
dance. If only she would unshackle her vivid ability to create

in terms of dance from the literary demands of her themes, she would produce a work as great as the themes themselves.

In *The Prospect Before Us* the choreographer has submitted herself to even greater demands from her thematic material, for she has written her book upon drawings of Thomas Rowlandson, from one of which the ballet takes its name, and a public account of the relationship and difficulties of two rival theatre managers: Taylor of the King's and O'Reilly of the Pantheon. Instead of treating her subject in the satirical manner of Rowlandson, however, she has resorted to burlesque and even some moments of slapstick. For those who have read about such great figures as Noverre, Didelot and Vestris, the ballet is naturally more interesting, although in the framework of such a burlesque de Valois has done little more than hint at certain outstanding characteristics of those figures. The irresponsibility and parsimoniousness of Noverre, for instance, become lovable, ridiculous attributes rather than serious impediments in a great master. Vestris walking through his part, on the other hand, and his autocratic behaviour towards his colleagues, is a more vivid if still slight attempt at characterization. Taylor and O'Reilly remain throughout two buffoons, the one morose, the other ribald, each a perfect foil for the other, with O'Reilly stealing all the laughs. Legitimate doubt has been expressed as to whether all the jokes really are either funny or appropriate: O'Reilly's skirt-lifting and other pranks in the street, when the public is being exhorted to produce financial aid, would scarcely be the right procedure for the manager of the leading London theatre. The answer, it seems to me, is that de Valois has not sought to develop any true representation of the style and manners of the period, but rather to use the rich material to produce a ballet abundant in fun and ridicule without making any comment whatever on late eighteenth-century theatrical history. In this she has undoubtedly succeeded, although I lament that she has not achieved her ends more frequently by purely choreographic means, as in the witty and ingenious dances of the lawyers.

Occasionally in small choreographic passages of this kind, whether of humour or some other emotion, de Valois seems to invent her movement under the compulsion of a rhythm which, although founded in the musical rhythm, yet transmutes that rhythm into a force all her own. The dance of the lawyers is a good example; others are the musicians' movements in the orgy scene from *The Rake's Progress*, the scene in which the gamblers await the arrival of the Rake in that same ballet, the dance of the pawns in the opening of *Checkmate*, and several dances in *The Gods Go A-Begging*.

These dances show de Valois as a great choreographer, when she has thrown off for a time the self-applied chains of literary and pictorial detail which bind her choreography tightly to earth in all but her most inspired moments.

Promenade was first produced in October 1944, during a long tour, at the King's Theatre, Edinburgh. Its purpose was undoubtedly the provision of some light-hearted escapism, framed in the terms of gay and romantic dance, built on the irrepressible Haydn dance melodies admirably arranged by the late Edwin Evans. For once de Valois has flatly discarded her 'book' and presented a series of inventive and developing dances unbound by literary considerations. The 'Rendezvous' number is worked out in the classical technique with a delicacy and a poignant expression which rank it very high amid the innumerable *pas de deux* of its kind. The solo 'Promenade', too, expresses the rapidly changing thoughts and emotions of an adolescent girl; the various day-dreams of love and ambition can all be imagined, if not traced with certainty, in these dances, as well as the flashes of coltishness which occur when she forgets her new and almost grown-up status. The 'Danse de Paysannes' affords interest of an entirely different nature, for each of the numbers was compounded of traditional Breton steps as shown to the choreographer by an authority on the folk dances of Brittany.

Not until 1949 did de Valois once again seek relief from the long round of administrative work in which the success of her efforts appeared to incarcerate her ever more securely year by year. Then, giving way to urgent demands to the effect that another ballet by her had long been overdue, she began work on *Don Quixote*, which was presented for the first time at Covent Garden in February 1950.

Some weeks before the event I purchased 'The Life and Achievements of the Renowned Don Quixote de La Mancha', by Miguel de Cervantes, and settled down in the long winter evenings to read the nine hundred pages of close print in which the famous Don's adventures have been recounted, at the same time registering a certain measure of gratitude to Miss de Valois and Sadler's Wells generally for compelling me to do so.

The more I read the more I wondered how such a character could be expressed in terms of ballet; and how the various episodes could be indicated without any attempt to vie with Cervantes' long and detailed descriptions. But I strongly believe that any artifact can itself become the source of inspiration for another original man-made product. The creative artist sees something with an intensity of vision denied to lower mortals and is thus able in his own medium to express a completely new reaction which will perhaps provide those who can tune in to his wavelength with an entirely fresh and novel experience.

As ever, de Valois chose her collaborators with great discrimination. Roberto Gerhard was really perhaps more than a collaborator, for his music had been composed some time before the ballet itself was put into production, and his 'book', I understand, was followed in considerable detail. The rambling Cervantes story is reduced to a few passages. This reduction would not matter very much if the choreographer had succeeded in establishing the character of the Don. At the outset it is surely vital to the development of the ballet, just as it was of the book, to show that the Don was crazed through reading hundreds of books on knight errantry. Yet all that we see is the Don, wearing a vacant expression it is true, sitting on a bed with an open book beside him. Much is made in the ballet of the robing of Aldonza, by which act she is transformed into Dulcinea, but I cannot see that this scene in any way illumines Cervantes' delightful account of the peasant's exaltation by the Don to the nobility. Read what he said:

> Near the place where he lived dwelt a good, likely country lass, for whom he had formerly a sort of inclination, though it is probable she never heard of it, nor regarded it in the least. Her name was Aldonza Lorenzo, and this was she whom he thought he might entitle to the sovereignty of his heart: Upon which he studied to find her out a new name, that might have some affinity with her old one, and yet at the same time sound somewhat like that of a princess or lady of quality; so that at last he resolved to call her

Dulcinea, with the addition of del Toboso, from the place where she was born; a name in his opinion, sweet, harmonious, extraordinary and no less significative than the others which he had devised.

All that I can say is that the above passage occupies less time than its relative scene in the ballet takes to enact.

The one episode by which the Don is known universally is quite ludicrous in the ballet. Again I quote:

> . . . he rushed with Rozinante's utmost speed upon the first windmill he could come at, and, running his lance into the sail, the wind whirled about with such swiftness that the rapidity of the motion presently broke the lance into shivers and hurled away both knight and horse with it, till down he fell, rolling a good way off into the field.

In the ballet the windmills have been made to look neither like that which they are in fact, nor that into which they have been transformed in the fantastic imagination of the Don.

Despite the lengthy programme note, the passage in which the metal pot of the itinerant barber is mistaken by the Don for the fabulous helmet of Mambrino would be completely obscure to anyone unacquainted with the details of this incident as given in the book. Each arbitrarily selected incident suffers in its enactment so that it remains no more than a bald and clumsily drawn shadow of the original.

Edward Burra's sets and drop curtain are original and dramatic, appearing to me to be influenced partly by El Greco and partly by Daumier. At any rate they succeed admirably in suggesting great space and the magnified distortions which fill the fevered mind of the Don. Flesh-and-blood dancers, however, cannot match either the size or the unreality of such settings, so that none of the Don's boundless chivalry or crazed foolishness is evoked in the minds of those who behold the ballet. Without such an evocation the work cannot in my opinion justify its existence.

Dame Ninette is an extremely busy and I imagine at times a harassed executive. I fear that the failure of *Don Quixote* will discourage her from again subjecting herself to the pangs of creation; and that would be a great loss to ballet, for I am convinced that she has as much to give in actual creation as she has given already in organization. She is not by any means prone to false modesty and in her evaluations of ideas, ballets, dancers, companies and repertories she displays remarkable insight coloured by no false sentiment or illogicality. Yet in her own ballets she seems frequently to rate her personal contribution of least importance, for except in but one or two works the choreography is stifled by literary demands and scenic decoration. De Valois has herself admitted the paramount influence of music in her own work; if she will once again allow herself to be inspired by the score and her own choreographic ingenuity, employing only the slenderest possible theme and insisting that the decoration takes second place, without at any time dictating the terms of her dance images, I am confident that she will give us some more great work. After all, de Valois was the first British choreographer as well as the first British organizer and producer of ballet. In recent years her work in the first of these two capacities has been sadly neglected; it is now high time for the smooth-running machine to receive less of her attention, so that she can devote more time to the creation of a work by which she will be remembered with as much esteem and admiration as for her work in other directions.

CHAPTER EIGHT

Frederick Ashton

IN 1930, Frederick Ashton wrote:

British choreographers should endeavour briefly to show the world the richness of our native endowments, and not be intimidated by the more colourful characteristics of other nations, for honesty to ourselves and our merits cannot fail to find appeal to a public as discerning and sensitive to good dancing as the British.

Innumerable members of that discerning and sensitive public to which Ashton refers will consider these words very much to the point today, for in the dilettante circles favoured by various immature choreographers credence is still given to the myth of the exotic; *Vive* Muscovy and Gaul and leave England to the Philistines! Later on most of these dilettante-inspired ideas believed to be *avant garde* are found to be out-moded by twenty years. But when Ashton uttered his admonition British ballet in the shape of the Rambert and Vic-Wells companies was being nursed by the Camargo Society. Memories of the Diaghilev Ballets Russes were yet rich and luxurious.

Since 1930 nobody has done more than Ashton to 'show the world the richness of our native endowments', for over a number of years he has been the leading English choreographer, mounting major works on one of the world's greatest companies. Further, he was the first to develop a national English classical choreographic style as distinct from the Russian school: just as Balanchine has developed a truly American style from the same source.

The differences between the Ashton and Balanchine styles do not lend themselves easily to facile literary explanation. Each is at its best in the creation of dance patterns untrammelled by plot or characterization. But whereas Balanchine employs endless new *enchaînements*, most of which bear a monotonous similarity to their predecessors to all but the few who have been educated in classical dance, as distinct from classical ballet, Ashton seeks less after originality of dance pattern than for intensity of emotional response, either to the music or to some nebulous theme. Balanchine usually displays and enhances the glamour of the female form, a typical and highly commendable American pursuit which many serious artists of all kinds on this side of the Atlantic appear to have given up; Ashton at times almost makes us forget that we are looking at men and women, but presents an imagery bereft both of sexual attraction and human conflict. Where Balanchine produces a slick, sometimes brilliantly humorous movement, Ashton seeks more after an English sense of fun, as in *Façade* and *Les Patineurs*. Both kinds can be subtle, both can be pointed; but each of them symbolizes a different ethos.

As is to be expected from a choreographer who considers that dancing should be the most important element in ballet, Ashton prefers to gain his inspiration from music. Like Balanchine he believes in dance which expresses nothing but itself. Unlike Balanchine, however, he also believes in the power of dance to evoke every kind of human emotion; and in the ability of each responsible member of the audience to react in a special and individual way.

'All through my life,' he says, 'I have been working to make the ballet independent of literary and pictorial ideas and to make it draw from the rich fund of classical ballet.'

Even Ashton's greatest admirers will experience some difficulty in equating that statement with the evidence of some of his actual works. *Les Illuminations, Daphnis et Chloe* and *Tiresias* may or may not possess great choreographic qualities, but if so it is scarcely because of their independence of literary and pictorial ideas.

Unfortunately, however, no choreographer can produce a continuous stream of successful ballets—successful either artistically or at the box office—which depend for their structure upon no more than the classical vocabulary. Works such as *Ballet Imperial, Symphonic Variations* and *Interplay* are rarities, for whatever expressive power they possess must stem directly from movement. Dramatic situations and human relationships can be presented only in widely generalized terms, and audience attention focussed solely on the dance patterns, whereas a strong plot will gloss over a lack of choreographic invention.

As choreographer-in-chief to the Sadler's Wells Ballet, Ashton could permit himself to wait for inspiration no more than the writer who depends for his living on popular short stories. If he is not to become unduly repetitive, the choreographer must fall back upon the structural assistance of plot. Despite his contention that it is possible to express every emotion through ballet, I do not think that Ashton can subordinate a literary plot to his own choreographic ends. Individual characterization, emphasis on dramatic climaxes and well-planned plot development must surely present insuperable difficulties to a choreographer who believes so passionately in the classical school.

It appears to me that this classical vocabulary is unfitted, just as the operatic aria and recitative are unfitted, either to express or exploit the human tensions inherent in a concrete plot. Any approach to realism exposes the pitiful inadequacy of the medium to express concrete ideas and individual reactions to a given situation. More and more I find that in the classical ballets I take less pleasure from the trappings and story enactment and greater pleasure from the element of pure dance.

Nevertheless plot cannot be abstracted from every ballet. In fact it can be dispensed with only in those few cases where the choreographer has been inspired either by some nucleus of movement from which to develop a series of purely balletic images independent of literary structure, or where he has been genuinely motivated by music. For the rest, choreographers must continue striving to usurp the prerogative of drama and literature. They can never wholly succeed, but sometimes they almost intuitively forge out of their problems a piece of highly charged dance.

In the selection of his themes Ashton has sought ideas from a wide field: from music, poetry, Biblical stories, from mythology and from an original libretto. Having studied his theme he next likes to imbue himself with the spirit of the period in which the work is to be set. 'See the modes and manners of the past through the eyes of the present,' he urges. He aims not at any kind of exact copy, of course, but at recapturing the essence of a period. In the tango from *Façade*, for instance, he has aimed at presenting a certain kind of social behaviour of the 'twenties as he saw it some years later. Let us not try to be too profound, especially in connection with *Façade*, but much of the pleasure in this work depends upon the choreographer's observation. Even today parts of it retain their point because they enable us to see a previous epoch with keener vision and thus to laugh at the social life of the past—always a safe and lucrative source of humour.

Ashton's Peruvian upbringing is sometimes said to have exerted a strong influence on his choreographic outlook. He has himself stated that he revelled in the rituals which attended the various Saints' days. On certain occasions he was chosen to serve the bishop at High Mass, holding the salver and other symbols of that office.

'I liked doing these ceremonies,' he is quoted by Beryl de Zoete in an article in 'Horizon' of July 1942. 'And I learned to time things rightly and to make effects at leisure, and the proper times for climaxes and the whole artful measure of things and the ecstasy of rituals.'

Doubtless this youthful experience has affected his outlook on the composition of ballet. In certain of his ballets it seems apparent that the ritual of dancing is allowed free play without heed to the ritual itself. The form of dramatic presentation of a ritual can frequently be appreciated more easily in its own right if we do not first have to decipher the signs and symbols from which it is made up. Most notable of the ritualistic features in Ashton's composition, however, is the lack of haste in the development of all his works and the manner in which his dancers pause and present themselves in immobility after each striking movement.

Partly through his interest in the dance itself, partly through his acknowledgment of the need to steep himself in the spirit of the period in which his ballet is set, and partly through his saturation in the music, Ashton is very rarely guilty of inconsistency in stylistic treatment. His choreographic patterns unfold in such a way as to unify the various elements of characterization, climactic development and mood into a choreographic design which is striking in its own right, regardless of its secondary purpose of the communication of purely theatrical ideas.

Up to 1939 Ashton seems to me to have aimed at entertaining audiences rather than attempting profound balletic statements or delighting in the complexity and abstruseness wooed by so many young men of letters, painting and music, more or less contemporary with him.

Right from the outset, with his early efforts in revue, his work with Madame Rambert, with the Rubinstein ballet and with Sadler's Wells, he sought to please—a by no means unworthy aim in an artist whose work depended to such a large extent on a loyal but sparse band of enthusiasts. Perhaps Ashton's youthful and extremely sensitive resentment of criticism contributed to this lucidity and absence of daring experiment from his early work; be that as it may, the ballets he produced were ideal for the nucleus of an English repertory. In 1940, however, and it seems almost too obvious to say that the war was responsible, Ashton abandoned his plea that he must always seek to entertain, and produced the first of a series of controversial works, although he has between times presented works which trade in light entertainment.

Another factor in his early compositions was the quality of the instruments upon which he had to play. The Sadler's Wells dancers of the early '30's were most of them possessed of no particularly outstanding technical ability. A composer scoring for a set of instruments each with a range of only a single octave, although he may well benefit in some cases by this limitation, will generally speaking be unable to exploit his creative gifts to their fullest power.

Through his marked preference for the classical technique, and through his skill in composing fluent *enchaînements* for both male and female dancers, whether of the ethereal brilliance of Markova or the first serious stage performance of a R.A.D. student, Ashton played a vital part in the moulding of our English style. His choreographic outlook and practice, together with Ninette de Valois' organizing genius, are jointly responsible for the ability of the Sadler's Wells Ballet today to be able to present an unsurpassed performance of the classical ballets.

Throughout his choreographic life Ashton has shown a profound understanding of the physical and emotional response of each dancer to his choreography and has thus been able to moderate his composition in accordance with the needs of each soloist. Fonteyn in the early years of her wonderful career benefited tremendously through this understanding. I intend not the slightest derogation of her personal greatness when I assert that this greatness would never have reached its present pinnacle but for Ashton's sympathy and almost intuitive appreciation of her individual needs.

In common with almost every one of his contemporaries, Ashton has sometimes resorted to hackneyed and derivative phrases. Who does not sigh 'Ah, Ashton!' when the ballerina is transported by her partner across the stage in arabesque, her *pointe* brushing the floor? Not quite so obvious perhaps, but clearly prevalent in an Ashton ballet, is the diagonal line of dancers broken at intervals by a soloist in mid-flight.

Such mannerisms may be regarded as fully justified signatures, however, and are indulged in by leading artists in all spheres. Less pardonable is Ashton's descent, fortunately very rare, into the composition of a work so hackneyed that thinking audiences are roused to wonder not only how such an important choreographer could have conceived it, but also why a great company should produce it. Happily the 'discerning and sensitive' British public clearly demonstrates their opinions through the box office and other ways, and the work is soon erased from the repertory. Pre-war audiences will remember the fiasco of *Cupid and Psyche*; and post-war audiences will remember *Les Sirènes* with its vulgar banality and knockabout humour.

The gap between mediocrity and brilliance is sometimes very small. The same series of figures in different *enchaînements* will obviously result in highly contrasted dance patterns. Whereas one *enchaînement*, made up of all the simplest and most obvious amalgamations, will be dated and banal, the same series linked together in new ways will provide an exacting audience with intense pleasure. Ashton and Balanchine are undoubtedly the most inventive choreographers in this kind of composition, although Cranko has betrayed signs in *Pastorelle* that he might well emulate them if he concentrates his talents for any length of time on this particular *genre*. It is therefore perhaps all the more surprising that both Ashton and Balanchine sometimes decline into such banality and plagiarism of their own previous efforts. Neither would have been permitted thus to fail himself under the eye of Diaghilev; and neither would either of them have produced inferior work had they been free from the need for pot-boiling which at times besets every ballet company regardless as to whether it is run by an enthusiastic philanthropist or supported by the state money-bags.

The fact that right through his early choreographic years Ashton composed for very few great technicians conditioned his style so that technique occupied a subordinate place. With more brilliant dancers in the company he would have been hard put to it to combat the pressure upon him to decline into long series of brilliant *pas*. Balanchine all too frequently does succumb, but with an effect not so serious as it would be on the romantic work of Ashton.

Through this absence of bravura in Ashton's compositions, his early and middle period works such as *Capriole Suite*, *Nocturne* and *Apparitions*, are frequently censured by the unperceptive as lacking in choreographic excitement. On the very few occasions when he has resorted to a form of acrobatics he has apparently used the tricks themselves to scoff at that which they represent, as for example the Blue Skater in *Les Patineurs*.

This early experience developed in Ashton his natural and sympathetic understanding of the physical and emotional powers and limitations of his dancers, and he has thus been able to compose to the best possible advantage for each of them.

Capriole Suite was the first of the Ashton ballets to earn a more or less permanent place in the repertory. Danced first by the Ballet Rambert, the Vic-Wells Ballet, and later Sadler's Wells Theatre Ballet, this work epitomizes the skill, the method and originality of the early Ashton. Despite the fact that Beaumont makes no reference to it in his monumental 'Complete Book of Ballets' and that Ninette de Valois ignores it in her 'Invitation to the Ballet', I still look upon it as a small work of great importance.

Capriole Suite is based on descriptions of various court and folk dances to be found in Arbeau's 'Orchesographie' of 1588. Of course Ashton did not seek an antiquarian reproduction, but has taken what after all were the progenitive steps of our classical technique and stylized them into ballet. What more suitable theme for a ballet could be found? Here were the dances of the sixteenth century; the gay and robust steps of the peasants, the stately eccentric measure of the court. Had he lacked subtlety the young choreographer might easily have fallen into the trap of overstressing the contrast, thus making a parody of both forms. Fortunately he was by no means lacking in subtlety and has obtained the most telling contrast, closely following his own maxim: 'looking at the past with the eyes of the present'.

Technically no part of the ballet is very exciting, but young dancers sometimes find that the dignified aristocratic poses in the court dances are a little beyond their mental grasp. These dances were generally performed to exploit the rich and extravagant costume of the period as well as to display a regal, well constituted grace of bearing. For the really perfect performance of such dances the dancers must try to project themselves into a strange world.

The folk dances require much more physical effort and less mental adjustment, and for these dances Ashton composed a series of energetic *enchaînements*, while for the court dances he has punctuated the slow and deliberate steps with frequent groups comprised of charming and well varied poses.

Peter Warlock's music helps to evoke the appropriate mood of each item, but I have never been able to conjure up any enthusiasm for the costumes. William Chappell, in common with both Ashton and Warlock, has sought to suggest the style and to contribute to the mood of the ballet rather than recreate the authentic costume. True, in this way he has been able to enhance the dignity of the nobles by contrasting the vertical design of their costume with the horizontal motif of the male peasants, the ruffs of the ladies with the caps of the girls. But there is no richness. In the court dances the steps and postures would show to far greater advantage in a more convincing, heavier material and more extravagant decoration. The colour of all the costumes too is of insufficient variety. Such a mass of pink and a material which hangs better for the short dresses than the long ones cannot help but mar the other elements.

Façade is another of the very few ballets composed by a contemporary choreographer which are included in the repertory of more than one company. *Façade*, indeed, is danced by Ballet Rambert who still cling tenaciously and, in the opinion of most, successfully, to the original 1931 version; by the Sadler's Wells Theatre Ballet, who have made certain alterations, and by the senior 'Wells' company, who brought the

Marjorie Tallchief and George Skibine in *Idylle*, one of the most successful ballets in the repertory of the de Cuevas company. GEORGE SKIBINE

Margot
Fonteyn
and
Alexander
Grant
in *Tiresias*.

FREDERICK
ASHTON

THREE
CHOREO-
GRAPHERS
Frederick
Ashton,
Ninette
de Valois,
and
Leonide
Massine.

Alice with the
King
and Queen of
Hearts in the
episode of the
Stolen Tarts
in the
Festival Ballet's
production of
*Alice
in Wonderland.*

MICHAEL
CHARNLEY

work on to the Opera House stage in 1951, again with certain divergences from the original.

Despite the very pointed commentary on the '20s, which forms an essential feature of several of the items in *Façade*, the ballet yet retains topical interest for present-day audiences, even though they may have been no more than babies in arms, or less, at the end of that hectic decade. There were times when certain types of audience sought associations between the ballet and Edith Sitwell's poems of the same title. Doubtless the sale of the poems received a pleasant boost, but anyone who could trace a resemblance must have possessed a labyrinthine as well as an ingenious mind.

The Scotch Rhapsody which opens the *divertissements* sets a light-hearted atmosphere, although anyone who refuses to be diverted from serious choreographic contemplation by frivolity will find here ample evidence that Ashton, thus early in his career, followed Massine's example in his ability to stylize folk dance. The Yodelling Song, in which a milkmaid goes through the motions of her occupation with the help of a most original cow composed of three young mountaineers who seek the maid's favours, looks original even today. The Polka is a charming dance—the more charming when performed in the original costume. I am myself especially attached to it perhaps because this was the role in which I first remember the young Fonteyn. It is a frivolous, gay number, danced on the *pointes*, and it requires wit and polish from its executant.

Critics and audiences of all classes and ages have found in *Façade* nothing but delight. Even the Americans, who differ so much from us in certain fundamental reactions to ballet, could find little but praise. John Martin, the very well-known dance critic for 'The New York Times', said: '. . . as fresh as the day it was made all those years ago. It is witty, light-figured and smart.' And Walter Terry, equally well known, said in the 'New York Herald Tribune': 'The evening's major joy was *Façade* . . . it is a delightful piece, fast of tempo, brief of scene and blessed with delightful ribaldries. Its humour is to be found not only in its ironic comments upon dance forms and human types but also in its use of the unexpected.'

The main differences in the 'Wells' and the Rambert versions have been concerned chiefly with sets and costumes. Why the original, rather natty dress of the Polka Girl was ever discarded for the far less attractive corsets and long bloomers is hard to fathom. Fortunately the original was restored after its successor had been subjected to a heavy and sustained barrage of disapprobation. The fluttering underclothes on the backcloth of the Wells' production is certainly no improvement on the original which, with its massively absurd Mrs Grundy in the window and its stable door, is in itself full of charming wit and gaiety.

The Tango is in my opinion still by far the most satiric of the items which comprise this ballet. A debutante dances with a Dago who ogles and dances like a gigolo attempting to outdo Valentino himself. The dance consists of a series of overstatements each of which burlesques various qualities of social dancing of the jazz age.

Still working on hedonistic principles, in 1933 Ashton made *Les Rendezvous*. Incidentally this is the first ballet he mounted for the 'Wells' when he was yet only a guest choreographer to that company. Constructed around Markova, *Les Rendezvous* typifies his handling of this particular style of classical *divertissements*, for it is strung together on a theme so slender that it can be entirely ignored for the benefit of choreographic ends.

Also in 1936, following *Les Rendezvous*, Ashton essayed his most ambitious work to that time: *Apparitions*. Forestalling Massine by a few months, he used the theme upon which Berlioz had constructed his *Symphonie Fantastique*, but avoided stealing more of Massine's thunder by going to Liszt for the music itself. The longest ballet in actual physical time he had yet created, it makes heavier demands than his previous efforts upon choreographic organization as distinct from choreographic invention. Further, he has quite clearly divided the ballet into separate periods of mime and dance. Both prologue and epilogue attempt a literal exposition in mime, proving once again the inadequacy of that medium for such a purpose; whereas the ballroom scene effervesces with alternate passages of serene and diabolic dance.

In a letter to Cecil Beaton, who had missed the opening performance of the ballet owing to a convention in New York, Constant Lambert left no doubt in the mind of the third collaborator as to its success. 'The Gallop in the ballroom scene is the most exciting thing I have ever known and the funeral procession was equally good in its way,' he wrote, and 'Ashton's choreography is the best that he has done—even better than *Baiser* and quite different.'

In the same year Ashton made *Nocturne*, a work which depends even more upon mood and less upon theme than *Apparitions*. In this case the choreography was governed by the well-known but by no means hackneyed 'Paris' Overture by Delius. The mood evoked is that of the late nineteenth century; drama and pathos are expressed through the contrast of the heartless, pleasure-loving attitude of a rich girl and the sad plight of a poor little flower-seller. Such a theme sounds almost good enough for a Ruby M. Ayres novel, but Ashton handles it with extreme delicacy, expressing the mood and style through a gay crowd of maskers who punctuate the ballet with telling frieze-like groups at each crisis. Their indifference to suffering and tragedy throws into high relief the subject of their indifference, thus saving the choreographer from the necessity of overstatement which could so easily have led to mush and melodrama.

Throughout the ballet Ashton resorts to symbols for the expression of various ideas and suggestions. Several of them evade immediate perception, but this hardly seems to matter, for the style and convention of pattern of the symbols in themselves are sufficient to convey the atmosphere and mood. He has expressed the casual, thoughtless behaviour of a crowd and the frigid ruthlessness of a woman after her prey, with some potency. But while the Onlooker raises his arms to the light of dawn as the curtain rings down, one experiences no sadness, no pity, no lump in the throat, for Ashton has been far more concerned with form than with statement. He has shown his mastery of construction without attempting to give life to the symbols he employs for his characters. Even Fonteyn as the flower-girl leaves me unmoved, for she is not one individual person in whom I can put my sympathy, but a mere abstraction —the representation of pathos rather than a living soul.

Many will regret the passing of this phase of Ashton's career, for they have powerful arguments on their side who believe that ballet should abjure profundity and seek only to delight and entertain. For anyone who seeks light entertainment in movement Ashton's next ballet, *Les Patineurs*, made in 1937, is a perfect example of its kind.

This ballet consists of a series of prettily linked *divertissements* founded superficially on the movements of ice skating, and firmly on classical principles.

The various parts are named as follows: *entree, pas de huit, variation, pas de deux, ensemble, pas de huit, pas de trois, pas de patineurs* and *ensemble.* To all intents and purposes Ashton has dispensed with groups and depends almost entirely upon continuous, non-stop classical dances of great style and variety. The spirit of the dance, coupled with the perfect choice of music and the best of Chappell's sets and costumes, gives the work a vivacity which infects all audiences. The wit and humour varies from the collapse of some novices to the showing off of an expert. With a company now possessed of some excellent technicians Ashton for the first time resorted to sustained passages of virtuosity. Even so, he distributed his fireworks in such a way that they are never in danger of becoming a mere firework display. The *fouettes* of one of the girls in blue and the expertness of the blue-clad male add tremendously to the zest of the ballet.

At this time the 'Wells' were beginning to attract a little fashionable support, although Islington hardly served to intensify the magnetism of this kind of theatrical performance. Further, Lord Berners and Gertrude Stein now became Ashton's collaborators in the making of *Wedding Bouquet*. Ashton and Stein had worked together in 1930-4 for the production of *Four Saints in Three Acts*, but unfortunately English audiJnces never saw the fruits of their labour, as this work was born and died in New York. From what he has himself said, and from other sources, it appears evident that Ashton found the collaboration a profitable one; that Stein's fantastication suited his own style, providing him with theme without undue definition of plot, literary context without banishment of fantasy or mysticism.

Wedding Bouquet has music, costumes and décor by Lord Berners. Although some complain that the costumes tend a little too far towards a ridiculous naturalism, it seems to me that this very naturalism in its absurdity adds to the humour and ridicule which the libretto, music and choreography seek to contrive.

Unfortunately, however, apparently in common with countless other members of the audiences on the other side of the Atlantic, I have never yet heard all the words, but only a snatch or two to whet one's appetite; as, for instance, when Julia is being carried away with her legs in the air, her negligible underwear plain for all to see, the words once resounded through the theatre, 'and for the winter she is quite unprepared'.

For the most part in *Wedding Bouquet* Ashton has relied more than usual upon situation as distinct from movement. There are, it is true, some delicious fragments of choreographic fun, but in the *pas de deux* between the Groom and Julia, and the Groom and his Bride, burlesque is contrived as much through mime and situation as through dance. Nevertheless the way in which the Groom is treated as a mere *porteur* by both the Insane Girl and by the Bride shows his dire helplessness in both situations. The drunken guest is a clear piece of undergraduate nonsense. In fact the entire ballet bears a somewhat adolescent air, which yet appeals to large audiences.

In 1938 and 1939 Ashton created nothing that has lived and nothing that has enjoyed a post-war revival. The work he did accomplish followed his well established formula: it was polished, highly entertaining—and insignificant. Then in June 1940 we were given striking evidence of a new strain which amounted almost to a revival within himself. The war made its impact upon most artists, and Ashton appeared to be particularly susceptible. Refusing on any grounds to plead for exemption, he went through the whole gamut of military discipline, frustration and futility which is so much harder upon the creative soul than upon tinkers, tailors and critics. But that was later. The rape of Poland at the outset had apparently affected him more than most Englishmen, who still remained cut off from the rest of the world by twenty-one miles of water. When he did *Dante Sonata* many of his admirers claimed that it symbolized the suffering of Poland. Fortunately Ashton denied this; had he not done so the ballet would probably have been damned thereafter with a procrustean theme. The actual programme note now makes quite clear the actual theme, which is the struggle of the children of light against the children of darkness.

Here, suddenly, is a new Ashton. No longer is his desire to

please allowed to predominate and even to censor his work. Now he aims, it seems to me, at the awakening of the public conscience—a troublous and wearisome task which seems at certain harrowing periods and during the holocaustic crises to give more concern to the artist than the priest. In such a work it is hardly surprising that Ashton deserts, or tries to desert, the style in which he had created so many more popular successes. I think he went unnecessarily far in robbing his dancers of their toe shoes, but his distortions of the classical technique, his mixture of Petipa and Martha Graham, certainly produced some striking and original effects.

Possibly he revolted against his previous rather reverent attitude towards his audience, for now it seems that he deliberately set out to shock them. The obvious reference to a crucifixion, the erotic content and the rather pointless grotesquerie which the ballet features, represent perhaps his desire to come to grips with reality in a grimly realistic epoch. Artists in various media were resorting to realism at this time. While people generally sought for escape, artists widened the gap of communication by exposing horror, violence and futility in terms forced out of them by loathing and revulsion. As the holocaust developed, a general feeling of excitement and participation in war led to a heightened pulse and alerted sensibility. Even the 'new art' found its sympathizers, although fortunately for the ballet countless thousands still sought to escape by means of gentle diversions which were not so closely in touch with reality.

That is why *Dante Sonata* encountered two diametrically opposed schools of thought. The escapist found it revolting and quite unsuitable for the ballet stage; while the realists rejoiced because it was the first major work to make contact with reality since *The Green Table*.

Dante Sonata continues to interest large audiences. Quite apart from its emotional topicality it is in parts moving and exciting in a highly dramatic way. Certain crudities must be condoned, for the choreographer was working under grave stress; on the other hand some of the mime seems to me to be so grossly exaggerated, particularly by the lowering, grimacing children of darkness, as to need ruthless emendation.

In the same year Ashton created *The Wise Virgins*, which had the advantage of a wonderful set of costumes designed by

Rex Whistler and a well-chosen piece by Bach orchestrated by William Walton. Owing to the reluctance of my commanding officer to display magnanimity in the matter of leave passes, I saw the ballet only twice, and can remember with any clarity only sufficient detail to encourage me into an urgent and persistent advocacy for the revival of the work. Fonteyn's saintly movements as the Bride were alone sufficient to justify a revival. I recall, too, some delightful dances by the Foolish Virgins, as well as some monumental groupings. With perhaps some small choreographic revision such a ballet simply could not fail to delight the present discriminating Opera House audiences.

1946 marks the presentation of Ashton's most talked about ballet, *Symphonic Variations*: the outstanding example of this kind of work from a British choreographer. Fragments of it are so complete in their abstraction that at certain performances the wonderful simplicity of the décor and costumes, by Sophie Fedorovitch, which are in perfect harmony with the choreography, exemplifies the effectiveness of decorative abstraction for dance abstraction. The fusion of the choreography with the music, too, is a revelation of the power of classical dancing to evoke romantic reactions. With great delicacy Ashton has paralleled the music's sweeping arc of tranquillity, failing in my opinion only in one short movement wherein he has sought too closely to fit minute steps to a rapid melodic line from the piano. Here he seems to have missed the mood by a too close observation of one strand of the music instead of the full score.

But this is a small criticism, for the dissonance between the visual and aural images lasts only a few bars. On the other side must be put a multitude of brilliant subtleties; subtleties that have been worked out not for their own cleverness but for the achievement of a near-perfect synthesis. One such invention are the statuary poses struck at the extreme edge of the stage while movement continues in the centre. If clumsily thought out this would have caused an irritating conflict of focus between the posed figures and those in movement. In fact the poses are so keenly felt that a sense of repose is impressed on the mind, the pattern of the moving dancers in the centre being superimposed upon it. One's eye wanders away from the statuary untroubled, for it is so definite that the eye returns at the merest suggestion of a renewal of movement. Ashton has included a similar device in *Valses Nobles et Sentimentales*, but has not achieved the same striking effect.

If *Symphonic Variations* is Ashton at his best, *Les Illuminations* is Ashton at his worst. It purports to deal with a French poet of the last century, Jean Arthur Rimbaud, a 'decadent' protégé of Verlaine. His life was adventurous and sordid to a degree, and Ashton has introduced sensationalism of several kinds on the stage. I can overlook the crude sensualities of a large part of the work, but I certainly cannot overlook the firing of a revolver on the stage amid all the pageantry suggested by Beaton's exquisite and unrealistic costumes and environment. When a choreographer has recourse to such a stunt, then I think his powers of subtle evocation—the essence of ballet— have for a time deserted him.

Daphnis and Chloe was added to the repertoire of the Sadler's Wells Ballet in 1951. From the outset is seems to me that Ashton's invention has been forced, his imagination absent for long periods. The dance contest between Dorkon and Daphnis, in which Dorkon is supposed to be hoplessly outclassed, is poor indeed. If the contest were genuine, and judged by unprejudiced authorities, then Dorkon would gain marks quite comparable with those of Daphnis. This is perhaps less surprising in view of the fact that Daphnis is for some unaccountable reason called upon to perform with a shepherd's crook across his shoulders. Lykanion's lust for Chloe is allowed expression more through melodramatic mime than actual dance, although Ashton has given her a wonderful movement in which she does a series of *ronds de jambe en l'air* through a number of turns. The three nymphs follow their nebulous ritual clad in diaphanous draperies suspended from a variety of unlikely portions of their anatomy.

In scene two the dance of the pirates is a mixture of *The Pirates of Penzance* and Fokine's *Prince Igor*. As Chloe, however, Fonteyn moves me to emotion at her plight. When her skirt is torn off I am quite sure that many male members of the audience are prompted to offer her their coats in order to save her modesty, so pitiful is her shame. The fact that a little later we are to see her, similarly clad, dancing joyously with little inhibition in the arms of her lover, is not her fault but just another example of the weak construction of the ballet.

The whole of Chloe's scene with the pirates is sadistic in a way such as ballet alone can express. Implication and stylization are more powerful media for the aggravation of sadistic reactions than the realistic illusion of sadism itself, for to most of us an act of cruelty is likely to revolt and thus stifle sensual reaction, whereas subtle suggestion might well evoke it.

In the group dances of the final scene some reference is made to the Circassian Circle, and more reference to the energetic 'stepping' of the grand finale of a musical comedy. The entire company prances first down stage and then retreats, arms waving in the air, wide smiles and 'personality' oozing over the footlights. Nevertheless, Fonteyn and Somes have a breathtaking *pas de deux* which almost causes one to forget for a while that Ravel's exquisite music has been bound to mediocre choreography and worse scenery and costumes.

Tiresias, the blind Theban soothsayer, plays such an important part in the mythology of Greece that he is associated in some way with innumerable events. After his death he was believed still to exercise his powers in the lower world. He lost his sight at the age of seven, various vastly different causes having been cited for his affliction. Ashton can hardly be accused of seriously falsifying history, however, when he causes the seer to be blinded by Hera for having proved her wrong in an argument with Zeus as to whether man's or woman's sex life provides the greater satisfaction. As Ashton has also taken one of the lesser known myths of Tiresias, which features his dual life as man and woman, the fairness of the question could hardly be doubted, no matter what one's views are upon such scurvy treatment for a disappointing answer.

Possibly the theme has within itself the source of a great ballet, but if so Ashton certainly did not find it. Set in a Cretan décor, the ballet starts in such a way as to suggest that it will become grand enough in conception to match the legend it seeks to express. But no. The warlike games of the soldiers after a few bars relapse into monotonous repetition. Tiresias himself is an impressive enough figure, and the tumblers afford a little light relief of lively movement, but the music and the décor suggest that something tremendous, something mystic, is about to be enacted. Instead we see banal groups and dances, an erotic writhing number by the two snakes, male and female, into which Tiresias is temporarily transformed, and an utterly unconvincing mime passage between Zeus and Hera which fails lamentably to suggest either the nature or the intensity of their fascinating argument. Finally the blinded prophet gropes his way off the stage, tapping his stick in what is presumably intended to be an impressive finale.

This work is the most boring ever to be imposed upon us by Ashton. It is far too long, lasting about an hour, with too little dance invention and insufficient incident. Perhaps the music, the last score by Lambert, to whom everyone concerned with contemporary ballet on both sides of the curtain owes so much, was partly to blame. Complicated in texture and rhythm, it yet lacks any of the sweeping grandeur needed for such a theme. Ashton found himself lost for invention in its very complexity, seeming for long periods to move his dancers about the floor merely in order to 'fill in'.

Homage to the Queen, 'The Coronation Ballet', possessed a certain emotional appeal, even before the curtain went up, in 1953. During the hectic days of that remarkable summer anything in the nature of a procession quickened the pulse of the people; fluttering flags, rousing cheers and a communal catch in the throat were a staple part of our daily diet.

As the national ballet's contribution to the Coronation opens, rightly of course, with a procession and closes on an apotheosis which glorifies The Queen, with, in between, several lesser glorifications of the queens of the elements, those who were not present at the Royal Opera House on June 3rd, 1953, will readily imagine the scenes of enthusiasm produced by this particular kind of topicality.

But today we view the ballet in a different light. Occasional processions are all very well, but now we are back to normal; in cinemas the audiences stampede before the final close-up in order to avoid self-consciously standing to attention and finding themselves at the end of the bus queue; a gently waving Union Jack no longer arouses wild enthusiasm, but merely curiosity as to why it is there.

Robbed of its topicality, no more an epitome of a national emotion, *Homage to the Queen* has very little left. Each of the four queens, after a 'Sleeping Beauty' like ensemble at the beginning, has only a hackneyed variation in which she makes a set of

movements vaguely suggestive of growing, swimming, flaming
or flying, as the case may be. Not one of these dances can claim
brilliant invention or excitement of any kind. The Queen of the
Earth, for instance, represents growth by means of an *arabesque*
in which the knee of the supporting leg is first bent and then
straightened. The Queen of the Air is carried 'at the double' by
her consort (usually the Queen is Fonteyn with Somes as her
partner) round the stage. Fonteyn is no heavyweight and Somes
no weakling, but nobody could run round the Covent Garden
stage in such a way without a slight buckling at the knees.

The costumes do not help. The headgear of the consorts
makes them look like 'swilled revellers' returning from a
carnival ball; the Spirit of Fire has little red ribbons at the end
of his fingers; and the background is set twinkling with stars.
Nowhere is there a trace of subtlety in choreography or design.
Only Malcolm Arnold's magnificent score gives the audience
credit for intelligence and even sensitivity.

Ashton's failures during the last few years have given
his admirers cause for alarm. Yet I am convinced that under
the right conditions his genius would flower as brightly as ever
before. Those conditions entail a completely free hand in the
planning of his work and, most important of all, the creation
out of inner necessity rather than expediency. His is not the
kind of talent that can be switched on merely because of Arts
Council policy or the Trustees' commission. Given the required
freedom, he is capable of producing a series of first-rate works
in a variety of styles—and of once again composing a part that
will enhance the greatness of that greatest of all ballerinas,
Margot Fonteyn.

CHAPTER NINE

Antony Tudor

ALTHOUGH TUDOR ARRIVED in the United States in 1939 the influence of that country does not appear to have become unduly marked on him until 1945, when he produced *Pillar of Fire*. It is perhaps significant that five of the works he created in England were subsequently taken into the American repertory; indeed his influence has been so strong that it can frequently be detected in the work of most of the younger American choreographers, thus serving as an excellent counterbalance to the Balanchine abstractions.

More than any other choreographer Tudor seeks to present individual characters rather than abstractions of the various human qualities and emotions. Massine has here and there succeeded in suggesting the individual instead of a generalization, but very rarely can any of the characters in his ballets be regarded throughout as individuals, for usually they are no more than puppets for the expression of his purely choreographic ideas. Tudor, on the other hand, sometimes strains the medium beyond its scope in his efforts to present a character in the round. Deploring the fact that dance cannot stand by itself, he is constantly attempting to enlarge its scope. 'Dance should develop from dance itself, a more conscious knowledge of the use of dance', he says. 'Why should we in the dance world be unable to develop from dance into dance, and indeed more dance?'

Always endeavouring to express subtle shades and nuances of atmosphere, Tudor builds a strong element of pantomime on to his foundations of classicism, but true to the Fokine principle he usually succeeds in welding the elements so closely together that there is rarely any danger of his work drifting into mimeo-drama. His male roles, generally no doubt because during his formative years as a choreographer he had to work under the handicap of a scarcity of male dancers, are provided with stylized movements as distinguished from dance. Further, his male protagonist, played by himself in early works, is as a rule dressed in a costume nearer to that required in the street than on the ballet stage.

In the construction of his ballets Tudor starts with a mood, a situation or a story and then, in his head, works out a type of movement by which to transfer it from his mind on to the stage. First he builds a framework by a series of movements which will become the highlights or climaxes of the finished product; then he fills in the movement, poses and groups which will link the many figures, seeking throughout a fusion of movement rather than a set of separate dances. When mounting the results of his mental travail on his dancers he shows limitless patience and consideration, and occasionally modifies or extends a phrase or pattern in order to do full justice to a particular dancer's dramatic potentialities. In this way he marries the *danse d'école* with his own original movement and stylized every-day gesture.

Lilac Garden, both in England and America, is the first ballet to attempt an expression of mental and emotional stresses and relationships as distinct from the physical conflict in certain Fokine and Massine productions. I have already compared Ninette de Valois with Christopher Marlowe, but I hesitate to accord to a choreographer the honour of comparison with Shakespeare, yet in this one respect Tudor does resemble him: just as Shakespeare was the first English playwright to search into the minds of his characters, so Tudor is the first choreographer, in the true sense of the word, to employ mime and stylized movement for the expression of mental and emotional states of mind as well as dramatic climax. The comparison cannot be taken any further, for Tudor is by no means the most poetic of our choreographers although, again like Shakespeare, he does seem to possess a more extensive vocabulary than his contemporaries.

The theme of *The Lilac Garden* is ideal for the exploitation of Tudor's method and style. During a party various tormented creatures 'take a turn in the garden', to be maddeningly interrupted from time to time by other strollers. Caroline, newly engaged to a passive and forbidding character fittingly described in the programme as 'the man she must marry', tries to take leave of the man she loves but is persistently frustrated in her quest for a private and intimate moment. Her fiancé also suffers embarrassment from an 'episode in his past'.

No programme note is necessary. Set in the environment of a suitably romantic garden, to which Chausson's poem for violin and orchestra adds the appropriate emotions, the characters mime and dance into clearly defined relationships and conflicts. The costumes for the ladies and for 'the man she must marry' are as naturalistic as the movement will permit, the lover alone being clad 'unnaturalistically'.

The work starts off with the unusual advantage of unity in time and place; further, the theme concerns four characters all of whom are at a climax in their lives. Emotional tensity is thereby the more easily developed and maintained. As the characters are the product of middle-class Victorian society they possess a superficial restraint, a restraint which Tudor expresses balletically by means of restricted movements of head, arms and shoulders. Paradoxically this physical restriction becomes highly and poignantly expressive, especially when it is preceded by a running leap by Caroline into the arms of her lover when they are momentarily alone. To express the restraint and reticence classical terminology is employed, but for the less inhibited character of the 'girl in his past', a broader and more realistic series of movements are brought into play. Throughout the ballet there are practically no fast movements and no beats, but a great variety of expressive turns and lifts.

Tudor, more than any other choreographer—or at least more consistently than any other—succeeds in producing a true and convincing form of dance-drama in which the conventions no longer obtrude between the audience and the illusion of reality. On the contrary, the effects and conventions become utterly convincing and even the less gullible ballet-lovers are encouraged to indulge in audience projection.

Faced with a great and overwhelming scene of slaughter or the phenomenon of a supernatural agency, the Greek dramatists wisely made no effort to reconstruct it in their plays, but used that effective device whereby the horrifying event is recounted by an eye-witness. Ballet makers could with advantage adapt this method for their own ends; too often is the medium stretched far beyond its limits, making ludicrous attempts to conjure up visions on the stage which are far better left to the imagination. In *Dark Elegies* Tudor has sought to make a ballet

on the mental and emotional stresses which follow tragedy
without any attempt to detail physical events.

Friedrich Rückert, a German lyric poet of the early nineteenth century, wrote a series of five poems following the death
of his two children in a cholera epidemic. In each of them he
expresses a different reaction of the father to his tragedy: in the
first he cannot understand why the sun continues to shine, in
the second he recalls the bright eyes of his child, in the third he
sees the mother enter the room and automatically look round
for the child, in the fourth he is oppressed by the quiet of the
house, and thinks momentarily that the children are out,
before the weight of his sorrow overwhelms him again. The final
poem is of a similar nature; aware of a heavy storm, he worries
because the children are out, then realizes that they are now safe
from storms, whereupon he at last grows resigned to his grief.

This series of poems was set to music by Gustav Mahler, who
naturally aimed at matching their mood rather than giving
aural support to their slender literary content. His own score
builds up from bitter grief to resigned acceptance, but without
any development of a major climax.

The simplicity of the costumes avoids any definite reference
to a particular people, although they are suggestive of peasantry.
From the small group dance images emerge which symbolize
first oppression, with the bowed head and bent back, to slight
relief through forgetfulness, back to despair and finally the
expression of calm courage. For the men there are virile movements and the solos stand out from the chorus in a more powerful rendering of a closely related movement pattern. There are
no classical steps, but *pointes* are given sparing employment.
As in *Lilac Garden*, Tudor again finds good use for the 'dead'
arms and restrained torso. Throughout the ballet it is evident
that he has taken his inspiration more from the music than the
poems themselves; for he does not seek any strong evocation of
the themes of any of the sonnets, although he does occasionally
vaguely symbolize certain physical events as they pass through
the tortured thoughts of the bereaved. For this reason the words
impede rather than add to the atmosphere of the ballet, for
there must always be a vague uneasy feeling that they have a
practical bearing on the dance patterns.

Despite Tudor's brilliant invention on such a deliberately

limited plane, *Dark Elegies* has never fully satisfied him as a theatrical presentation, for the simple reason that there is no coherent development running through the ballet; neither is there any real dramatic climax, for the work rests on a few deliberate modifications in emotional reactions to a tragedy which has already occurred. The mental and emotional adjustment to this tragedy is I think one of those subjects which can be treated successfully only in terms of those concepts which lie within the power of words to express. Even if that expression must retain all the vagueness of words it is, nevertheless, a subject which no other medium can legitimately treat.

In London Tudor's *Judgment of Paris* appears to be regarded by most as a trifling burlesque and by a few as an example of that kind of obscenity which can be presented in the ballet theatre only because it is not subjected to scrutiny by the censor. I can find only a handful of candid spirits to agree with me that this work, despite its snatches of Rabelaisian humour, expresses with great poignancy the most sordid of human tragedies. In the more permanent literature of the ballet in the United States I can find scarcely any detailed criticism at all except in Grace Robert's 'Borzoi Book of Ballets', whose allegiance I am delighted to quote: 'It ought to be very funny, but there is an underlying mood that renders it not much more comic than a death-bed scene'.

Set in what has been variously described as a brothel and a clip-joint, *Judgment of Paris* unfolds its simple and sordid theme by an elegant language compounded so skilfully of mime and movement that not one discernible break appears. Perhaps I can clarify this point by comparing dance and mime with poetry and prose as employed in T. S. Eliot's *Family Reunion*. Here, as the playwright admits, the poetry draws attention to itself as poetry, thus causing a break in illusion. In a verse drama, too, prose should be used very sparingly, for the audience is called upon to make a rapid adjustment with each change from one to the other. Similarly in a dance-drama, pure dance, by which I mean dance as distinct from stylized natural movement, must be employed, if it is to be employed at all, with the utmost discretion.

Out of their context each of the dances would appear no more than a piece of barren tastelessness, for Tudor makes his point

LEONIDE MASSINE seen here with Alexandra Danilova in an early production of *La Boutique Fantasque*.

Two scenes from *Carmen*, each showing Renée Jeanmaire as Carmen and Peti as Jose.

Roland Peti.

in this work first by presenting his three prostitutes as pathetic creatures, all of them in their different ways sick of the life to which evidently they have been brought by inveterate sloth and lack of will. Juno, youngest of the three, dances before the drunken customer with still a shred of shame. Her gauche, unpractised movements and the clumsily arch manipulation of her black lace fan gain scarcely a glance from the customer, who continues to order what must be a more potent liquor than that usually obtainable in such places, for he rapidly becomes well nigh incapable. Venus, with a mop of uncontrollable tow hair and a ghastly blue satin dress, next takes the floor, insinuating herself with no small difficulty through a couple of hoops, sighing with relief rather than triumph at the end of each repetition. More sophisticated than her young sister, she executes a kind of *ronde de jambe* movement to draw a brief flicker of interest from the solitary onlooker—the cadaverous and utterly blasé waiter cannot be included among the audience—sinking breathlessly into her seat with a scruffy-looking feather boa, too tired and hungry even to conceal the fact. Determined not to waste her energy, she bends over the customer's table and shows him with her fingers the nature of the choreographic virtuosity she is about to essay. Her efforts to perform the splits show that she has long passed the time when limbering exercises could be of any use to her, and she knows it. Very soon she must sink into a deeper degradation that will require not even the shallow formality of this kind of performance.

The customer chooses Venus, but falls into insensibility before taking his prize; whereupon the three women and the waiter dive frantically for his pockets. Before she hides it away in her bosom, Venus listens to his watch to make sure it is still ticking.

The situation itself is, of course, sufficient to evoke sympathy and even pity. But if the various dances were composed without subtlety and in a spirit of mere burlesque, the effect of the situation would soon wear off to be replaced by ribald amusement or disgust. Perhaps the poor reception of the work by English audiences is due to a still widespread reluctance to admit that such a sin as prostitution exists here at all. I don't know. To me the work can lay just claim to recognition as high art.

Gala Performance is another work to be included in the repertory of both an English and an American company. The manipulation of its theme enhances the expressiveness of the choreography and provides ample opportunity for great variety. The Russian ballerina specializes in *pirouettes* which she performs with great energy and determination. The Italian remains aloof, almost as though her audience did not exist. Employing the Cecchetti method, she balances in *attitude* with a cold indifference to time, either that directed from the conductor's baton or that required by the chronometer. The French girl effervesces with gaiety and flirtatious charm and, quite unlike her Italian colleague, remains extremely conscious of her beloved admirers out front.

The opening scene back-stage has often been criticized on the grounds that it is too static, that its wit and satire are secured solely through mime and not by dance. This criticism is certainly based on a valid assumption, but the wit is so pointed and the entire scene so well balanced and developed to the climax before the ascent of the curtain that it seems to me to form a perfect introduction to the scene which follows.

In the final scene the three ballerinas are seen in a constant state of antagonism. Each of them does a series of fevered and spectacular steps to draw attention to herself. Not content with that, one pushes in front of the others to their chagrin and our delight.

The entire work consists of overstatement, but its wit and humour are the more pungent for being well and truly founded on aspects of character which we still like to believe belong essentially to the species ballerina.

The Prokofiev music to which the work is performed is claimed by some to be inappropriate, but I find its persuasive rhythms and occasional tinkle completely apposite to its context.

On both sides of the Atlantic *Pillar of Fire* is regarded as the most remarkable of all dance-dramas. The plot itself grows and develops out of Hagar's own character, out of her struggle to adjust herself to a given situation and out of her reaction to the modes of behaviour to which she becomes subject. Hagar, a lonely and sensitive soul, is out of tune with the life she is expected to live by her puritanical elder sister, and humiliated by her younger sister, who wrests away by her superficial charms the Friend to whom Hagar looked for comfort and escape. Sitting at the front of her house, Hagar sees in her imagination the earthy love-making which goes on in the house opposite. At the same time horrified and attracted, she readily falls a victim to the lustful attentions of one of the inmates of that house. But mere sexuality, far from solacing her for the apparent loss of the Friend, brings self-disgust and an inconsolable feeling of guilt. Now she suffers humiliation from her own set and is spurned by the loose-living outcasts in the house opposite.

The younger sister returns from a walk with the Friend and the elder sister calls the family indoors. But Hagar then sees the creatures from both her worlds and is again scorned and rejected, her sister failing to recognize her. She flies in abject shame from the Friend, only to be restrained and taken into his heart with love and understanding.

Tudor has composed the choreography for the expression of this plot with his customary ingenuity. The Lovers in Innocence employ a kind of dance which makes liberal use of classical terms, whereas the Lovers in Experience give expression to more earthy and sensual movements. Hagar has two kinds of *pas de deux*, one with the Young Man and one with the Friend: the first contains some typical Tudor lifts and stresses the sexual relationship between man and woman; the second is gentle and calmer in nature, showing Hagar's emotional conflict with herself, her abasement and finally the new understanding between her and the Friend.

The closing scene alone gives rise to censure and perhaps to a little ridicule, for as the couple walk towards the brighter future the curtain comes down in a flood of false sentiment reminiscent of Hollywood at its most banal.

Apart from this end the plot is conditioned by the characterization. Although the events of even a Tudor ballet deny realism, the reference to every-day movement, together with costumes which make many concessions to normal apparel, do stake a claim for the expression of contemporary life through the medium of ballet.

As *Undertow* has been seen in England only very few times, I will summarize its plot in the hope that a recollection of the movement and pattern of the work itself will thus be prompted in the minds of those who saw it. Cybele, mother of the Gods, gives birth to a son. Early in his life the son is injured in mind and spirit when his mother rejects him and goes to Pollux, as a result of which the world becomes saddled with yet another Transgressor.

Next time we see him at the dockside of a large city, together with a young companion. Volupia, a street-walker, attempts to attract his attention too. Although disturbed by her presence, he successfully wills himself to ignore her. Then follows a number of incidents between Volupia and two Sileni who, according to the ancient myth from which all the characters in the ballet derive their names, are the sons of Hermes and one of the many nymphs with whom he enjoyed sex relations. Other sons, the Satyrisci, boisterous adolescents, make a stormy appearance, as do various other mythical creatures, all presumably to express some symbolical and psychological aspect which I remained unable to interpret. Ate, spirit of evil, nearly suffers strangulation at the hands of the Transgressor, and finally, to bring the sordid tale to a conclusion, Medusa is murdered by him after providing him with what is presumably his first sexual experience.

An epilogue shows the Transgressor awakening from deep slumber. As the actors point accusing fingers at him he marches bravely forward to meet the consequences of the sins which Fate had decreed he must commit.

Undertow has been described as a psychological case-history expressed in terms of dance. Whatever it is, much of its inference is so bewildering that only a trained psychologist could unravel it. Nevertheless, in parts naturalistic movement and gesture are intermingled with easily recognizable ballet steps in such a way that the work bears the unmistakable Tudor signature. Volupia seeks business on her *pointes*, evidently quite certain of her power and destiny, but the Transgressor develops his character by means of movements which are as incoherent and confused as a drunkard's speech. Medusa, far from turning the Transgressor into stone, raises him to passion and uncontrollable desire, first to possess and then to destroy her.

Following his customary style, Tudor resorts very rarely to anything remotely approaching a fast movement, although he does exploit the sudden and spasmodic gesture and convulsive movement of the body. Frequently he ignores the actual beat of the score, matching his choreographic patterns against the pattern of the sound itself. Despite its 'realistic' theme and its attempt to interpret and expand various states of mind and conflict between the Transgressor and those with whom he comes into contact, *Undertow* contains a surprisingly large element of true dance.

Naturally this particular kind of ballet is not to everybody's taste. There are many who believe that ballet is a completely unsuitable medium for the expression of a state of mind; others even go further and urge the renunciation on the ballet stage of anything but the classics and modern works which conform with the requirements of a sort of effete musical comedy. They may be right.

After Fokine's first shining example had formulated the pattern of twentieth-century ballet, others took his pioneering experiments further. Nijinsky groped for a wider scope in balletic expression; Massine found yet closer harmony between dancing and mimetic gesture as a means of expressing dramatic action and to enlarge the physical vocabulary of dance; Balanchine brought the classical idiom into touch with contemporary life in a development of style which truly but inexplicably be described as American; Ashton has done the same for England; and Tudor has pioneered a form of dance-drama which seeks not merely the exposition of dramatic action, but the mental and even psychological impetus underlying such action.

CHAPTER TEN

Walter Gore

APART FROM HIS Scottish birthplace, Gore's background, unlike that of so many choreographers, undoubtedly encouraged him in his pursuit of ballet. His father was a violinist and musical director of distinction, while both his mother and maternal grandmother were women of the theatre. Once in the Marie Rambert organization he found himself in conditions of unbounded balletic fertility. Soon he grew eager to make a ballet, but not before 1938 did he find an opportunity. Then, using scenery and costumes originally designed for Ashton's *Valentine's Eve*, he presented *Valses Nobles et Sentimentales*.

In 1939 four more works stemmed from his active imagination, but from then, throughout the war, he served with distinction in the Royal Navy, returning in 1945. In that year he devised *Simple Symphony* for the Ballet Rambert, and in the next few years added considerably to that company's repertory, both in the number of productions and in their variety. Following the inauguration of Ballet Workshop in 1950, he also made ballets for that admirable institution, as he did for the very short-lived New Ballet Company in 1952. In 1953 he gallantly and perhaps foolishly refused to be deterred by the pitiful history of so many ballet companies that have sprung up since the war, and with his wife Paula Hinton started his own compact and modest little group.

In composition Gore depends largely upon music for the development of his structure. Possibly for this reason he dislikes the strict form of much eighteenth-century music. Throughout his career he has employed mostly the music of living composers, choosing accompaniments which lay down a complex fabric of rhythm but with no overbearing melodic theme. Professedly impatient of the discipline, convention and formality demanded by classical ballet, he nevertheless relies very strongly on the classical vocabulary. In common with most of his contemporaries he modifies and distorts this classicism to his own ends, as well as seeking a greater expressive power by the employment of a variety of styles of movement together with naturalistic mime and gesture. His works can be divided into three groups: (1) exercises in pure dance inspired by reference to games and folk dances; (2) dramatic themes expressed chiefly in terms of dance; (3) narrative dance-drama expressed chiefly in a compound of quasi-naturalistic and highly stylized movement. In the first group are included ballets such as *Simple Symphony*, *Pastorelle* and *Hoops*, in the second *Mr Punch* and *Winter Night*, and in the third, *Confessional* and *Tancredi and Clorinda*.

In his essays in pure dance Gore dilutes his facility of invention, his flowing and vital movement images, with too much repetition. Frequently an exciting piece of dance structure is followed by a series of formless, hackneyed steps. In fact these abstract works often seem to be no more than the choreographer's rough notes for a ballet. Every single work of this nature which Gore has put on the stage, or so it appears to me, needs rigorous and even ruthless pruning, extensive replanning, greater cohesion of choreographic pattern and in many cases far firmer stress on the actual climax of dance.

In his second group, Gore is perhaps most effective; at any rate he certainly achieves a far greater theatrical appeal, although here one must be careful, for whereas in the first group visual effectiveness depends solely upon the choreography, now the plot or situation has in itself a measure of interest. Provided he has not chosen too strong a drama, therefore, Gore does succeed in developing an intense dramatic appeal in his own choreographic terms. Sometimes, in common with all choreographers who are working in the medium of dance-drama, his plots overwhelm him. At such times nothing but a direct verbal statement or action, stylized only enough to fit it or the stage, is either adequate or suitable. Bereft of verbal language, and by the conventions of his medium denied the use of naturalism, Gore resorts to a futile compromise, when his mummery of a highly charged situation becomes as ludicrous to modern theatre-goers as a piece of Victorian barnstorming.

In the third group Gore has so far made two essays. To the accompaniment of a narrative poem, read either off or on stage, the dancers interpret and express sometimes the mental reactions of the characters to a given situation and sometimes a semi-naturalistic imitation of the physical actions which the poem describes. In principle I am strongly opposed to the idea of translating poetry into movement. It is, I think, both permissible and even logical for a choreographer to interpret his reactions to a poem into his own terms; whatever one's opinion of John Cranko's *Harlequin in April* or Jerome Robbin's *Age of Anxiety*, these two choreographers can hardly be accused of attempting to clutter the stage with visual translations of the poems which form the source and inspiration of these two works. It is also a different matter, of course, if the poet intended a visual realization of his images, as Milton did with 'Comus'. There the choreographer can work with confidence in the knowledge that if he accomplishes his own task well enough, the visual and the aural images will complement each other. The whole point about a great poem, not so intended, which disqualifies the choreographer is that free of any counter-suggestion the mind is at liberty to react to the poem as it will, soaring into the highest imaginative summits, impelled by the intense and evocative power of the words, the images and the rhythms.

However, Gore possibly agrees with the theory of Leonardo—a theory with which Lifar also concurs—to the effect that poetry is severely limited in its imaginative scope. If so he is fully justified in attempting to enrich the narratives with an accompaniment of his own lively invention. But the artist who seeks to enlarge the expressive power of any other work by marrying it to a creation in his own medium is on dangerous ground: it is one thing to use an existing work as a source of inspiration for another work, but quite another thing to translate that work into a new medium. The creative artist must be influenced in his choice of subject-matter through the very nature of his medium. It can of course be argued that many ballets set to already existing music seek to translate patterns of sound into patterns of movement, but I submit that there is a fundamental difference between the choreographic translation of music and poetry. Music is not usually bound to any literary theme, whereas poetry invokes visual images even when treating in spiritual or metaphysical concepts. The poet seeks to conjure up in the mind of his audience a series of images; if these images are provided by the choreographer the audience is given somebody else's imagery, somebody else's reactions to the poem; reactions which are themselves trammelled by the limitations of the human body. The beholder then has to transfer his imagination to the visual patterns and conceive in them something beyond their actual physical enactment.

So far Gore has attempted this translation of two poems. His first essay was in 1939, when he set his movements to Browning's poem, 'Confessional'. The poem represents Browning in highly dramatic and emotional mood. Its theme is concerned with a girl who is persuaded into betraying her lover for his own good to the Spanish Inquisition. But too late she finds she has been duped and sees her lover burnt at the stake. While the poem is read off-stage the girl performs stylized passages of mime and gesture, expressing her reactions to the various situations the poem describes.

In all probability this work will never again appear on any stage. In 1952 Sally Gilmour finally left with her husband to live in Australia. Madame Rambert made one of her typical and delightful gestures and presented her with the costume; for Sally had been the only interpreter of the role since the ballet was first produced in 1941 and 'Mim' decided to pay her the compliment of removing it from the repertory with her departure.

Tancred and Clorinda develops from *Confessional* in that an extract from Tasso's 'Jerusalem Delivered', together with the music by Monteverdi, composed as a setting for the words over three hundred years ago, is chanted on stage. Apart from the fact that in *Tancred and Clorinda* two characters each play an equally important part, the work follows an identical formula; the two fight their prolonged duel, each armed with a sword. But in this case the poem describes such extreme physical violence and such unbelievable human fortitude that all is far larger than life. Overwhelmed by the images conjured into the minds of the audience by the words, the movements of the dancers become so inadequate as to be ridiculous.

Simple Symphony, set to Benjamin Britten's music in 1944, soon after Gore was demobilized, has been described by Lionel Bradley as follows:

One of the best *divertissements* in the history of English ballet, with a spontaneous gaiety and fine invention of steps and a strong sense of pattern.

Gaiety, invention and pattern the work certainly does possess, yet for a large part of the ballet's duration the dancers appear to be motivated by no logical impulse, but only by a desire on the part of the choreographer to see them expressing gaiety on the stage. Certain folk-dance movements are suggested and discarded; an incipient game floats across our vision for a few moments, and various references are made to human pursuits; but mostly the work remains pointless, the gaiety lacking in reason.

Antonia is compounded of elements from each of the last two groups. An intensely dramatic theme is worked out by means of expressive movement and descriptive gesture. There is no spoken narrative, and the short theme is abundantly clear, so that the dance can be expressive without being explanatory. The programme note reads:

> It is the story of Raphael and his passionate love for Antonia. It begins in the darkness of his room where his tortured brain sees her continually before him as he first believed her to be and then how he discovered her to be, a faithless, worthless wanton.

The opening *pas de deux* with which Gore seeks to express the imaginings of that tortured brain is conceived in gentle and even tender terms, throughout providing an excellent contrast to the sensuality of the later *pas de deux* of Antonia with her lover, Sebastian. In the first passage Raphael and Antonia dance without touching each other, the tempo is slow and the movements soft and flowing, with no hard stresses or accent. In the movement devoted to the portrayal of Raphael, however, quick nervous footwork appears allied with heavy and exaggerated arm and body rhythms. The effect is as potent an expression as is possible in ballet of such a neurotic character who is prone to self-dramatization. His pursuit of Antonia through a Carnival seems to me to be a concession to Ballet with a capital B: the outmoded belief that ballet must contain spectacle. Here the spectacle is hardly worthy of the name and would have been better omitted, for it is incongruous to boot.

When the two finally come to the dance which forms the

climax, however, a very real tension has been developed, for they move simultaneously for several bars, Antonia carrying out her evasive action, the while Raphael gradually, relentlessly, draws nearer and nearer. To enhance the effect here Gore employs the rhythms of the dancers' feet to heighten the effect, although I heard one member of the first-night audience say that the choreographer had been compelled to invent an extraneous rhythm because he had chosen the wrong music in the first place. It is a point of view, but the Sibelius score is in many ways highly appropriate: its undertones, and its stresses, its solemnity and mild romanticism, support the theme and choreographic plan without overwhelming them.

Before Raphael at last gets his hands on the girl and strangles her, she exposes, through some of the frankest dance passages seen on the English stage, the full extent of her sluttishness. Here there is no attractive movement, but the negation of all which the adherents of ballet have come to regard as beautiful. Indeed, Gore has evidently used his knowledge of the classical idiom in order to work out this almost horrifying antithesis of it.

This kind of ballet is well worth attempting even if to permit a school of imaginative choreographers to stretch the expressive power of movement to its limits. Philosophical, psychological and even aesthetic arguments aside, however, Gore has undoubtedly produced in *Antonia* a telling piece of theatrical dance in which he has attempted to give, in that most expressive yet most limited language of dance, an original statement resulting from his own perception and imagination.

Gore is by no means the first choreographer to discover that drum-beats undiluted by other orchestral sound can offer great aid in the accomplishment of dramatic effect. I cannot, however, remember the drum being used more skilfully towards this purpose than in the opening of *Crucifix*. The music, by Samuel Barber, was provided with a specially composed percussion introduction by Michael Hobson.

A girl (Paula Hinton), suspected of being a witch, is pursued, baited and beaten by a mob. The drum rhythms, brilliantly conceived in relation both to the dramatic considerations and the choreographic form, add power and pathos to the semi-naturalistic movements by which the girl communicates her plight; the lighting, concentrated in areas of light and dark, together with a backcloth consisting of severe 'cut-outs', each contribute their share, and the mob looks ten times as big as its actual number, becoming a symbol of insensate sadistic violence.

A priest who comes to the rescue keeps the mob at bay only by constantly shoving his crucifix into their faces. In her terror the girl kills the priest and herself grabs hold of the crucifix for protection. But she is taken by force and tried in the people's court before a judge no less terrifying for his imperturbable mien and a jury with gargoyle faces, with prosecuting and defending counsel influenced in their advocacy perhaps by *The Green Table* and Paul Draper. Following which the girl is bound and led to the stake—a macabre and telling set, this last, with the cruel wooden pillar lit by a single illuminating spot.

The final moment set us talking. The fire is kindled and the girl suddenly lets out two horrifying bloodcurdling screams as the curtain falls.

Mostly the ballet succeeds in its aim to thrill and to shock. The climaxes are perfectly spaced and skilfully developed. Paula Hinton as the central figure throughout mimes, acts and moves in a way which brings out every intonation of the choreography, although even she could not conceal one or two surprising weaknesses in a work otherwise so well devised. But in my submission the gravest breach of all lies in those two screams.

In *Street Games* Gore has made an effort to marry his three styles, with emphasis on the dance element. Children play balletic hop-scotch, they divert themselves and some members of the audience with a rubber ball, some boys indulge themselves in a game of rugby and fight the sort of duel beloved of imaginative small boys the world over. They play statues and they dress up. Adolescents emerge from a cinema and mildly emulate the celluloid figures of their adulation by an exciting and ecstatic tango, together with a little harmless and a trifle self-conscious love-making.

Free of the slightest trace of pretentiousness, *Street Games* possesses some moments of charm and more of wit. But, like so many other Gore essays, it is not a finished ballet. Skilfully though the dances are worked out and pieced together, there is no illuminating climax, no highlight of exciting dance to make the work memorable.

Hoops is another work compounded of children's pleasures. All the dances are carried out by dancers who hold wooden hoops and who are reminiscent both in movement and costume of circus entertainers. As usual the movement contains much that is original, much that is ingenious; one dance for the leading girl, executed with a completely expressionless face, is notably effective in its wit. But the joke is dragged on, and throughout the entire ballet, which is not unduly long, there is far too much repetition, far too much dead wood that should ruthlessly be cut away.

Mr Punch is exactly what its title indicates—a balletic version of the apparently imperishable fairground and seaside entertainment. Despite the sometimes lamentable sophistication of children today in their outlook towards entertainment, despite the standards set by film and television, Punch and Judy rarely fail to draw a crowd. For the little ones undoubtedly the most attractive element is the uninhibited whacking which goes on throughout the performance; whereas for older children the sense of participation is a point in its favour.

But Gore's version was made for adults, and the music was specially commissioned from Arthur Oldham. This was Gore's first work to a specially commissioned score and it was presented with some flourish in 1946 before Ballet Rambert's trip to Australia.

Lionel Bradley, apart from his singular accuracy as to facts, especially chronological ones, was noted for his admiration of the Rambert company, and especially for his sympathetic interest in all those choreographers who have developed under 'Mim's' influence. Bradley wrote very little, but in an appraisal of Gore he claimed that *Mr Punch* was a 'masterpiece of comic ingenuity'.

While inclined to agree with this glowing verdict, I feel that Gore has tied himself too tightly to the plot. Instead of presenting a new outlook on the Anglicized version of the old story, he has been content to put certain well-known actions and episodes into choreographic terms. These terms are I agree both comic and ingenious, but they add nothing whatever, it seems to me, to the version which we see in fairground and holiday beach, either in characterization or in plot development. Once again he has found vivid expression for the obvious. Such a work undoubtedly has a certain amount of entertainment value, but does not advance its creator very far in his choreographic career.

Winter Night falls between the first two groups of Gore's ballets, for although it has a theme, it is the kind of theme which lends itself admirably to interpretation by means of a series of dance episodes practically undiluted by mime. This theme is as follows.

> *Robert:* 'We have loved, Felice, and now . . .'
> *Felice:* 'And now?'
> *Robert:* 'There comes the parting. Life consists of meetings and partings. How else is life?'
> *Felice:* 'This parting is the winter night of my despair.'
> *Aimée:* 'It is for me the bright summer now beginning.'

Founded on Rachmaninov's Second Piano Concerto, this ballet to a certain extent parallels the musical structure. All the chief characters, backed by a *corps de ballet*, are given dance which accords with one of the musical themes: the first represents the tragic figure, Felice; Robert is the main theme, with Aimée, who interweaves her way among them, sometimes taking part in one and sometimes another.

Naturally in a work of this length and complexity Gore has not sought to maintain anything like an exact parallel. When the musical themes develop and become more and more involved he abandons the parallel, but not before the sentiment in each of the themes is firmly related to the movement of each character. The *pas de deux* of Robert and Felice, Robert and Aimée, and a *pas de trois* with the three main characters, are very effective passages. Each is in strong contrast with the others, yet each has much in common with the *pas de trois*. Each of them, too, typifies the definite quality of each character and each of them advances the logical action of the ballet.

What Gore really needs is a Diaghilev: a trite remark, perhaps, for I can think of no choreographer except perhaps Roland Petit who would not benefit from the influence of the founder of modern ballet. But Gore needs more than most the sharp discipline as well as the taste of a Diaghilev for the control and development of his particular talents. His choreography possesses as a rule both a well-marked visual pattern and a strong sense of musical rhythm; he betrays poignant flashes of tenderness and sympathy; occasionally he sketches the outlines of a powerful character; but inevitably these promising beginnings are dissipated into weak and discursive ramblings. The inventiveness, the vitality and the sensitivity need a control and discipline which Gore seems to be unable to give them. His known impatience of discipline and the formalities of classicism are in themselves both an advantage and a disadvantage; while he is thus encouraged to compose in a contemporary idiom, he is also liable to ignore the need of formal elements to such an extent that his work becomes quite shapeless. But one day Gore will produce a ballet of the highest possible class; it will contain both great entertainment value and wonderful choreographic invention; its characterization will be vivid and intense and the entire work will hang together and develop in the perfect shape of its individual movement as well as in the form of its overall structure. All this will most surely come about if only Gore will subject his talents to a director of the most profound sensibility or alternatively develop a discipline of discrimination within himself.

CHAPTER ELEVEN

Robert Helpmann

H ELPMANN'S ATTITUDE TOWARDS the making of a ballet
is best summarised in his own words:

Ballet is essentially a theatrical art. The man in the
street may not understand technique, but he does understand and will react to a dramatic situation.

Throughout his long career as a dancer—the first male
dancer with English as his native language to become a well-
known figure outside the balletomanic circle—and his much
shorter career as a choreographer, Helpmann has remained
an enigmatic and highly controversial personality. His efforts,
both as dancer and choreographer, would have been far more
readily understood and appreciated had these words of his,
uttered to a large gathering of teachers when he delivered an
annual address to the Royal Academy of Dancing, and subsequently published in 'The Dancing Times' (September 1942),
been assimilated by all who have tried to assess his work.

Many times he was accused of overacting and even of
parodying and burlesquing his roles. Critics of widely contrasting points of view took him seriously to task on innumerable
occasions. But Helpmann the actor, robbed of the power of
speech, obviously could not resist the temptation to compensate
for this disability by stressing his remaining, highly mobile,
means of communication. Perhaps he was wrong, but I suspect
that the corpus of ballet-goers, if reluctant to admit it in public
because warned so often of his exaggeration, have been strangely
unmoved by his successors in such roles as Dr Coppelius, Tom
Rakewell, Mr O'Reilly and The Stranger. In each of his five
ballets, all he has created and all in the repertory of Sadler's
Wells, he has expressed himself by statements as direct as the
language of ballet will allow and has again been accused of
corrupting the beauty of that language by the introduction of
naturalistic mime and gesture. Had his dance-dramas treated
subjects of a lighter nature, and therefore more generally

ery Pagava and George Skibine in the first production of *Night Shadow*.
GEORGE BALANCHINE

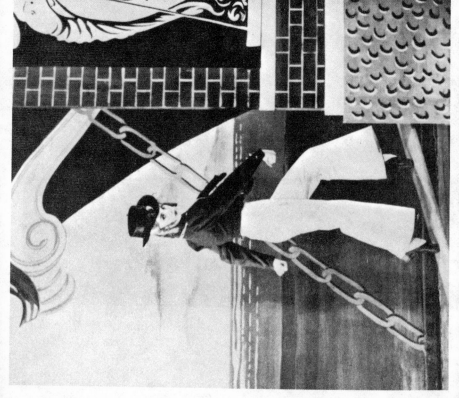

acceptable in the ballet theatre, perhaps his style and method would have received less harsh criticism.

Helpmann's formative years in Australia were spent under a strong influence of the legitimate theatre and no direct influence of ballet at all. Undoubtedly this interest in drama led him to seek dramatic themes for his ballets. His firm conviction that ballet is a theatrical art, and that its appeal must be made to the theatre-going public rather than to a specialized audience, conditioned his style so that the dance element and naturalistic movement were married in such a way as to convey an illusion of reality.

Every one of Helpmann's ballets is compounded of stylized natural movement, occasional dances which either advance the action or express a mental state of one of the characters, and emotionally significant groups. In all these constituent parts mime plays an important part. 'Mime is as legitimate an element in the medium of ballet as dancing,' says Helpmann. 'In fact, what distinguishes choreography from an arrangement of dance steps is its concentration on the composition as a whole—not merely the dance movement but also the mime.' Unlike several other twentieth-century choreographers, Helpmann in his actual work has always tried to put his own theories into practice. In his efforts to combine the elements of dance and mime for the purpose of a strictly theatrical effect, he has evolved a type of mimetic movement readily comprehensible to a modern theatre-going audience. Intolerant of those who assert that his ballets contain too little dance, he says: 'Every movement made on the stage by a dancer must be dancing.' On first acquaintance with them, works like *Miracle in the Gorbals* and *Adam Zero* do appear to contain long passages of more realistic action than any other choreographer has put on to the stage. This delusion is due entirely to the cunning method of their composition, for in fact not one passage bears any real resemblance to everyday movement. He does, however, evoke a strong impression of realism and expresses many mental states commonly experienced in the twentieth century.

But anyone who tackles Helpmann too vigorously on this question of dance in ballet is likely to be repelled by a withering and typical reply: 'There is less dancing for the male in the classical ballets, except *Giselle*, than in most of the shorter modern ballets.'

Produced during the war, his first major work, *Comus*, provoked even at that uncritical time a storm of controversy. The silence accorded to the ballet stage, demanded just as rigidly if not for equally good reason as in the Reading Room at the British Museum, was shattered by the voice of Comus (Helpmann), uttering two long quotations from the wonderful Milton poem. The fact that the work was described in the programme as a masque was insufficient grounds, according to many balletomanes, for the breaking of the golden rule.

The stage spectacle, accompanied by the magnificent Purcell/Lambert music and decorated by suitably fantastic Messel scenery and costumes, was wholly exciting. The enactment of the Lady's adventures by means of solo movement punctuated by a series of highly inventive and beautiful tableaux, plus the quotation to which Helpmann gave perfect utterance, formed a work so satisfying that I was unconcerned as to whether it should be called a ballet or a masque. Checking my memory now with the aid of a pile of photographs, I am struck again by the composition of the groups, the slow majestic development of the action, the delicate hints of characterization, the Lady in particular living fully up to Milton's 'Virtuous mind that ever walks attended by a strong siding champion, Conscience' and the abundant invention in all the elements.

Heartily I agree with Caryl Brahms: 'A notable early work by a man with a great instinct for theatre.' The only drawback is that Helpmann alone possesses the necessary qualifications to play the title role. If the masque is revived different arrangements will have to be made for the spoken words; unless, of course, Helpmann plays it himself, or a new and phenomenal personality springs up from somewhere.

The opening of the ballet *Hamlet*, so dramatic and so vivid in its imagery, should make quite clear even to those who possess only a rudimentary knowledge of the play that they are now watching not 'Hamlet without words', but one person's conception of what Hamlet might dream in his 'sleep of death'. For in the ballet or dance-drama, call it what you will, the beginning is the end of the play, but with an important difference: the apparently bodiless head of the prince already takes on the appearance of an uncovered skull; and when the corpse is lifted its bearers are not four captains but four somewhat nebulous

monks. No fighting man or brutish slaughterer, Hamlet gives
himself after death a hint of religious justification.

The programme note, consisting merely of those highly
charged lines from the soliloquy:

> For in that sleep of death, what dreams may come,
> When we have shuffled off this mortal coil,
> Must give us pause.

is sufficient indication of the subject-matter of the ballet. Yet
such a distinguished critic as Cyril W. Beaumont has written
that it is a 'well-staged and well-dressed play, the words of
which are drowned by the music'. A far less important member
of the audience, according to Caryl Brahms, who herself has
discussed the ballet brilliantly in her war-time book on Helpmann, proclaimed that 'the play had always been ruined by
words, anyway'. Miss Brahms has recorded other equally
pungent fragments of alleged overheard conversation, some of
which I suspect are in fact the fruit of her own lambent wit.

The choreography of *Hamlet* employs symbols and direct
statements. Every passage of stylized movement advances the
mood and action, and each solo dance springs naturally from
the context, so that there are no digressions. Of course not! A
man of the theatre could not countenance digressions, no matter
how brilliant or beautiful. As Helpmann himself explained during a broadcast, 'there are many symbolic movements and
actions, but it is unlikely that anyone, even those with a perfect
knowledge of the play, will fathom more than a few of them.'
Why are they included? Because in the view of the choreographer
they contribute to the general atmosphere without creating an
impression of obscurity. Nevertheless, without a fair but not
necessarily profound knowledge of the play, the ballet will remain
obscure. Is Helpmann then justified in presenting it to a ballet-
going audience?

The question is not an easy one and I am conscious of the
flaws in my own answer, but I think that certain broad principles can gain a broad measure of agreement. Let us widen the
scope of the question. If Helpmann is to be justified in presenting
Hamlet, has de Valois an equal right to present *Don Quixote*?

In my opinion everyone who sets foot in the theatre, no
matter if the ballet theatre takes most of his money, ought to be

acquainted with the play 'Hamlet'. Perhaps more than any other Shakespearean masterpiece, 'Hamlet' is an integral part of British theatrical tradition. Several young ballet-lovers have admitted to me their gratitude to Helpmann as much for coercing them to study the play as for their pleasure in the ballet. Despite its long programme note, the ballet *Don Quixote* contains a number of baffling incidents for those who have not read the Cervantes romance. Yet no matter what our opinion of the ballet, the choreographer cannot possibly expect her audience, except the critics, to possess a knowledge of the book unless it is of the Windmill scene and possibly a hazy notion that has somehow persisted since school-days of one or two other outstanding fragments. Briefly, then, I urge in the making of ballets upon existing works that the choreographer assumes a knowledge of those works in the audience only in very rare cases: 'Hamlet', yes, 'Romeo and Juliet', yes, but 'Don Quixote', emphatically no.

In his next ballet, *The Birds*, Helpmann employed a theme in which he felt justified in exploiting the classical technique; but in an entirely Helpmannesque style, for not once did he cause his dancers to dance for the mere sake of dancing, every turn, every *fouetté* and every *arabesque* growing out of the thematic development. The *fouetté* served excellently as the song of the nightingale, the Doves flew softly and flutteringly by means of a series of classical steps and made ample use of *pointes*; and all the birds hovered in flight most pertly and sometimes most wittily by the aid of a variety of *arabesques*. And what a brilliant idea for the Hen to disguise herself as her rival the Dove by using a similar *batterie*.

Nevertheless, despite its many excellences, I do not recall experiencing the same measure of excitement over *The Birds* as over Helpmann's two preceding ballets. Notwithstanding the sophistication woven into the simple tale, notwithstanding the skilful simulation of flight (ballet dancers are not birds!), I found myself pondering on the physical limitations of human bodies and speculating how much better Disney, whose influence I suspected every now and then, could have worked out this very theme.

The problem of dance-drama is to present a series of convincing dramatic situations in a medium which normally denies dramatic conviction. If this problem is resolved, the cry of 'Not enough dancing' is raised in a loud clamour; and if the problem is avoided the work is dismissed as 'lacking in theatrical appeal'.

Of *Miracle in the Gorbals*, Helpmann's fourth ballet, in which he aimed at theatrical illusion more definitely than in his previous works, 'The New Statesman' said: 'But isn't slap-up melodrama, however well mimed and put over, a waste of this company's talents for dancing?' 'The Times' was even more dogmatic:

> From the first note of Bliss' powerful score it is plain that ballet has once more set itself the task of enlarging its subject-matter, deepening its dramatic appeal, and aspiring to the rank of tragedy—but it will not do. Ballet has not grown up to the magnitude of such a task. It discards the majesty of language and limits its own technique in pursuit of this mistaken ideal.

It seems that the writers of these criticisms—and there were several others of similar opinion—cannot accept the absence of words in a work which seeks to present a significant and dramatic action. Probably the contemporaneity of the theme—although it is really ageless—militates yet further against the power of such a work to convince any but those who are sympathetic and sensitive to the expressive qualities of movement. Nobody can possibly gain the maximum pleasure from any kind of ballet unless they do possess a keen physical apprehension of movement together with a sensitive emotional response.

Right from the outset, with the disclosure of the ship and the idle dockyard in the drop curtain, interest and sympathy are held and stimulated by a close collaboration between all three elements. The atmosphere of worklessness gives way immediately to the evocation of a slum district which epitomizes poverty, with the fried fish shop and gin bar by which the inhabitants try to forget their woes. The appearance of the beggar with his shifty glance and furtive walk makes us stir a little uneasily in our plush seats. The gathering crowd complete a more pictorial summary of the social history of a workless community in the early 'thirties: the influence of diluted negroid rhythm on the girls, the effects on impressionable minds of tawdry films, the shrewd wit and incipient savagery of children brought up on a semi-starvation diet, the vice, the despair, the tenderness, and the failure of the Church. Each of the thirty characters on the stage is the essence of a type but holds our interest and sympathy as an individual.

Contained within a short ballet the intensity of the drama is tremendous, yet it is all contrived by a composition of dance and highly stylized movement. It is frequently claimed that certain episodes, for example the way in which the prostitute lures her gentlemen and the murder of the Stranger, are too realistic; but those who do make such a claim for the 'Magdalen' have evidently never enjoyed a nocturnal stroll in Piccadilly; nor seen a murder carried out with broken bottles.

In Arnold Haskell's book 'Miracle in the Gorbals' there are twelve large photographs of the ballet, starting with the drop curtain and progressing through various stages to the beggar holding the dead Stranger in his arms. Every one of these photographs, particularly those of the groups, makes a powerful impact, for in an essentially balletic manner and in the most economic terms possible, are expressed the qualities and fundamental outlook of each character. Here is the character of the Stranger, in the creation of which Helpmann was influenced by El Greco, the majestic movement of the hands and arms suggesting an authority endowed by a power beyond this world; the relationship of the community one with another; the evil power of the prostitute; the scandalmongering; the tenderness and innocence of the young lovers; the drama of the Suicide; an excited wonder at the revelation of God; the worldly jealousy; the frailty and impotence of a Minister of the Church, and the ironical conclusion with the beggar, the attempted suicide and the prostitute, the only ones who mourn the death of the Stranger.

Obviously several morals can be drawn from such a ballet; and it has been condemned on the ground that ballet is not a suitable medium for the preaching of a moral. It is equally obvious that Helpmann did not aim consciously at such preaching; but as the ballet achieves its purely theatrical end in treating such a theme with magnificent theatrical effects, exaggerated balletic conclusions and theories are almost inevitable. It should be judged purely on its merits as a theatrical production, and viewed in that light it is as significant a work as any dance-drama yet created, marking a definite advance in the form itself.

With growing confidence and experience Helpmann now tackled his most ambitious work: *Adam Zero*. This was his first ballet made especially for the spacious stage of the Royal Opera House and evidently he revelled in making full use not only of the space but also of the various effects which were out of reach in the making of his previous works.

Adam Zero can be said to be an allegory on man's life related chiefly of course in terms of stylized movement and tableaux. But now Helpmann has gone further afield for his vocabulary, even including a certain amount of unalloyed classicism which he interpolated judiciously so that it did not conflict with his main form of expression.

The presentation of birth on the ballet stage is by no means a novel idea, but here Helpmann in his own original terms gave this miraculous if everyday event a majesty and mystery which evoke both the power and mysticism of Man as well as the puny stature of the individual. Clad in unidentifiable vestments—the symbolic act of dressing being carried out by three characters who are to be his life-long shadows, Designer, Wardrobe Mistress and Dresser—Adam quickly grows to man's estate. On the stage when he is born a group of exhausted dancers remain quite unmoved as the process of nature reaches its climax under their noses. Gradually the empty stage is filled with scenery, an enormous cycloramic backcloth suggestive of astronomical distances unfolds across the stage and the activities of Adam are presented in such a way as to represent both the microcosm and macrocosm of contemporary life. At the summit of Adam's career a spectacular classical ballet sequence epitomizes the grandeur with which man endows himself and the complete ineffectuality of his achievements. Brief episodes which pretentiously proclaim their symbolism convey the futility of politics and the baffling, insensate brutality of man to man. The Church, represented by a senile prelate in rich robes smothered with mystical designs, sleeps amid world-shaking events.

All this symbolism, and there is much which is less easily understood than that I have mentioned, can well have been eliminated, but it does not mar one whit the exciting and constantly changing spectacle; nor does it clog the action or rob the struggle of Adam with his heredity and environment. The final scene, in which Adam at first combats Death before resigning himself and then actually courting her, is magnificently presented on a huge expanse of stage, with Death in flowing crimson robes and Adam back in the clothes of his beginning. In this scene symbolism also comes into the climax, for Death is the mother who had also been his partner and mistress. But once again Helpmann showed himself too much a man of the theatre to allow his preoccupation with symbolism and monumental spectacle to deprive him of the humble and intimate anecdote; one of the most touching scenes in the entire work is that in which his cat and dog are the last to leave him in his old age.

Nobody could justly accuse Caryl Brahms of having a dull brain, yet of the first performance—in common with everyone else—she confessed her inability to solve all the riddles, a confession which carried with it a strong condemnation of that aspect of the ballet. She wrote:

> . . . like all Helpmann's work, it is of the very bone and sinew of good theatre. I would hazard a guess that the work will not wear well. And I would leave it at that. But if I am to believe my programme note, I must confess myself at sea. 'Philosophy of timeless oracles' forsooth!
>
> And so I propose to concentrate greatly on what I know I saw, rather than on what I fear I missed.

Better advice would be hard to find: Ignore the symbolism and live vicariously in the exciting dramatic expression of a theme in language compounded of every kind of human movement conceived by a choreographer who is steeped in the theatre.

So far *Adam Zero* is the last of the Helpmann ballets. Now that he has left the ballet stage and embraced more closely the legitimate theatre, there seems little immediate prospect of his returning to create another ballet. It is to be fervently hoped, however, that either his friends or his own urgent need for expression will persuade him to return, for English ballet needs the originality, the vitality, and the contrast which he can give to our choreographic achievements. Paradoxically, but by no means I hope an inexplicable paradox, the severing of his intimate contact with his contemporaries at Covent Garden would perhaps endow his work with even greater originality and more intense theatrical appeal. From a choreographic point of view that kind of appeal is in more urgent need now than ever, for the ballet and the theatre appear at times to be growing further and further apart. The widening of the breach between them can serve only to rob each of them of power. America possesses several choreographers who will at least diminish the breach if not close it. But can England boast of only Helpmann? A few other of minor stature are perhaps following his footsteps, but only Helpmann possesses a major genius in this particular field. Yet at present, as I have already said, not one of his works is on view! Whatever the reason, such neglect is unfair both to ballet audiences and to the ballet itself.

CHAPTER TWELVE

Andrée Howard

SUCH IS THE NATURE of their composition that some creative artists leave us undecided as to whether they have added to the expressive power of their medium or whether they have merely uttered a weak paraphrase of somebody else's original work. Andrée Howard is one of the few who have been privileged to devise works for the Sadler's Wells Ballet, but it seems to me that since her early creative urge under the compelling influence of Marie Rambert, her creative genius has gradually degenerated into a familiar and uninspired formula. A brief consideration of all her works shows clearly that she has never advanced the expressive power of ballet but has employed her own compound of dance and melodrama, together with skilfully chosen music, costumes and décor to create a particular kind of illusion and atmosphere.

In common with choreographers, such as Gore and Ashton, Howard has alternated between intense dance drama and pure dance. She followed *Mirror for Witches* for example with *Veneziana* and before that had preceded *Mardi Gras* by *Assembly Ball*. Her ability to take the plot of a novel and extract the essence of it such a way as to provide both the stimulus and the fabric on which to build an entirely new work is quite remarkable.

Nevertheless this very ability at times betrays her into a presentation of inexpressive mime and dance which is little more than a poor re-enactment in balletic terms of a work which is far more powerful in its original form.

Andrée Howard ballets can be divided into three groups, in the same way as those of Gore, with a considerable amount of overlapping between divisions. First come works based on a strong plot, often even on the bones of a novel. Second comes the mood ballets, of which perhaps *La Fête Étrange* is the best example. Here the choreographer mixes all her elements, sometimes with great skill and sensitivity, to create a romantic and often melancholy mood, the entire work depending for success on its power to set up this mood. The third group comprises the ballets built up on pure dance, *Assembly Ball* probably being the best example. In this group I think Miss Howard has had both great success and dismal failure.

The works based on a strong plot are headed, in time, by *Lady into Fox*, which was first presented in 1939. For the narrative element Miss Howard took David Garnett's novel and extracted the main climaxes together with atmospheric and background material. Beaumont describes the result as a 'skilful adaptation' and Bradley as 'a skilful combination' and both to me seem on the one hand less and on the other hand more than adequate. The choreographer has not in any strict sense of the word adapted the novel. Rather has she absorbed its extraordinary air of fantasy, which is mingled almost inextricably with actual physical events, and then attempted to translate it into her own medium. No matter how strongly one reacts against the interpretation of a novel in terms of ballet, Miss Howard is here on firm ground. Words are not, in the opinion of many, including several who employ them with great professional skill, the best means of expressing fantasy, whereas ballet has more than once been claimed by leading choreographers to be only really at ease in the expression of fantasy.

Beaumont has with complete justification described the ballet as a 'sustained *pas seul*', although the choreographic construction is rather more complex than it would seem from that definition. In the first scene the simple, perhaps repressed, dance of the guests, together with the Huntsmen's vigorous solo and the bustle of preparation for the hunt, all heighten the tension and serve as far more than a frame for the revelation that all is not well in the mind of the hostess.

The trick of Mrs Tebrick's rapid transformation from a woman into a fox has sometimes been praised beyond its due. Many adherents of ballet are not content with the normal potentialities of theatrical illusion, but actually condition themselves to succumb to an illusion where none actually exists. A far greater measure of illusion could have been obtained without straining the resources of the theatre, but I submit that such an illusion would have destroyed the choreographic aim. In a ballet of this kind no suggestion of physical magic is sought, but an indication of mysterious forces at work, and the effect of these forces on human character. Anyone who goes to see such a ballet in the belief that an attempt has been made to depict the actual physical change of a woman into a Vixen will find little but the limitations of a short ballet in dealing with either the supernatural or with vivid characterization. Instead the ballet traffics in a mental and spiritual tenseness, a struggle against vast unknown forces, expressing the conflict with telling pathos and suspense.

The argument against the ability of the short ballet to express character has been cogently advanced by Richard Buckle, who claims that within the space of thirty minutes it is not possible to create sympathy for a particular character, and that the plot development and climaxes shed much of their effect if the audience is not greatly touched by the conflicts and duress suffered by the leading characters. My own view is that the choreographer must try to kindle our interest and sympathy in a character by means of a definite outline and vivid fragment of dance or a potent symbol.

After all, the limitations which beset any form of expression are at the same time a strength of that form. Great short-story tellers from Tolstoy to H. E. Bates have all employed the short form to create living, exciting people; I see no greater difficulty in one than the other. In fact, present-day choreographers would gain much by a studied construction of certain short stories by distinguished contemporary writers.

Be that as it may, Buckle could if he wished have quoted *Lady into Fox* as a striking example in support of his argument. At the opening of the ballet little attempt is made to excite sympathy either for Mrs Tebrick or her Husband. In the novel the character of both, and their interrelationships, have been brilliantly described and illuminated. Obviously this method could not be followed in a thirty-minute ballet. Therefore the choreographer should have sought different means. As it is, only a superficial sentimental attachment is indicated, greater stress somewhat naturally being placed on Mrs Tebrick's strange and alarming malady. If the choreographer felt unable rapidly to develop audience sympathy for the Tebricks, then in my submission she should not have essayed the ballet at all—unless of course she assumed that every member of the audience would become familiar with the novel before going to see the ballet.

Perhaps the weakest of all Andrée Howard's works to be based on a strong plot was *Twelfth Night*, composed in 1942 especially for the late lamented International Ballet. This ballet not only robbed Shakespeare of his words, but turned the various situations, farcical even in the original, into a ridiculous romp completely lacking in any of the qualities necessary to a successful theatrical presentation. Fortunately, as that work is no longer being seen, there is no need to discuss it.

The next definitely 'literary' ballet came in 1947 with an adaptation of another of David Garnett's novels, this time *The Sailor's Return*. Now, however, the choreographer took more details of the plot and developed them by means of a cunningly blended mixture of dance and mime into one of the finest dance-dramas in the English repertory. To me the ballet is far more satisfying than *Lady into Fox*, for its characterization is developed to a higher degree, the climax more keenly stressed, the mood and atmosphere growing in power through a gradually mounting hostility towards Tulip and a sense of impending tragedy.

Generally speaking, choreographers do not like to be stringently rationed as to space. In most ballets the décor is limited to a back-cloth and wings which are strictly prohibited from encroaching onto the stage. It was therefore strange that in London at about the same time Les Ballets des Champs Elysées produced *Le Jeune Homme et la Mort* and the Ballet Rambert, *The Sailor's Return*, for the décor in both these works trespasses seriously on what is usually regarded as territory sacred to the dancers. On this occasion the spatial limits thus imposed actually added to the expressive power of the choreography, so that the inn scene remains a vivid example of the ability of ballet to treat in emotional terms that atmosphere which Garnett himself has to a certain extent left to the imagination. By a recapitulation of the story during the last scene, a recapitulation made for the benefit of William's brother, the drama itself is thrown into a new perspective, for the audience now sees it through other eyes. The dance of William's brother in this scene, although rich in humour, displays a dim sense of foreboding. A strange belief exists among certain types of playgoers and in certain inferior playwrights, but not yet fortunately in choreographers, that tragedy and suspense must be relieved at well-spaced intervals. The idea upon which this belief appears to be founded is that tension cannot be maintained throughout a play and that this tension must therefore from time to time be released by a gust of laughter. If this be true, then a dramatist who is able to tighten up the tension of his atmosphere by high art and theatrical craftsmanship must also waste his effort by unwinding the spring.

In fact the great dramatists from Shakespeare onwards have used laughter as a sort of safety-valve which relieves tension without dissipating it, in order to develop an equal or an even greater tension once again, proceeding by means of harmonious and rhythmic contrast. Laughter of the wrong kind, laughter too strong, or laughter that threatens to get out of hand, destroys in a flash any atmosphere appropriate to the general development of plot and characterization.

In this inn scene, at no time, even when William's brother reaches a climax of gaiety and Tulip is a happy carefree child, is that sense of evil ever completely dissipated.

As is customary with Miss Howard's ballets, the music enhances and stresses the choreographic climax as well as remaining throughout completely harmonious to the mood. A specially written score seems vital to the success of such a work. Ballets which depend upon purely atmospheric development or upon dancing alone are perhaps better served by existing music; indeed it is by no means unusual for the source of inspiration of such a ballet to come from the music. Dance-drama can hardly be expected to thrive by superimposition on a ready-made score, for the aural accompaniment must not only support the general overall mood, but must also give point to each and every twist and climax of the plot.

Yet another Howard ballet to be composed from a literary work is *The Mirror for Witches*, which used Esther Forbes' novel of seventeenth-century New England for its plot and source. Once again evil forces are at work, but this time the structure is more complicated, there being constant alternations between natural and supernatural forces so that at times a great whirl-pool of emotion floods all the characters and the audience is subjected to a series of highly charged scenes in which it is frequently impossible to unravel the real from the unreal.

The opening scene, in which victims of a witch hunt (old

style, even though it did happen in America) are rushed on their
stakes across the stage, with the mob worked up to a state of
frenzied excitement at the prospect of the spectacle of torture
and death shortly to be enjoyed, has been condemned for an
excess of realism. Such nonsense! In fact the obloquy seems to
to be an unintentional form of praise, for whereas there is little
illusion of physical reality, the effect of the reactions are so
intense as to make at least certain members of the audience
suspend their capacity for disbelief.

The effect of this opening scene sets the tempo of the ballet
as well as establishing the savage lust for revenge and indulgence
in superstition which both the novel and the ballet in their
vastly different ways so successfully portray. Neither Miss
Forbes in her book nor Miss Howard in her ballet has determined whether Doll is a witch or not. As a result there is of
course a certain amount of speculation. Lionel Bradley, writing
in 'Ballet' (May 1952), was I think the first to commit a
definite opinion to print. He said:

> I think myself that Doll is innocent and that her belief
> that she has inherited her mother's power is due to her
> solitary life with no real affection, except from Bilby, in
> the strict Puritan atmosphere in which she finds herself.
> And that is why she cannot accept the timid life of Titus
> when it is offered to her. And the lighting of the super-
> natural scenes suggests that we are to regard them as
> imaginary.

Later in the same long and discerning article Bradley
states emphatically that this work is Miss Howard's best.
Certainly she has succeeded in expressing various outstanding
human qualities; also she has sustained the tension of the
prologue—no easy task—and has skilfully employed her
abundant capacity to work with her collaborators. It seems
evident to me that part of her choreography, especially that
required for characterization, springs from a vision of her own
ideas and the dancers called upon to exploit these ideas.
Further, here again I agree with Bradley, who said it first,
she has used her crowds significantly. Although the dance
element is in itself not original, the main points are made
legitimately by means of movement, the trial scene in particular
being worked out in terms of highly charged and well-contrasted

dance accompanied by natural movement, a limited vocabulary from the classical form, and some naturalistic gesture.

Selina is a ballet which does not fit perfectly into any of my classifications. It is constructed on a fairly strong plot, which owes its origin not to a novel but to a romantic ballet of the first half of the nineteenth century. In fact the work opens more or less as a romantic ballet of that period, with a heroine made up partly of Giselle, partly of La Sylphide and many other creatures of earth and heaven. Following loosely the structure of a romantic ballet, Miss Howard soon begins to poke at times delicate and at times heavy-handed fun at that period's expense. *Giselle* in particular comes in for parody and regular ballet-goers revel in a game of detection, tracing as many choreographic fragments as possible back to the original. Showing through the light-hearted vein are some well-conceived dances, so that what might well have degenerated into balletic slapstick very rarely falls below the level of burlesque and occasionally rises to subtle and gentle satire.

With her essays in pure dance, Miss Howard, like most of her contemporaries, has had mixed success. In this *genre*, *Vis-à-Vis* mounted on the Walter Gore Company (as though that small group did not have enough difficulties to contend with during its London season) in 1953, was one of the worst ballets ever performed by an English company on the London stage. Another, the pattern of which has now happily faded from my memory, was *Ballamento*, produced by the ill-fated Metropolitan Ballet in 1949. All that I can find to say about either of these two mistakes—although more so about *Vis-à-Vis* than the other, because I have not yet been able to obliterate its ineptitude, its choreographic boggling, from my mind—is that with their utter lack of invention, their torture of the classical technique and their apparent reluctance to attempt any relationship, however distant, with the music, they ought never to have been presented on the professional stage.

What a different story when we come to the mood ballets. Sometimes, as in *Assembly Ball*, mood is so tenuous as to be indiscernible, but it seems that the creative spark in Miss Howard needs just that much in addition to the music upon which to erect her choreographic structure.

As we have already seen, even in those works which are based

w York City Ballet's production of *Lilac Garden*; Tanaquil Le Clerq as The
oman in His Past and Hugh Laing as the Lover.   ANTONY TUDOR

impressive and significant group from *Miracle in the Gorbals* with Helpman
e Stranger) in the centre.   ROBERT HELPMAN

John Gilpin, Anita Landa and members of the Festival Ballet in one of the many joyous scenes from *Symphony for Fun*.

MICHAEL CHARNLEY

on a firm plot, she is still at her best, as every good choreographer should be, in expressing the emotion arising out of the
occasion rather than the occasion itself.

It is true, as has been asserted by more than one critic, that
Miss Howard's style frequently appears to be very similar to
that of Ashton. It is true also, I think, that her invention
suffers by comparison with that of Ashton, especially in the
development of choreographic tensions and stresses. Further,
again by comparison, her dramatic effects are obtained by
means less choreographically pure than those of Ashton.
Nevertheless, some of her mood ballets make definite advances
in the ability of British ballet to find expression for that which
cannot be expressed in other terms.

One of her fairly early essays in this *genre* was *Death and the
Maiden* in 1937. This ballet follows a rather obvious pattern in
which the characters both of Death and the Maiden each react
to the melodies with which they are identified in the music.
There is also a procession in which a figure is carried by a group
round the stage, an episode that has led for some reason to a
comparison, unfavourable of course, of this work with Ashton's
Apparitions—as though he were the only choreographer before
1937 to design such an episode. There is nothing particularly
original or striking about the choreography; indeed, a description of the Maiden's *enchaînements* makes the actual dance
arrangement seem quite banal. Yet in some mysterious way the
whole becomes far greater than the sum of the parts, with the
result that the ballet develops a strong feeling of relentless fate
and the overcoming of a passionate but futile resistance.

La Fête Étrange is claimed by many to be Miss Howard's
finest work. Although once again her source of material came
from a novel, in this case Alain Fournier's 'Les Grands Meaulnes',
the drama is entirely different from her other ballets founded on
a literary basis. One episode of the book has been abstracted,
an episode in which the author has evoked a highly unusual
and delicate mood. Beaumont has perhaps summed up the
essence both of the original source and the ballet in his 'Supple-
ment to Complete Book of Ballets'. He says:

> The tragedy of sensitive adolescence, symbolized not only
> by the circles of events but by the gradual though pro-
> nounced change of mood; anticipation leading through

increasing happiness to ecstasy, which needs depend fades into suddenness and dissolution.

Again, if the dance arrangements were to be coldly dissected into their component steps we should be faced with but little evidence of greatness. Apart from some lovely sustained poses, including what is by some critics said to be an excess of *arabesques*, some well-disposed groups, and some effective if rather obvious contrasts in the movements of the main characters, we are presented once more with nothing excitingly new and much that really ought to be dull and ineffective. But again, analysis is totally misleading.

Fauré's haunting, melancholy music, skilfully selected by Ronald Crichton, is used as an integral rhythmic part of the dance so that the two become one as nearly as in any ballet of my experience. Sophie Fedorovitch's simple sets and the beautifully clean-cut lines of her costumes, set off by their dark pastel shades, also integrate with the other elements in this work which is notable for its restraint but yet builds up to a highly charged emotional climax.

Much has been said about the songs which sometimes accompany *La Fête Étrange*. Bradley insisted that they add to the emotional effect, but I consider that they jar slightly on the poise and mood of the ballet; further, there seems to be no reason for their interpolation.

During the skilful harmony and varied dance in the scene on the terrace of the château, a strange building up of tension is contrived in the simple game of blind man's buff. The frozen stillness used with similar dramatic ends as in Tudor's *Lilac Garden*, at the moment of the climax, is worked out brilliantly if not with originality. This cessation of movement works gradually through the group, but instead of minimizing the final effect by anticipating it, suspense is heightened as we wait for it all to dawn on the young chatelaine. Her reaction as she gazes across at her lover is more moving than any of the 'transverse conversation' with which some of the Florentine painters give dramatic emphasis and unity to their groups.

Assembly Ball starts at a great advantage as far as I am concerned through the joyous, exciting music (Bizet's Symphony in C) which accompanies it. The work opens excitingly with a short, vigorous, unaccompanied bout of leaping and turning by the male soloist. Following that, it develops by means of a series of dances to match first the gaiety of the score, then its general sentimentalism and finally its rousing finale. In the solo movement the violin and oboe melodies form a perfect background for a charming *pas de trois* between the ballerina and two cavaliers.

When Miss Howard returned from the U.S.A. she did perhaps indulge in too many lifts. It seemed that she could not find enough ways in which to swing the ballerina up aloft and have her transported across the stage. Perhaps in the slow movements there is a little too much of this kind of transportation, but the idea has been worked out so delicately and the lifts and mid-air movements of the supported ballerina are so picturesque, that no undue straining for effect is perceptible.

Throughout each of the four movements a definite mood and atmosphere are developed, each in some contrast to the others, but each related, perhaps rather slenderly but sufficiently to unify the parts into a ballet and not leave them in isolation one from the other in a series of *divertissements*.

No greater balletic contrast can be imagined from one choreographer than *Assembly Ball* and *Mardi Gras*. Whereas one is gay and vivacious, redolent of good clean fun and innocence from introspection, the other is murky and probing, employing symbols that evoke feelings of evil and horror. A young girl becomes lost in a fantasy which seems to me to be compounded of Miss Howard's own nightmare of *Mardi Gras*. A colleague of mine found it a 'mystery of apparently unrelated elements'. But that surely is exactly what happens in many a nightmare. As far as the form, patterns and dynamic development of the ballet itself are concerned, each 'element' and incident grows at least with sufficient illusion of inevitability out of its forerunners as to evoke quite a variety of emotions.

Possibly because this ballet was mounted on a company that had been formed only a few months, possibly because the members of the company were nearly all extremely youthful, and possibly because many ballet-lovers—and others for that matter—are of the opinion that their favourite theatrical entertainment should come into contact only with the lighter and even more frivolous aspects of humanity, the ballet was condemned in certain quarters solely because of its theme. Such condemnation completely ignores the excellence of its production, the highly charged choreographic passages and brilliantly contrived theatrical climaxes. The various small parts are firmly drawn in by a few deft touches, but the girl herself is perhaps not firmly established. This may well be because she herself is the subject of the nightmare, and her own character is thus intended to be revealed through the creatures of her imagination. But this means that insufficient sympathy is cultivated in the audience if the protagonist and the choreographer are faced with what might well prove to be an insoluble problem. As far as I am concerned with this ballet, however, the problem can be filed away, for I find myself continually harrowed by the girl's terrifying experiences. Some of the theatrical tricks, to wit the transmogrification of those high dignitaries of the Church, might be expected to fail after several viewings of the ballet, but I have not found this to be the case. Now that I know exactly what is coming I experience the horror of anticipation rather than the original horrifying surprise. My heart goes out more and more to the girl in her pitiable plight.

In this particular episode, as in several others, one can find, if one is of that particular disposition, hidden meaning and heavy symbolism: the failure of the Church to provide sanctuary for tortured souls; the ultimate and awful dissolution of faith— and so on. But when you think you are being extremely clever in translating symbols and abstractions, the existence of which the choreographer is very likely completely unaware, remember that every single human relationship, either with fellow humans or with systems and organizations, can be resolved in terms of the individual or of the whole of humanity.

I seem to be progressing by contrast. In 1953 Miss Howard composed her second work for the Sadler's Wells Ballet: *Veneziana*. This work consists of a series of dances by masked ladies and their cavaliers, harlequins, colombines, pulcinello, tarantella dancers, and La Favorita.

Writing about it in 'The Observer', Richard Buckle described Miss Howard as 'the Virginia Woolf of choreographers'. 'She is so shy', he said, 'of committing herself to any violent statement.' Although I think he has over-stated his case, for Miss Howard surely proved herself capable of violent statement in *Mardi Gras*, it certainly is an inspired comparison, for *Veneziana*, built up on a selection of Donizetti melodies in the form of a *divertisse-ment* and some mildly attractive ensembles, flows smoothly and rhythmically along with no highlights, no climax, and in fact no suggestion of a raised voice or ejaculation to rouse the audience from a not too impolite torpor. Apart from a number in which La Favorita deigns to dance majestically with her cavaliers, and a solo in which Miss Howard confounds those among her critics who accuse her both of an inability to compose male dance and a lack of a sense of humour, *Veneziana* is no more I think than a piece of extravagant mediocrity. As Annabel Farjeon wrote in 'The New Statesman':

> A little outline music combined with dominoes and masks is certainly not sufficient to conjure up a vision of the Venetian atmosphere.

The earliest existing Howard ballet is *Mermaid*, which was composed in 1934. This story of a prince, in love with a princess, who is bewitched by a mermaid, provided an ideal theme for her to strive after that expressive evocation of mood which were to form the keystone of her choreographic motives. Content to suggest superficially the underwater movements of the mermaids, Miss Howard succeeded in arousing strong sympathy for such a strange genius. Perhaps the group movements are today somewhat hackneyed and lacking in force, but the impact of the work, resolved in simple terms, remains valid and sincere if a trifle weak through a certain outmoding in style.

When the *Mermaid* was shown on television too many concessions were made to a rather absurd quasi-realism. The mermaids were seen among real fish and various other deceits peculiar to film and television were employed. All of them had the effect of stressing the artificiality, robbing the work of illusion rather than investing it with verisimilitude.

I believe that Andrée Howard possesses the ability to compose many more ballets of a nature well contrasted to the work of her contemporaries. Perhaps one day she will abandon fantasy as a scaffolding for her compositions and create a work out of a current problem, whether a mass emotion or a less obvious reaction by a smaller group. By paring down the 'literary' interest as far as is compatible with intelligibility, she will not weaken her structure but on the contrary will endow the work with greater coherence and expressive power by trading in terms in which she ranks among our most satisfying choreographers: the terms of mood, emotion and subtle conflict between characters expressed by means of a flowing stream of images, naturalistic gesture playing an ever diminishing part. In such a progression she will most certainly become 'the Virginia Woolf of choreographers'.

CHAPTER THIRTEEN

Eugene Loring and Agnes de Mille

THE HISTORY OF American ballet opens towards the end
of the eighteenth century. Several native dancers in
the next hundred years gained international fame, but
not until the beginning of the twentieth century did a continuous
development become discernible. Although they were not the
first classical dancers to cross the Atlantic, Pavlova and
Mordkin did most at this time to plant the sometimes delicate
and frequently capricious plant of the Russian Imperial tradition in this vast and still extremely youthful country.

After a successful four-week season in New York in 1910 they
appeared again the following year under the imposing title of
The Imperial Russian Ballet, with Pavlova announced as the
prima ballerina assoluta and Mordkin as the *premier danseur
classique*. In spite of such titles, however, the company was
quite a small one and the ballets probably far below the
quality of the Diaghilev company which was then startling
Europe out of its balletic torpor. During this second visit a
long tour was accomplished, at the end of which Pavlova and
Mordkin parted company, both of them subsequently returning
with their own groups.

From 1913 to 1925 Pavlova's was the only company making
regular and extensive tours of the country. Her approach to
her art was that of the Leningrad school, softened and
westernized only through her past interest in the reforms Fokine
had been trying to carry out, and through the necessity of
making liberal concessions to her audiences. *The Dying Swan*
perhaps symbolized both her style and technique as well as her
artistic outlook. This slight work she danced everywhere, of
course, together with other works of varying and never super-
lative quality. But the power of Pavlova the dancer was enough
gradually to win for a modified form of Russian Ballet a large
and enthusiastic audience.

Mordkin, after returning to Russia, visited America again
with a company in 1923 and for two years toured the United

States with a small group of Russian artists. At the end of this tour he opened a school of ballet in New York, rapidly gaining a reputation as a great teacher. Several years later he once more formed a company which included many of his own pupils, including Lucia Chase and Viola Essen. But this company, although chiefly American in personnel, remained Russian— pre-Diaghilevian Russian, at that—in spirit; further, it had to compete with the de Basil company at the height of its triumphs, with the result that, without unlimited funds, it could not continue. But Mordkin's efforts were far from wasted, for his company was used as the nucleus of the first truly American full-scale professional company—Ballet Theatre.

Diaghilev also left his impact on early American ballet, although it seems that he resisted the attractions of a visit until for one reason or another in 1915 it became necessary for him to go in order to save his company. Although, owing to the war, he was unable to take the best possible group of artists, the works presented undoubtedly exerted a strong and lasting influence. If most members of the audience were perhaps unable to appreciate this choreographic subtlety and originality, they certainly could rise to the miracle of Nijinsky's dancing and to the most exciting series of theatrical spectacles ever to appear in that country.

Gradually the easily traceable thread became transformed into a tapestry. After Diaghilev, came de Basil and then both de Basil and Massine together, the pattern of the programme remaining Diaghilevan in character despite the appearance from time to time of new ballets with titles such as *The New Yorker* and *Saratoga*. But in 1934 Lincoln Kirstein opened the School of American Ballet. Among its aims was one to 'preserve and further the tradition of classical theatrical dancing in order to provide adequate material for the growth of a new national art in America'.

This school has certainly played its part in the accomplishment of that aim. But had Kirstein not devoted his patronage, his scholarship and his tremendous driving energy even more unreservedly to the establishment of ballet in America, in all likelihood the story would have been less glorious. Altogether he has formed four companies: the American Ballet, Ballet Caravan, Ballet Society and the New York City Ballet—the last-named in collaboration with Balanchine, with whom he has worked closely right from the outset.

The tale was not one of continuous success—of unparalleled enthusiasm and a stream of 'House Full' notices. Far from it. It is a far more interesting tale than that; indeed, I consider it one of the most fascinating and exciting tales in the whole of dance literature. There are several accounts, the best in my opinion appearing in a modestly produced little book entitled 'Ballet: the Emergence of an American Art', by George Amberg. Published by the New American Library, it is unfortunately not obtainable very easily in England.

Perhaps Balanchine, a Russian, was the creator of the first American ballet when he produced *Alma Mater* in 1934. Certainly none of Massine's works would ever have qualified for an American passport. But the first truly American ballet created by Americans was *Billy the Kid*, with choreography by Eugene Loring, a young man from Wisconsin. Produced in 1938, its 'book' was by Lincoln Kirstein, its music by another American, Aaron Copland, and décor and costumes by yet another, Jared French. Unfortunately it is the only Loring work to be seen in England, so we on this side of the Atlantic cannot discuss Loring as a choreographer with any confidence or authority.

Billy the Kid is certainly an outstanding work and obviously the creation of a pioneer, for its influence can be detected without difficulty—or imagination—in a number of ballets which have followed it. It contains various subtleties of composition which at first sight are not easily discernible. The nature of these subtleties suggests, however, that Loring has observed at very close quarters the methods and style of Fokine and Massine. For example, in the opening scene, when the Kid's friend leads the march of the pioneers, stylized versions of various characteristic movements of the frontiersman, amounting at times to mere suggestions of the action by which they have been inspired, are introduced. First comes the driving of a wagon, the breaking of a path into unknown territory, a hand extended in friendly gesture to the Indians. Incidentally I must confess that the breaking of the path movements and that of the extended hand would certainly have defied my understanding had I not first read Grace Robert's brilliant account of this ballet in 'The Borzoi Book of Ballets'.

The Street Scene is again made up largely of stylized suggestions of 'the activities of a frontier community'. Indeed, as Miss
Robert says, the riding and roping pantomime has been imitated
time and time again in musicals ever since. Rather amusingly she
suggests that as the sequence is sometimes used without any
acknowledgment to Loring, it has now perhaps attained the
statue of a classic, 'to be quoted as freely as one quotes Hamlet'.

Billy's solo dance employs stylized classical steps, with *tours
en l'air* and *pliés*, together with hand movements which certainly
reminded me of Gary Cooper in an exaggerated version of
'The Plainsman'. The card game and the appearance of the
posse after the murder I find too little stylized for my taste.
The multiple repetition of the men in formation imitating the
firing of a gun holds up the action instead of tightening the
tension. Nevertheless the structure of the scene is excellently
contrived. Similarly I consider the closing scene, in which the
Kid is stalked by his friend Pat, lacking in the intense dramatic
effect aimed at through undue reliance upon the silence, the
self-consciously dramatic and very improbable lighting of the
cigarette, and even the call. Each time I saw the ballet at
Covent Garden I felt relief as the company swung into the
march which ends the ballet with a repetition of its beginning.

These mild strictures, purely personal and minority views at
that, serve only to point the excellence of an American classic
which, despite its strictly national roots and local environment,
makes a strong appeal far beyond American frontiers. This
appeal may or may not be universal, but it certainly won
acclaim in England among audiences who are probably not
among the regular patrons of western films and might therefore
have been excused for failing to rise immediately to its regional
theme, style and movement.

As John Martin, a pioneer among American dance critics,
has said, 'Loring is the first really original artist to arise in the
field of the American ballet'. Influenced strongly by an early
training as an actor, he brought to this composition an obvious
determination to avoid superfluous dances or even details which
did not contribute directly either to the development of his
theme or shed light on one of his characters. In the works of
the Ballets Russe which he had seen, the thematic development
was frequently held up for a dance *divertissement.* Such holding

up of the action must have exasperated the young American, but in revolting against it he might well have made too many concessions to naturalism and thus presented no more than a mime play. Far from this, although I have quibbled at the insufficient stylization in certain parts of *Billy the Kid*, he succeeded in creating a new form of theatrical presentation. For the first time ballet had been brought into contact with life, perhaps not exactly with contemporary life, but at any rate with live and plausible characters. For the first time ballet had demonstrated that it could make a clean break with fantasy and make-believe and yet endure. It was to be several years before Robert Helpmann did as much for Britain with *Miracle in the Gorbals*—and even then some may contest that despite its contact with living people, Helpmann's work still traded in the supernatural.

Agnes de Mille's *Rodeo* did not appear until four years later. Because of a certain similarity in style between the two works, because *Rodeo* was the next major ballet in the same *genre*, and because it was immediately seen to be firmly rooted in the lives of real people, some excuse is permissible for those who suspected de Mille of plagiarism. In fact, and for those who did not see the performance reviews appeared in various periodicals, she had produced a public performance of a work in 1938 in which were employed several of the movements and gestures later to be transferred to *Rodeo*.

But factual evidence aside, no intelligent ballet-goer would accuse such an outstanding choreographer of deliberate plagiarism. Many times in the history of art two pioneers, each striving in complete isolation one from the other, have found a common means of extending the communicative power of their medium. Is it then so strange that de Mille and Loring should each find this means in an outstanding and almost idiosyncratic movement and gesture derived from the community in which their works were founded?

De Mille herself has said: 'It would be odd if contemporaries working as they do under the same roof did not handle similar problems in a manner reminiscent. The more astonishing fact is that using the same dancers and rubbing elbows one with the other hour after hour they preserve their own styles to such a marked degree.'

Rodeo depends on a theme of far less dramatic intensity than *Billy the Kid*. In fact it is a commonplace story of a tomboy who turns into a beautiful girl to get her man. A rodeo scene contains a remarkable choreographic stylization of cowboys riding on and tumbling from bucking broncos, with the Cowgirl vying with the men at their own game. For contrast there is the 'refined' young lady who has come out to watch the fun and to engage in mild flirtation.

Miss de Mille's graphic account in that exciting autobiography 'Dance to the Piper', which in my opinion ranks in the same class as Karsavina's 'Theatre Street', of her efforts to teach a group of classically-trained Russian dancers to simulate the movements of the cowboy—a phenomenon they had probably never seen—are illuminating as well as uproariously funny. The keen observation, the 'feeling' of a particular character had first to be interpreted in terms of movement and then transferred without loss of expression on to young men who had been highly trained to do everything in the greatest conceivable contrast to that which they were now exhorted and cajoled into contorting themselves.

> For two hours I rolled on the floor with them, lurched, contorted, jack-knifed, hung suspended and ground my teeth. They groaned and strained. I beat them in impact, resilience and endurance. I broke them to my handling. I broke them technically, which was where they lived and worshipped. At the end I suggested we walk. We what? We walk like cowboys. They look at me in dumbfoundment, their clothes matted to their bodies, their hair all on end and dirty from the floor. They walked. 'Not that way', I shouted.
>
> By this time I was feeling pretty frisky. Crotch-sprung, saddle-sore, with rolled-over high heels and sweat-stained leather, ill at ease and alien to the ground, unhorsed centaurs.
>
> 'Look,' I said. 'The sun in Colorado beats on your eyes like blows. You can't hold up your heads that way in the sun.'
>
> 'Why, that's right,' said a couple nodding in recognition. They began to squint, their gait slowed, they grew hot and dusty and weathered before me. One could almost, as my sister said later, smell them.

That quotation I think gives a better idea, not only of some of the vivid physical details of the actual translation of the movement on to the dancers, but also of the aim and high purpose of the ballet itself. The choreographer evidently set out to express the life of one particular, identifiable community.

In addition to the characteristic stance and movements of the cowboy, the dance pattern of *Rodeo* is made up largely both in its steps and floor patterns of country dance. As well as a lively example of a running square dance there is also a processional number. By means of these cohesive patterns, into which are woven brilliant stylizations of the movements of deeply observed types, the audience is given a rare insight not only into the life of a particular community, but also to rare flashes of individual character. The number of ballets to achieve so much in the twentieth century can be counted on the fingers of one hand—and with fingers to spare.

Miss de Mille's earliest extant work is *Three Virgins and a Devil*. First performed in London in 1934 as a revue, it was at that time mounted on music by Walford Hyden. In 1941 it went into the repertory of Ballet Theatre accompanied by far more suitable music in Respighi's *Antiche Danze ed Arie*. When Ballet Theatre performed it during their 1946 season at Covent Garden most of the English critics dismissed it as a trifle. One said 'It is not much more than a frolic'; another that it hardly merited consideration as ballet at all. In the Crush Bar I was in a very small and ridiculed minority who found it an outstanding and even brilliant composition. For once, however, the American critics were ranged on my side. Amberg said in the book from which I have already quoted:

> The story is related in the broad and deliberate manner of the Flemish masters, reminiscent of Breughel in its sensuousness richness of life, love of the grotesque and attention to detail. The three virgins, the Priggish One, the Greedy One and the Lustful One are sharply characterized and there is a truly dramatic tension in the Devil's changing tactics as he pursues and eventually catches each one in turn.

Grace Robert in 'The Borzoi Book of Ballets' expresses a highly favourable verdict, and John Martin—well, as the choreographer said herself, 'Martin was just plain dandy'.

Although Miss de Mille refers to the ballet as 'her morality play' this is surely a tongue-in-cheek definition, for the plot is worked out in terms of gusty and pungent balletic farce, relating how the Devil lures the three strongly contrasted virgins into hell. Conveniently, hell, in the form of a cave, is situated close to a church to which the Priggish Virgin drags her two sisters to their devotions. When the Devil plays a fiddle all three are compelled to dance in anything but a decorous manner. The Priggish One is utterly horrified at an inexplicable inability to control her indecently wriggling hips, but the others put up much smaller resistance. Soon, for the ballet is short, each of the Virgins is either lured or tricked into the mouth of that awful cave.

The movement which in my opinion so piquantly enhances as well as relating this moral tale is, like the music, a continuous flowing rhythmic stream. But its atmosphere is lighthearted rather than macabre, a contradictory feature which stresses the farce as well as facilitating some uproarious choreographic humour. The Virgins' dances are mostly compounded of well turned out and slightly grotesque figures, together with a delightfully exaggerated walk which is perhaps very loosely based on the postures of dancing groups painted by Flemish artists of the fifteenth and sixteenth century. The Devil, on the other hand, employs a large number of distorted classical figures including beats, *pirouettes* and some *tours en l'air*.

But the ballet, in common with all ballets which trade in this particular form of humour, demands first-class performance by first-class humorists. Again I quote de Mille:

> *Virgins* became a staple of the comedy repertoire until it was withdrawn at my own request. The ballet requires five star comedians and very few companies boast this many at one time.

Tally-ho, another comedy ballet, is set in the period of Louis XVI. The plot concerns a genius who neglects his wife until roused to jealousy by her flirtations with a prince. As a background we have the amorous adventures of the gay young people of the court. Again this work possesses an impulsive overall rhythm which is completely infectious. The choreography appears to be not too studiously based on the court dances of the period. This style enables the young wife to provide a vignette of charm, coquettishness and beauty without in any way clogging the satirical and witty commentary upon the life and morals of the time.

Agnes de Mille's sense of humour is so acute, her observation of comic human weakness so keen, and her facility for choreographic comedy so intense, that I feel disappointed when a work stems from her fertile brain which is not at least dappled with laughter. Before the curtain rose for my first view of *Fall River Legend*, that American tragedy of Lizzie Borden, I expected that despite what I had read of the ballet the working out of its awful theme would occasionally be relieved by that most wonderful of all humour—the inward chuckle begotten of choreographic means.

But no. The tragedy is worked out graphically, the frustration and oppression of the girl by her stepmother being developed and communicated by the choreographer in a number of brilliant movement images. The whole success of the ballet depends upon this evocation of sympathy, of profound pity for the girl's plight, for failing that we should not be the slightest bit interested in her. A 'flashback' method usually associated with the cinema is employed to reconstruct the circumstances of Lizzie's life which have led up to the murder; and although every detail of the action centres on her, the roles of her friends, and even of those who are merely curious, all contribute firmly to the establishment of her character.

The appearance of a real axe on the stage, towards which at one time the whole action is drawn as though to a magnet, was a dangerous—I do not mean that the dancers lay in any physical danger, of course—but fully justified expedient. The introduction of scenic naturalism in ballet, especially an instrument with such obvious associations, is likely not only to disrupt the realism within the fantasy of such a work, but also to turn every stylized movement and gesture, every detail and situation, into an obviously spurious illusion rather than a highly dramatic theatrical presentation. In fact the axe stresses the drama and at one time the entire mental and emotional output of the ballet are recharged by a concentration on its stark outline. To the girl it is a symbol of the finality which is no finality; to the onlookers a symbol of horror and wonder— wonder at the mazy turn of a brain which could put the instrument to such use.

The Harvest According, made in 1952, is based on some lines from a Walt Whitman poem:

> Life, life is the tillage
> and death is the harvest according.

The choreographer has worked out her theme in three simple and clear-cut scenes: Birth, Games, The Harvest.

Since Balanchine's *Apollo* in 1928, human birth has been enacted, symbolized and interpreted in several ballets, sometimes with delicacy and sometimes without. De Mille interprets the Mother's travail by means of movements which look as though they have been strongly influenced by the Central European school, but may have been a purely personal interpretation of certain mental and emotional impulses. The arrival of a number of girls and women I took to represent the support of American womanhood for its Mothers, but perhaps I was imagining too much.

In the Games episode the choreography adopts the familiar form of stylizing a number of 'show-off' tricks by the boys in front of their girl friends and some delightful suggestions of folk dance.

The Harvest symbolizes that aspect of the Civil War in which the men depart and the women wait. Inevitably the woman in whom we are most interested loses her son. While the others dance to celebrate the return of their men she is lost for a time in sadness but then stoically joins the others, for life must go on.

Miss de Mille has at times been a little derivative in her composition, but she has also employed her own distinctly personal style. In previous works she has very rarely used *pointes*; here she does so sparingly, with telling effect, and throughout expresses simple emotions by simple means.

The other elements of the ballet also employ simple terms. Virgil Thomson's music is made up of a number of formal melodies which surely find their roots in American folk-lore. The three backcloths by Lemuel Ayers are simplified landscapes, each in strong contrast with the others and each highly susceptible to the subtle changes in lighting to which it is subjected. These backcloths have too the power to draw attention to the dancers and at the same time provide the perfect environment.

Whatever success the ballet has gained lies then in the close integration, as well as the simplicity, of all its elements. That it is

The Corregidor (Jack Hart), the Miller's Wife (Margot Fonteyn) and the Miller (Massine) in the *Three-Cornered Hat*.

LEONIDE MASSINE

Moira Shearer, Margot Fonteyn, Pamela May, Alexis Rassine and Michael Somes in *Symphonic Variations*.
FREDERICK ASHTON

not a great work is due to the fact that it contains no strikingly original statement; and no vivid disclosure of a profound perception.

Neither *Fall River Legend* nor *The Harvest According* is leavened with humour. Perhaps the choreographer felt that she was treading on such thin ice that even the slightest temporary easing of tension in the development of the plot would ruin the cumulative effect. Nevertheless I am still of the opinion that so matchless is her ability to create subtle comedy and humour in dance terms that no de Mille Ballet should be without it.

Quite apart from her ballets, the name of Agnes de Mille and her work are better known to the world at large through her dance arrangements in musicals. I hold an opinion which is difficult if not impossible to prove that by her work in this *genre* she has added considerably to the ranks of ballet-lovers. Before the war most musical shows sought popularity through lavishness. Spectacular sets and large numbers of dancing girls brought stage musicals into unfavourable comparison with Hollywood Technicolor all-star, all-singing, all-dancing billion-dollar productions. Which was silly, for most of us do not go to the live theatre to be stunned by such gargantuan entertainment.

In *Oklahoma!* Agnes de Mille firmly established a new style. Now no attempt was made to present a lavish spectacle, but instead the dance element was closely integrated with the rest of the action. The idea was by no means new, but with *Oklahoma!* it was introduced, at any rate to London, for the first time in a full-scale musical. Its success is now a matter of history. In later musicals to come here the style has been continued, and in some cases homage by imitation has been paid to *Oklahoma!*. The dream sequence in *Love from Judy*, which enjoyed a long run at the Savile Theatre, is a case in point. Although the dance pattern is in a definitely individual style, the same scheme of integration is followed. Indeed, since *Oklahoma!* I can think of no first-class musical which has not employed the dance element for its development rather than, as in the old days, to hold up the action. Other brilliant choreographers such as Michael Kidd and Jerome Robbins are now employed to provide this dance element; and for *Kiss Me Kate* a distinguished 'expressionist' or 'modern' dance arranger, Hanya Holm, composed the dances. Indeed, the producers considered the accuracy and complete integration of the movement into the whole so important that Hanya Holm herself was engaged to reproduce the dances exactly for the London production. For this purpose she brought with her a director of the American Dance Notation Bureau, Ann Hutchinson, who had notated the original American production.

Agnes de Mille has, since *Oklahoma!*, been responsible for the dances in several other musicals. *Paint Your Wagon* is perhaps the best example. In this case, although again the dances were a vital part of the plot development, one of them, which became known as the *Pony Ballet*, was considered of such outstanding artistic merit in its own right that it was included in the Royal Variety Performance.

I sincerely hope that Agnes de Mille, despite her wonderful success in this field, will continue to make occasional ballets for American companies. The discipline and the necessity to create in terms of dance which are completely self-supporting and fully expressive in their own right, the freedom from 'box office' considerations, and the challenge of creating a ballet worthy of a first-class company, are all vital elements in the growth and even the maintenance of the great choreographer's creative urge.

Agnes de Mille has done more than any other post-war choreographer to keep ballet in harmony with the common touch. She has also done more to raise the level of the common touch. Add to this the creation of several ballets of great value and then ask yourself: what could any choreographer want more? I doubt whether even Agnes de Mille herself could answer that one.

CHAPTER FOURTEEN

Jerome Robbins, Michael Kidd, John Taras

ALL AMERICAN CHOREOGRAPHERS have come under some sort of outside influence, for they have had ample opportunity to become thoroughly well acquainted with the work of the Diaghilev-Russian choreographers, as well as that of Tudor and Ashton.

The formative years of Robbins, Kidd and Taras were spent in America under the direct influence of Balanchine, if not always under his tutorship; and this combination has undoubtedly produced the first essentially American choreographic style. Balanchine freed the traditional classical technique of its remoteness as well as its grandeur, transforming it into a more personal style, with a new and youthful dynamic appropriate to the character and individualism of young women whose aim on stage was not to appear sexless and saintly, but feminine and approachable.

On this basis the rising generation of choreographers in and around New York were brought up, again choreographically speaking, of course, during the war, when outside influences were reduced to a minimum and when a national emotion had America in its grip as never before since the Boston Tea Party. Of the three who have produced the most outstanding work, Jerome Robbins, Michael Kidd and John Taras, the first two have remained completely American in outlook, producing ballets and dance arrangements which clearly and forcefully express aspects of the American character, and even at times the American way of life. Taras, on the other hand, partly because he has spent several post-war creative years in Europe mounting ballets on non-American companies, and partly because of his especial style, does not always betray his nationality.

Although he had begun to create a few years earlier, Robbins' first major work was *Fancy Free*. At its first presentation at the Metropolitan, New York, in 1944, it was immediately described as a smash hit—this epithet for once not proving an exaggeration. London did not see it until the first season of Ballet Theatre in London, at the Royal Opera House, in 1946. We Londoners came out of the theatre dazed but excited. This was something new in ballet. Something to give it a new impetus. This was American, and that was what we wanted to see.

In all probability the libretto for *Fancy Free* is the most detailed ever to be written for a short one-act ballet. Judging by the expressiveness of this libretto, its economy and the evident discernment of its author, Robbins will one day write an autobiography comparable in style, intensity and wisdom with Agnes de Mille's 'Dance to the Piper'. It seems strange that these two Americans possess such literary ability while not one of our younger contemporary choreographers has written anything of importance whatever. At least, if they have, such writing has been kept a fast secret.

After briefly indicating the theme of the ballet Robbins issues equally brief instructions about the costumes and décor—instructions which have been carried out to the letter but with a wealth of free imagination by the designer. Then he moves into action, making notes in the left-hand margin as to the line to be followed by the composer of the music. Yet nowhere does he actually lay down definite dance movements. The libretto is the foundation upon which he has built up the choreographic structure. Evidently he had so thoroughly absorbed the theme, the atmosphere and the characters, their relationships and conflicts as individuals as well as symbols, that when the time came for him to start composition he was able to concentrate on the invention of movement appropriate to the action, untrammelled by any other considerations. The libretto appears in full in George Amberg's book, from which I have already quoted. Here are the opening directions:

Music and Mood:
Fast, explosive, jolly, rollicking. A bang-away start.

Action:
Three sailors explode on to the stage. They are out on shore leave, looking for excitement, women, drink, any kind of fun they can stir up. Right now they are fresh, full of animal exuberance and boisterous spirits, searching for

something to happen. Meanwhile
they dance down the street with
typical sailor movements—the
brassy walk, the inoffensive vulgarity, the quality of being all
steamed up and ready to go. They
boldly strut, swagger and kid each
other along. This section should
serve as an introductory dance as
well; bright, gay, fast and happy.
One should feel immediately that
the three are good friends, used to
bumming around together, used to
each other's guff . . . that they are in
the habit of spending their time as a
trio, and that under all their rough-
and-tumble exterior there is a real
affection for each other, a kind of
'my buddy' feeling.

Notice that the exact form of the dance is never
indicated. It seems to me that having once decided on the
plot and incident, and become intimately acquainted with his
characters, Robbins depended upon his own reactions to
express himself in the richest conceivable mixture of dance,
stylized natural movement, mime and gesture. In addition to
this strong foundation for his ballet he also had the benefit of
a wonderful score by Leonard Bernstein. From those annota-
tions to Robbins' libretto it is clear that Bernstein has followed
them with the utmost fidelity, but that he has also fired them
with his own vivid imagination. Similarly the artists responsible
for the set and costumes, Oliver Smith and Kermit Love
respectively, have meticulously carried out the choreographer's
instructions, at the same time adding tremendously to the value
of the work by insinuating their own creative offerings. In this
way each element of the ballet, while remaining strictly within
the terms of reference laid down by Robbins, plays a vital
part not only in support of the choreography but also as a
positive creative element in its own right, yet without obviously
asserting this right.

There are those who, while admiring the ingenuity of
Fancy Free, its flowing rhythms and expressive dance, cannot

bring themselves to admit that a work based on three gum-chewing, girl-chasing sailors, and their feminine affinities, can possibly be a great ballet. But many of the greatest works of art in all forms conceal by their outer brilliance and common humanity the very essence of their greatness.

Throughout the ballet Robbins and his collaborators have achieved an apparent spontaneity. I cannot recall any other ballet which, after so many viewings, retains for me such spontaneity. The dances have been worked out in the most minute detail, yet, particularly in those 'show-off' numbers in which the sailors vie with each other in front of the girls, they always seem to me to be completely extempore. Incidentally, for students of technique these dances are of particular interest, for they have been compounded out of the classical technique, Indian dance, Latin-American ballroom dancing, stage dance and other varieties. Yet nowhere are there any obvious joins; on the contrary the dance flows smoothly—although that is perhaps not the right description for the short Samba—and naturally, as an integral part of the ballet.

Although the ballet in modified form has been employed with ecstatic success in more 'popular' entertainment, both on stage and film, beneath the excitement of its immediate appeal lie subtlety and even profundity. These sailors are the prototypes of their kind. Avoiding the mawkish sentimentality to which lesser Americans give way so frequently in their art forms, Robbins establishes the comradeship beneath their bantering façade, the deference which controls their lust. The girls, too, notwithstanding their sexy walk, their brassy confident manner, in which they make it quite clear that they can easily handle and exploit to their own ends the natural bent of the sailors, are vivid characterizations which have not been surpassed in the medium of ballet. Under the very uniformity of the sailors' costumes, their single-mindedness of purpose, the equally manifest purpose, no matter under what subterfuge and concealment, of the girls, each stands out not perhaps as an individual character but certainly as an individual symbol.

I have no hesitation in declaring that *Fancy Free* is one of the few really great ballets in the contemporary repertory.

Interplay, Robbins' next ballet, started off as an item in Bill Rose's 'Varieties', but soon gained artistic promotion to the repertory of Ballet Theatre. Perhaps it is because of its first environment that several American critics stress its superficiality. Denby regrets that such a lovely composition should be limited to a purely formal statement of such little expressive power. I find this opinion a little difficult to understand, coming as it does from one who has a boundless admiration for the work of Balanchine. Amberg agrees with Denby, yet adds:

> But the little ballet is a theatrically effective, choreographically inventive and highly entertaining combination of sport, party games, jam session, physical exuberance and artistic discipline. It provides the same exhilarating and electrifying spectacle as an athletic championship, the same satisfaction as the display of physical prowess and superlative technical mastery, and particularly the same moment of suspense that stems from friendly competition.

Although *Interplay* has no plot, at least in the same sense that *Fancy Free* is based on a strong plot development, it does possess very definite human relationships—relationships quite apart from Balanchine's insistence that no ballet is 'abstract' for it cannot exist without human relationships. The ballet is built upon a sort of continuous game in which eight American adolescents, four girls and four boys, provide a stylized epitome of their physical life. They play games, they dance an old and dignified dance with respect to its form but amusement for its anachronism, they indulge in puppy amorousness, they dance with abandon for the sheer fun of being alive. Says Edwin Denby:

> Not of serious ballet quality is *Interplay*'s specific dance technique. Robbins does not show the resource of deploying the body unselfconsciously, of a sustained and natural soaring and sailing; the foot positions are only approximate and this spoils the buoyancy and sharpness of floor contact and of phrase construction; he tries for vivacity by again and again overspeeding *pirouettes*; his jokes are sometimes too coy; he does not distinguish between the timing of pantomime and of dance gesture; and the accents of the dance are likely to be energetic thrusts expressing a shot-in-the-arm vigour rather than an individual response to a dramatic moment.

Robbins employs the same idiom for *Interplay* as for *Fancy Free*. The main difference is that in *Interplay* he has called upon a more continuous dance, compensating as it were for the absence of plot by setting up close relationships between his dancers solely by means of ingeniously integrated dance patterns which develop sentiment, tensions and climaxes, just as surely as in a well worked out plot ballet. Instead of developing one particular theme, however, he has taken a number of adolescent reactions and relationships, exploiting and expressing each one by his own eloquent language, each playing its own part in the composition of the striking, exciting, overall pattern.

The English language is made up of many tongues and it is possible for the layman as well as the philologist to state in numerous obvious cases which word comes from which tongue. Yet in some well expressed sentences a writer employs words of Greek, Latin and Saxon origin, and others which have even insinuated themselves into the English dictionary from a modern foreign language. The skilled writer, whether of poetry or prose, welds this polyglot army into a powerful unified force. Similarly the skilled choreographer calls upon dance and movement forms, as well as upon his own formal vocabulary, from all over the world. By moulding them together he avoids disjointedness and expresses himself in a style notable for its absolute homogeneity. The choreography of *Interplay* can be dissected into a great variety of dance forms, including classical ballet, Latin-American, ballroom, free or expressionistic, Spanish, Oriental, early court, acrobatic, modern stage, and others. Yet nowhere is there an ugly join, nowhere a vestige of incongruity. At certain places one particular style is chosen as the most appropriate, but even then it is mingled with other styles, and soon merges into the larger vocabulary.

Yet with this international language Robbins has composed a ballet which is utterly and completely American. I remember remarking to Anatole Chujoy, the distinguished editor and publisher of 'Dance News' of America, that when I first saw *Fancy Free* in 1946 I felt that this was in every way a really American ballet, both in conception and in realization. 'Yes', he said. 'But only a part of America. It hasn't been influenced to the slightest degree by the life of, say, Kansas, or any of the other inland states.'

He was absolutely right, of course. So many English people forget that there is more to young America than that which we

saw expressed in that ballet. *Interplay* is far more truly represent-
ative of the whole country, if it is possible to express the tempo,
the rhythm and even the ethos of such an enormous and
variegated people in one work. To me this ballet expresses
perfectly the sentiment and style of twentieth-century America:
its speed, its accent on youth, its determination to say what it
thinks, its destruction of shibboleths, even the vigour and the
occasional gaucherie of its language.

It was inevitable that a choreographer so closely in touch with
contemporary life would attempt a ballet with a serious theme.
In *Facsimile* Robbins conducts a flirtation between an idle woman
and two idle men. But the motive power is sex, not affection,
with idleness sapping purpose, so that all give way to small
desires which thus grow to uncontrollable magnitude. The ballet
is founded on an Eastern proverb:

> Small inward treasure does he possess who, to feel alive,
> needs every hour the tumult of the street, the emotion of
> the theatre, and the small talk of society.

On this concept Robbins has developed a series of dance images
which stresses the dependence of one such individual on the
others, the emotional disturbance, frustration and futility which
is their lot.

Despite its vastly different theme, the ballet is treated in very
much the same way as *Interplay*. On to a basis of classical dance
the choreographer has grafted his own expressive movement and
gesture language. One emotion is developed and stressed by the
dance harmonies and tensions between a small number of
characters, each emotion gradually giving way to another,
which grows out of it. Throughout, the insecurity of each character is emphasized by remarkable choreographic invention.
Possibly because of sympathetic chords and similar roots of
psychological experience, it became very easy for me to feel
for these three characters. Although they remained without
individual character, the weaknesses they expressed are so
universal, so contemporary, as to strike immediate chords of
sympathy. At the climax of the ballet the woman in her anguish
vents a choking cry which for no logical reason is as valid and
legitimate as the shriek in Gore's *Crucifix* is lacking in those two
qualities.

In *The Guests* Robbins again formulated an ideal theme. Now he sets up his tensions between two groups; the larger of them is accepted in the social environment in which their host seems to be the leader; and the smaller is treated with overt hostility. Obviously the working out of such a theme allows interesting and stimulating scope for expressive choreography. The theme, but not the movement pattern, is complicated by a certain amount of symbolism in which masks are handed to the privileged guests by their host. Such a symbol can mean exactly what each member of the audience wants it to mean; as it is not an obtrusive symbolism as far as the choreography is concerned, it is of small importance. Despite a very definite segregation of the two groups, however, a girl from the smaller and a man from the larger are drawn together by some relentless force, expressing their love for each other by tender and impassioned *pas de deux* in strictly neo-classical terms.

The dance movements and the overall patterns of the groups suggest a very definitely laid down code of behaviour. Code and convention seem to have robbed the larger group of initiative, turning them into a stereotyped community organized in thought and deed by some hierarchy. The smaller group, although less stifled by codes and conventions, also suffers from clearly manifested taboos. Neither group will accept the lovers, who thus seek escape from a blind and senseless universe.

Despite a degree of repetition, and at times an insufficiency of contrast, the choreography of *The Guests* is marked by telling phrases of intense emotional power.

If anyone, no matter how thoroughly acquainted with Auden's 'Baroque Eclogue', were to see Robbins' *Age of Anxiety* without first glancing at the programme, they would by no stretch of imagination suspect that the ballet had been inspired by the poem. Auden's original aroused considerable discussion, for while it demonstrated his almost incredible mastery of words, his skill in versification, his great intellect and in places his uncanny insight into the hidden corners of human character, few of his images are such as to render themselves amenable to translation into terms of movement.

The poem takes the form of a conversation between there men and a woman, first in a bar, and then in an apartment, both in New York, on All Souls' Night during the war. As the title indicates, Auden is concerned with insecure people. The opening words, in prose, are:

> When the historical process breaks down and armies organize with their embossed debates the ensuing void which they can never consecrate, when necessity is associated with horror and freedom with boredom, then it looks good to the bar business.

After introducing his characters, Quant, Malin, Rosetta and Emble, with terse, vivid prose, Auden opens the poem with the thoughts of each as they lounge at the bar. For instance:

> Malin was thinking.
>   No chimpanzee
> Thinks it thinks. Things are divisible,
> Creatures are not. In chaos all bodies
> Would differ in weight. Dogs can learn to
> Fear the future.

Of course Robbins has not attempted any sort of literal translation in balletic terms, but has sought to parallel the conflicts, the tensions, and the broad emotional impact contained in the poem. The characters discuss the seven ages of man, their imagination ripening as they help 'the bar business'. The seven ages become seven stages of escape and each of them grasps at a joy which is not joy, coming at the end to some kind of peace through the revelation of their own insufficiency.

In fairness to Robbins I must add that his work is based not only on the poem but also on Leonard Bernstein's Second Symphony which is itself based on the poem. Taking his inspiration first from one and then the other, he does succeed at times in presenting a crude, generalized concept of an age of anxiety. On to his usual compound of pure dance forms he has grafted a number of perfectly natural gestures: the nod of a head in recognition, a pat on the back, even a handshake. He has also employed symbols: the father image and dancers whipping their other selves. By every possible means he has sought to express the overriding philosophy of the poem. Too great a choreographer to fail completely, he has however failed in his main purpose, succeeding only in short passages to convey anything but obscurity. Auden too can perhaps be accused of obscurity, but the poem is abundantly rich in wonderful images, in perception of minute human truths, in practical philosophy and a profound knowledge of a diversity of characters:

> So fully conscious of the attraction of his
> uniform to both sexes, he looked round him slightly
> contemptuous when he caught an admiring glance, and
> slightly piqued when he did not.

or

> Where country curates in cold bedrooms dreamed of
> Deaneries till at daybreak
> The rector's rooks with relish described
> Their stinted station.

Every page holds passages of equal power and brilliance. Auden's ultimate obscurity, if it is obscurity, lies in a mass of brilliant word pictures and profound wisdom; whereas the obscurity of Robbins is an obscurity which is only enlightened here and there with a telling passage. In fact, reading the poem I feel that any obscurity lies in my own inability to understand; whereas the ballet is no more than a misguided attempt to stretch the medium beyond its limits.

In *The Cage* Robbins has created a superficial suggestion of insect life as a setting for a brilliantly conceived erotic *pas de deux*. A Novice is accepted into a society of insects represented by female dancers in flesh-coloured tunics. A male enters and attempts to possess her, but she viciously and effectively disposes of him. For this success she is highly commended by the leader of the group, but soon another male appears, and this time a far greater struggle ensues. The couple twist and turn in an erotic dance in which many classical figures can be identified until gradually the Novice yields and the encounter now becomes a complicated chain of embraces. But the other members of the society of insects have evidently kept close watch on the proceedings, for they now conduct a mass attack and bear their victim to earth, the Novice herself making the kill by digging her fingers into the victim's sides.

All this is highly sensational, theatrical, effective—and unpleasant. Its excitement cannot be denied, and Robbins has certainly accomplished his aim. But the aim was not high and the target was a sitting one.

At first glance *Jones Beach*, in the making of which Balanchine and Robbins collaborated, would seem to be very far removed from *The Cage*. Boys and girls in sleek swim suits besport themselves on the famous Jones Beach and indulge in all the antics usually associated with such an environment. But in fact, apart from some ingenious stylizations of beach games and some luxurious sun-bathing, the centrepiece of the ballet is again an erotic—although perhaps erotic is a little too strong a term—*pas de deux.*

This *pas de deux*, however, is far more brilliant and original than that in *The Cage*. A boy saves a girl from drowning and then proceeds to practise his knowledge of artificial respiration. The resultant dance is abundant in extremely beautiful passages punctuated by wit and fragile charm as the girl gradually comes to and of course falls for her rescuer. This *pas de deux* ought to be kept alive, no matter what happens to the ballet.

The Pied Piper is another example of a perfect theme for the exploitation of Robbins' lighter invention and young American dancers. It is constructed on Aaron Copland's Concerto for Clarinet and String Orchestra. At the rise of the curtain a clarinettist strolls on to the stage and begins to play. The stage, bare to the walls except for bits of scenery lying haphazardly around, is lit with a directional beam, which changes later in the ballet to throw grotesque shadows of the dancers on to the back wall. Everything appears to be spontaneous.

Dancers in practice kit enter two by two, breaking into movement as the rhythm of the music gets hold of them. The first couple perform a simple *pas de deux*, wander off and are replaced by another couple. Then, with the opening of the concerto's next movement, a group of dancers take the floor and improvise to the modern rhythm now being played. Gradually it becomes more and more apparent that the dancers are acting completely under the compulsion of this modern counterpart of Hamelin's famous benefactor. Led by one dancer, with whom the group dance in counterpoint, the dancing grows wilder and wilder, the huge stage seeming to be filled with an animated mass of dancers who surge towards the piper, recede, and surge again in an ever more uncontrolled paroxysm of dance. At last, in a final series of leaps and contortions, they all collapse together, like the one-hoss shay; there is a flash, a bang, a burst of smoke and the musician disappears.

The Pied Piper may be dismissed as a light and inconsequential bit of nonsense. Nonsense it certainly is, but inspired nonsense.

The dancing gets hold of you and one feels what the modern jive dancer must feel as his feet and hips begin to oscillate to hot music from his favourite band. It is all within the realm of human experience.

Robbins, in common with all his pan-American colleagues, has arranged the dances for several musicals; he has also created other ballets which have not yet crossed the Atlantic. So far he has not only remained completely American, but has also expressed himself in purely national terms. A test of his greatness will come when he is invited to make a ballet for our national British company. If he can compose a work in more universal terms, and mount it on dancers whose style and impetus, wit and tradition are so different from the instruments with whom he has worked so far, then his vision will be enlarged, his scope extended far beyond its present limits. Further, I think that the Sadler's Wells repertory is likely to receive wonderful enrichment.

Of the other young American choreographers—and there are several producing work of charm and originality—the most popular with English audiences are Michael Kidd and John Taras. The success here of Michael Kidd is attributable to one ballet, *On Stage*, which captivated and enchanted us during the first wonderful 1946 season of Ballet Theatre at Covent Garden.

His first major work, *On Stage*, is another of the several brilliant American compositions to get off on the right foot with a perfect plot. A rehearsal on stage is interrupted for an audition. A little girl, dressed in pink, whose diminutive stature and timidity captures our immediate sympathy, fails lamentably because of nerves in front of the company. A handyman attempts to comfort the girl while the rehearsal proceeds and together they watch the rehearsal, each day-dreaming that they are dancing in the star parts. When the rehearsal is over the handyman with his broom entertains the girl with some eccentric pranks and soon she begins to dance, all trace of nerves and timidity now vanished. The handyman finds the ballet master and drags him back to watch; members of the company also stroll back as the little girl, oblivious of them all, dances a brilliant solo. At its conclusion everyone applauds, and she is led triumphantly away. As she goes she casts a grateful glance back at the handyman, who conceals his own ambition in delight at her success—a typical American touch, this last bit of hackneyed but nonetheless piquant sentiment.

Apart from Kidd's own highly amusing eccentricities as the handyman, *On Stage* is by no means notable for the originality of its dance content. The solo which forms the highlight consists largely of a long series of rapid *bourrée* turns and *pirouettes*, performed with *brio* and abandon. First in Janet Reed and later in Alicia Alonso, whom we saw in London in 1946, Kidd found the two ideal interpreters of the role. None but the dynamism of the U.S.A. blonde or the classical but equally vital attack of the Cuban brunette could have produced such excitement from such a commonplace *enchaînement*. But there, partly at any rate, lies the secret of Kidd's success. He is not so much an outstanding choreographer as a producer of exciting if low-brow theatre. Judging from this ballet, he obtains his effects by creating a play which, because of the skilfully worked out plot, just does not happen to need words. In fact a few words are actually spoken, but only for atmospheric purposes to establish the rehearsal environment and perhaps to provide a mild shock in order to avoid boredom in a longish passage leading up to the highlight.

John Taras first gained our admiration for his *Designs with Strings*, which he mounted on an English company, the talented Metropolitan Ballet. This is an abstract work set to Tchaikovsky's Trio in A Minor. Taras has composed a series of softly flowing passages for eight dancers, first one and then the other forming the kernel round which the images are formed, the patterns resolving and dissolving in rapid succession. The style is neo-classical and a delicate amorousness, together with a sentiment highly appropriate to the Tchaikovsky score, pervades the ballet. Not surprisingly a strong Balanchine influence is evident, for Taras has come directly under Balanchine's tuition. Rapid changes of impetus in the dance are noticeable, as is the flowing pattern in which the arm plays a highly complicated and vital part. There is also a sort of limping step which is typical of Taras' master.

In *Piège de Lumière*, for the Grand Ballet du Marquis de Cuevas, Taras has created in a very different style. Unlike the majority of his American contemporaries he has employed a libretto from the brain of another, Philippe Heriat. The theme is as simple as it is original: escaped convicts, joined at the opening of the ballet by a young newcomer, band themselves together in a forest and eke out an existence by the clandestine sale of snake skins, rare stuffed birds, and exotic butterflies. In order to catch the butterflies a light trap (*piège de lumière*) is set up in the forest. The programme note continues:

> The lightest of them all, an Iphias, and the most beautiful, a Morphide, arrive last. Even their love for each other cannot save them from this mortal attraction, and the massacre of the butterflies begins. The young convict captures the Morphide, but the Iphias sacrifices himself to save her. She escapes, but leaves behind the pollen from her wings which turns the convict into an insect.

The ballet opens in a forest clearing, with the escaped felons frisking about in some sort of balletic game. Here I was reminded forcibly of Agnes de Mille's deep understanding of the cowboy character and her careful observation of his movements: 'Crotch-sprung, saddle-sore, ill at ease and alien to the ground.' By contrast Taras' convicts never for a moment cease to be ballet dancers. In their gestures and movements there appears no vestige of furtiveness or fear; nor the cunning which crime and prison life inevitably engender in a man. Their walk and their bearing, far from suggesting their situation, is that of young men who have been trained to move with far more grace and assurance than those of us unfortunate enough to have lacked a training in classical ballet.

Apart from its all-male composition, then, in which a few athletic dancers mildly enliven the proceedings, this scene is by no means worthy of a skilled choreographer. The brilliant and fantastic scene which follows would have been enhanced had this opening possessed a little more realistic conviction.

When the light trap is set up moths of every kind and description flutter towards it. Here the choreographer and the composer, Jean-Michel Damase, must surely have worked closely together, for the growing urgency of the action is dramatically backed and even impelled by the mounting tensity of the rhythm. First in a long diagonal beam of light, various kinds of moth are lured to the flame. Next they are seen flattened, fluttering and struggling against the frame which prevents them from burning. In a striking tableau which constantly changes its

...e three sailors and one of the girls in an imaginative shot from *Fancy Free*.
JEROME ROBBINS

...e scene which begins and ends *The Green Table*.
KURT JOOSS

Lucia Chase as the Greedy One and Eugene Loring as the Devil in *Three Virg*
and a Devil.
AGNES DE MIL

A moment in *La Création*. Jean Babilee is on the extreme left, Leslie Caron a
Natalie Phillipart are at the 'barre' and Tatiana Riabouchinska is on the rig
DAVID LICHI

pattern they evoke that feeling of insensate futility which one gains from looking at moths against a flame. There is also a striking *pas de trois* between the young convict, the Iphias and the Morphide, and a suggestion of the pageantry of these insects in the entry of the Morphide. Next comes a wondrous and singular procession, in which the dead moths are carried in an amazing variety of poses slowly across the stage by their victors. There is a mild sense of tragedy here, even the gait of the convicts having a melancholy air, as though lamenting the loss of the frenzied gaiety of the insects.

Perhaps the ending is symbolic, but if so I have not yet been able to fathom its meaning. The young convict who has lost his prey now apparently imagines himself transformed into a moth; the curtain comes down as he leaps wildly into a growing madness.

The ballet is a trifle too long, for the impact of each of its startling surprises fades long before the next in a mass of choreography which is too repetitive to sustain interest through to the next climax.

For a company of outstanding soloists, both male and female, of which he is the ballet master, the creation of a ballet presents other problems in addition to those normally attendant upon the process. The de Cuevas company is not so much a company as a collection of individual artists, with all the advantages and disadvantages which go with such an arrangement. It means invariably that the choreographer has to create with certain definite dancers in mind. For some this provides a stimulus to creative activity; for others, and I classify Taras among them, it is a disadvantage. Taras, I think, needs the even temperament of a perfectly integrated company with a cohesive style in order to facilitate his dance invention and the realization of his flowing patterns.

CHAPTER FIFTEEN

Roland Petit

ALTHOUGH PARIS of the twentieth century has played a noble part in the development of ballet, Petit is the first French choreographer of the century to gain any large measure of popularity outside his own country. Some small part of his fame can be attributed to the sensationalism in his work—a quality which makes names but not necessarily great ballets; part to the unusual and even bizarre themes upon which his ballets are founded; part to the remarkable scenic backgrounds which sometimes almost obliterate the foreground dance content; and part to his own original choreographic treatment.

The occupied Paris of the last war in which Petit developed obviously had no contact so far as ballet was concerned with the rest of the world. At the Opéra Petit grew up under Lifar, chafing under the regime before he reached his majority. As remains apparent in his work, however, he benefited a great deal under the influence of Lifar, learning to base his invention on the classical idiom no matter to what extent he distorted and added to this idiom by means of his own special dance images. Every outstanding choreographer signs his compositions with his own impetus and rhythm, which lie quite outside the control of the temporal conditions set by the music. Frequently the signature is obscured to such an extent as to be indecipherable, but occasionally it stands out with luminous clarity; then it is possible to discern the dynamic differences between the work of one choreographer and another, no matter how closely they follow each other in theme and style. As Petit absorbed the style of his master, so he learned to impose on this style the stamp of his own personality.

In England we first came into exciting contact with this personality in April 1946. Our own national company, of which we had now become so proud, opened its first season at the Royal Opera House in February of that year. Already we had seen that wonderful and lavish production of *The Sleeping*

Beauty, Ashton's spacious and fluent neo-classicism in *Symphonic Variations* and, almost clashing with the opening of Les Ballets des Champs Elysées at the Adelphi, Helpmann's *Adam Zero*.

To compare with all that Petit gave us *Les Forains*. In place of all the mechanism and the brilliant employment of the Royal Opera House stage effects, a few strolling players saunter on with a wheel-barrow and erect a tattered red tent. Weary and depressed, they sink on to the ground to snatch a little sleep before giving their performance (the comparisons with *Adam Zero* were in places quite extraordinary); a small crowd gathers round, the players go through their routines, a whip-round with the hat produces practically nothing, the onlookers wander away, the players pack up their gear and more weary than ever begin their trek to the next pitch.

The performance consists of a dance for Siamese twins, a veil dance after the manner of Loie Fuller, an acrobatic dance, a conjuring turn worked out in terms of dance, a clown number and The Sleeping Beauty. None of these items bears undue resemblance to the real thing, but each is stylized and satirized in such a way as to arouse pity for these pathetic creatures in their tawdry costumes (brilliantly designed by Christian Bérard). The opening of the ballet depends upon the music to establish the mood. This Sauget has done by taking a 'hurdy-gurdy' waltz and developing it into a tender and sentimental evocation, not of a circus or fairground proper, but of that sympathy and affection we all have for performers in this environment. Petit takes over as this atmosphere becomes established, amusing us with his effective stylizations and his choreographic wit, but at the same time playing on our sympathies, at the end perhaps laying on the sentiment a trifle too thickly when the little girl, drooping with fatigue and hunger, comes back to find the dove that has been left behind.

During the interval which followed *Les Forains* on that first London occasion I remember Marie Rambert in the vestibule running from colleague to colleague, and even to acquaintances, stretching her diminutive figure by clutching at men's lapels, and proclaiming, 'Isn't it wonderful! Isn't it exciting!' Very few would have dared to join issue with her, but some of the English professional critics were not so fortunate as Madame Rambert in being able immediately to rise to the phenomenon. One said that

she objected to acrobatics on the ballet stage, and another that
the company was 'undisciplined'. Fortunately, however, others
were not so insular. Writing in 'The Evening Standard' after
the first performance, Caryl Brahms said:

> The abiding effect of the evening is one of elegance, wit
> and taste. And it is to be hoped that these qualities will
> quicken the theatre arts of this country, for too long
> isolated from the Continental stage.

Later, although I cannot remember the exact quotation,
Miss Brahms compared the French and the English companies
as *soufflé* to roast beef. After all, both dishes are a great asset to
the menu, and act as a complement one to the other.

During the first season of Les Ballets des Champs Elysees,
Petit was responsible for the choreography of five out of the
total of ten ballets: *Les Amours de Jupiter*, *La Fiancée du Diable*,
Les Forains, *Le Déjeuner sur l'Herbe* and *Le Rendez-vous*. Apart from
Les Forains and *Le Rendez-vous* these works did not live very long.
Petit is of a volatile nature; no sooner has he completed a work
than he appears to lose interest in it. Whereas another creative
artist, given equal opportunity, would most certainly have kept
such a ballet as *Les Amours de Jupiter* in the repertory, Petit's
creative urge impels him constantly to seek new ideas which he
produces with the frequency, the speed and the facility of a
Leonardo making rough notes for a painting. Occasionally he
finds such an immediate creative impulse in his theme that he is
able to present a finished work in one deft sweep of his hand, as
it were; then he gives us such works as *Les Forains*, *Carmen*, *Les
Demoiselles de la Nuit* and *Le Loup*; at other he produces a slick
and sophisticated piece of work, redolent possibly of the music
hall, which all of us, especially himself, can enjoy and forget
after glancing at the press notices.

In an interview with Peter Williams which was charmingly
and illuminatingly reported by the latter in 'Dance and Dancers'
(November 1953), he said:

> I want to do just what I want in life—have a company;
> make ballets just how and when I feel like it; perhaps work
> on a musical; then go and live on a Pacific island for a
> year. I hate being tied down to anything, that is why I
> could not stay at the Paris Opéra or with the Champs
> Elysées Ballet. Perhaps one day when I am an old old man

I shall have a really big company and then it will be time to settle down and make three-act classical ballets. But that sort of thing is for old people and there is plenty of time.

Few will disagree with Williams when he himself says of Petit, in the same article:

His attitude is just what is needed in an art that is starting to kill itself by taking itself too seriously.

But few also will fail to regret the passing of certain Petit ballets into oblivion. Of that first London season's crop, for example, I should certainly like to see again *Les Amours de Jupiter*. As its title will imply to anyone with a small knowledge of mythology, the 'Jupiter' ballet concerns the love affairs of the Earthshaker when he sometimes abandoned Juno to make merry elsewhere. Aided by his messenger, Mercury, he enjoys affairs in his various 'disguises' with Europa, Leda, Danae and Ganymede. Each of the scenes was realized with typical Parisian wit, daring and charm. Particularly memorable was the Danae episode. Brought into her prison by three jailors, Danae expressed through wonderful movements first frenzy at her captivity, and the then ecstasy of her seduction by the golden rain. Each of the incidents was realized in striking contrast one to another; and all were linked excitingly together by Mercury, who by an apparently simple arrangement of *brisés* and *jetés* appeared to be travelling through limitless space. The final episode saw Jupiter forgiven by his wife in a moving piece of dance imagery.

Le Rendez-vous is in very different vein. The libretto, by Jacques Prevert, is the longest yet to appear for a Petit ballet. From it, together with a few notes on the dance style employed for its expression, a good idea of the ballet is obtainable. Incidentally, this libretto is typical of the modern French method in which the bare details are coloured by emotional comment:

two loving children exchange kisses during the night . . . A young man, born under an unlucky star, has a rendez-vous with Destiny, irresponsible and solemn, indifferent and menacing, is preparing to cut his throat officially and quietly, because that is how he feels about it, that is how it is written, the despairing young man, finds in the energy of his despair, the strength to lie to Destiny and to tell him a story. . . .

. . . Evoking, at the moment he is menaced by Death, the great love which he has dreamt of like so many others. . . No, truly, it is impossible to cut his throat like a pig, to strike him down like a dog, when he has a rendezvous that very night with the most beautiful girl in the world, the star of his most beautiful days, the light of his life.

Destiny shakes his head. 'Is that the truth you are telling me?' he asks, and lets him go . . .

. . . And the young man, happy at getting out of his predicament and of having so easily got the better of Destiny, continues on his way with his hands in his pockets. . . .

. . . Suddenly, he perceives, motionless before him, She whom he has described, the most beautiful girl in the world, the light of his life . . .

. . . He does not believe his eyes at first, but as she abandons herself, living and warm, into his arms, he kisses her and she returns his kiss, he caresses her and she allows herself to be caressed . . .

Then the young man is happy and fascinated for the first time in his life, when a whistle is heard in the night and the most beautiful girl in the world cuts the throat of the young man who falls bleeding to the ground, and like a prostitute she rejoins Destiny at the corner of the street, who becoming impatient, had put his fingers in his mouth and whistled a second time . . .

. . . And the young man dies without even realizing it, and the two loving children pass in front of him stop a moment and kiss each other, then go on their way without having noticed him.

The setting for this ballet is one of the less salubrious districts of Paris, somewhere near the Seine. The ballet opens with the human spindrift which one expects to find in such a district, wandering across the stage, the two loving children oblivious of them all. The young man in whom we are chiefly interested touches a humpback for luck, and the humpback becomes attached to him to such an extent as to serve almost as his shadow. In every movement fate and menace are evident. Destiny appears suddenly from out of the wall, a tall cadaverous figure with a trace of clownishness in his battered top hat and tight trousers which finish above his ankles. Destiny, in Petit's young life at that time, was apparently a figure of fun which nevertheless expressed inevitable, relentless and cruel fate. He cannot be said to express these qualities by means of dance, but rather by the staccato gesticulations of his long lean hands, which poke like twigs out of sleeves that reach not much further down than the elbow.

The girl remains an enigmatic figure, stressing the evil and inhumanity of her character by means of a steely walk on *pointes*—the influence of Lifar is clearly manifested here—and an angular distortion of both classical technique and natural movement.

After the first performance in London of this work there were many who asserted with some asperity that such a sordid subject was totally unsuitable for ballet. Did they then expect an intelligent and sensitive young man who had so recently known war and the German occupation to content himself always with the froth and frills of ballet? The very people who take ballet too seriously all the time are those who with equal consistency urge that it shall not become embroiled in sordid subject-matter. As though any art form can live by isolating itself from life.

But Petit fortunately appears to be little concerned with the opinions of others. His is a creative spirit. When Les Ballets des Champs Elysées returned to London in 1947 he had already added several new works to his rapidly growing score. Now experimenting with great freedom and daring originality, he presented a season which provided constant excitement and ample scope for controversy.

Undoubtedly the most sensational work of this season was *Le Jeune Homme et la Mort*. The idea for this ballet came from Jean Cocteau, who is also said to have assisted with the choreography. We are told that it was rehearsed to jazz music before Bach's great Passacaglia in C Minor was 'applied' to it for actual performance in the theatre. A box set of imaginative realism without naturalism was designed by Wakhevitch, who also provided the two dancers (always Babilée and Philipart) with a sort of neutral costume appropriate for a starving artist in his garret and his girl friend.

On his sordid iron bedstead the artist impatiently awaits the arrival of the girl, who at last makes her entry on hard steely points; nobody is left in doubt for a moment as to her venomous power and relentless cruelty. Movement on the ballet stage is as remote from natural movement as poetic drama is from prose drama. To be successful, in common with poetic drama, dance-drama must be dramatically convincing, and not consist merely of a series of significant but undramatic dance images. This achievement of drama through movement is the obvious but seldom resolved problem of every choreographer in this *genre*.

Pleading and grovelling, the artist is first spurned and then savagely and repeatedly kicked by the girl, who remains nevertheless cold and sadistic. When she leaves him he hangs himself; whereupon the set rises to expose the roof-tops of Paris. Now in masks, the woman leading, they glide slowly over the roofs. Is it to Hope, or is it to Life? Whatever it is, the pair have evidently found affinity and beatitude. There is symbolism here which each can solve according to his own psychology.

The anonymous but doubtless distinguished ballet critic for 'The Times' made his attitude quite clear; he found the ballet:

> . . . a brutal tale of sex antagonism and suicide, with a kind of symbolical epilogue that sat upon it incongruously. It was an outrage to choose Bach's great and noble C Minor Passacaglia for organ as the music for this ignoble and sordid story. It neither fitted the development of the plot nor was the pattern of the dance fitted to its recurrent theme. . . .

This critic went on to admit, however, that the ballet 'unde-niably has strong dramatic tension . . .'. Peter Brook in 'The Observer' held an almost diametrically opposed view. In the expression through dance terms of sordidness and violence he found 'not naturalism but poetry, not the dance-destroying movements of the commonplace; but the great line of real dancing'. Of the music he said:

> The seemingly outrageous use of the Bach music is also a complete success. It is a logical step in Cocteau's eternal quest for the affinities that underlie apparently wide differences of idiom and period.
> . . . At the climax there is a remarkable fusion of incon-gruities into a moment of theatrical truth.

I found the exultant renewal of faith so powerfully expressed in Bach's music perfectly appropriate to the theme. The surge, vitality and inevitability of the work left no feeling in me of sordid ugliness, but one of ultimate triumph and perfection.

The dance idiom employed for the artist is a compound of central European, acrobatic and classical. The girl uses very little but a distorted version of a limited number of classical exercises. Instead of that boundless outflowering of a movement which is so vital to the classical style, however, she represses her movements into a significant angularity; the spacious *épaulement* of classicism is thrown aside, so that each momentary pose is either exhibited in profile or full face.

In the depth and power of its expression, in its style and rhythmic force, in its daring innovation, I consider *Le Jeune Homme et la Mort* one of the greatest dance-dramas of the twentieth century. Some who have admired it qualify their admiration with the reminder that Petit depended very largely upon Babilée and Philipart, and that without them the ballet would have been nothing. But is a choreographer less great because he creates deliberately with specific dancers in mind? I cannot understand this point of view, which is raised periodically in connection with several choreographers. I rate Petit the greater for his ability to use the special qualities of such dancers as part of his own creative process. We shall lament if in their absence the work cannot be performed, but far better, surely, to experience greatness that possesses no continuity within itself than mediocrity in a never-ending chain.

Another new work presented in 1947 was *Le Bal des Blanchisseuses*. In addition to the delightful novelty of its décor of washing hanging up to dry, this work displayed another young French dancer, Danielle Darmance, in some enchanting and exciting acrobatics-*cum*-classical technique. Again Petit composed especially for a specific dancer, and achieved great success in the process. We have an errand boy, a wandering clarinet player and some *blanchisseuses* who were evidently better trained as dancers than as washerwomen. The melodies of the clarinet are quite irresistible, and the entire stage is filled with a mounting whirl of movement, Danielle Darmance supplying a wild and thrilling climax.

In 1949 yet two more important works issued from Petit: *Les Demoiselles de la Nuit* and *Carmen*. He had then left Les

Ballets des Champs Elysées, after creating for that company the bulk of its repertory. Now, having formed Les Ballets des Paris, he took unto himself even greater freedom of control than before, including the responsibility of artistic direction as well as of choreographer-in-chief. Losing his two leading dancers, Babilée and Philipart, who remained with Les Ballets des Champs Elysées, he found others of an entirely different style and composed works ideal both for their technical ability and their temperament.

Les Demoiselles de la Nuit is concerned, not surprisingly, with cats. In three highly appropriate sets by Léonor Fini, and to wailing cat music by Jean Francaix, Petit develops the Anouilh-elaborated tale of a cat turned woman for love by means of some beautiful *enchaînements* in which feline gestures are welded to classical figures. The first scene, a cat party in a disused mansion, sets the mysterious atmosphere; the second consists chiefly of a moving love *pas de deux* in which the cat is torn between her half-human love for the man and her burning desire for true feline freedom on the roof-tops. Burning desire gains the victory, so that the final scene presents a chase on an extremely naturalistic sloping roof. Obviously, there could hardly be a happy end to such a story; add that factor to Petit's flair for tragedy, and it will seem hardly surprising that the cat loses her life. Incidentally she is the first cat I have ever heard of, although I do not claim to be an authority on cats, to lose its life by falling from a roof.

Some criticism was levelled at the set for the third scene, as a sloping roof, dormer windows and chimneys were hardly conducive to freedom of movement. I found little cause for complaint in the effective choreographic style in which Petit evoked the excitement and the taut nervousness of the chase. I did however condemn such a surfeit of realism for a lack of consistency; when the cat fell to her death she could tumble, owing to the unavoidable limitations of the stage, to say nothing of the safety of her own limbs, a maximum of two feet. This, the climax of the entire work, thus lost its point. I was reminded, not incongruously I think, of Satan falling from heaven in *Job*. Such a purely and obviously physical act must be realized with great imaginative skill on the ballet stage, not merely represented. The ballet-going audience will accept more obvious deception than an audience of children; it will do its best even to deceive itself, but if you give it naturalism to such an extent as in *Les Demoiselles de la Nuit*, then this naturalism must remain a consistent quality throughout the ballet.

Apart from this blemish I consider the ballet to be among Petit's most powerful efforts. The leading role was created especially for Margot Fonteyn, interestingly enough a lover of cats and owner of several, who danced the role, as guest artist of course, unfortunately only once or twice in Paris. For the London season and later it was taken over by Colette Marchand, for whom it might well have been composed in the first place. Since that season she has put on a certain amount of weight, but then she had a distinctly streamlined, feline air, with an assurance in her movements, and with the perfect certainty of a cat, even on the sloping roof.

When the filming of ballet has made many advances, when director, choreographer, composer, scenic artist, dress designer, and cameraman have really learned the craft as well as achieving perfect collaboration one with another, and when the final editing is done by director and choreographer acting as a single perfectly co-ordinated mind and heart, then I hope *Les Demoiselles de la Nuit* will subject itself to the treatment. With its compound of realism and fantasy, its long stream of highly charged dance images, its demand for rapid transformations, it could as a film vie with such Cocteau fantasies as *La Belle et La Bête*, and yet be even more truly cinematic in its more complete reliance upon movement—the treatment of which is surely and essentially the cinema's business.

Of all the ballets presented in London since the war *Carmen* has undoubtedly caused the greatest stir among audiences far outside the specialized group known as balletomanes. Because of its sensationalism, because of its exciting theatrical appeal, because of the vivid personality of Renée Jeanmaire, who played the title role and won more national publicity than any dancer for many a long day, and to a lesser degree because of the controversy that waged briefly around the production, theatre-goers of almost every kind, from front-row habitués of the Windmill to connoisseurs of the Old Vic, paid at least one visit to the Cambridge Theatre. Many went again—and again.

Merimée's story is followed to such an extent as to be easily identifiable by those familiar with the opera; although there are several divergences from the original. Clavé sets the pace with some remarkably effective sets, each of which charges its particular scene with the appropriate atmosphere. Outside the cigarette factory José receives a fatal glance from Carmen, but not before that charming young lady has enjoyed an encounter with a fellow worker in which kicking, biting and scratching are not so highly stylized as to rob the scene of a vivid expression of the sort of people among whom we have wandered. The second scene transports us into a café of doubtful reputation. Here José, now abandoned to pursuit of Carmen, indulges in a habanera to the music of Carmen's castanet dance, while the crowd in the café croon a chorus. The third scene, consisting entirely of a few cartwheels of various sizes, some hanging and slowly swinging in space, others leaning untidily against a few poles, is obviously a fitting place for robbery with violence. Goaded on with malevolent seductiveness by Carmen, José commits murder by knifing a man in the belly. The victim falls stiff, flat on his face. Perhaps Petit had never seen a man knifed in such a way, but though the fall was certainly not copied from nature it was at any rate highly theatrical. The gang run gloatingly off with the loot, leaving the murderer to follow, after which comes a bedroom scene. The morning sun streams into a room which despite its tawdry furniture, its disorderly appearance, and its suggestion of illicit love, yet possesses a charm which is brilliantly in keeping with the relation between these two unusual people. Carmen dances a piquant solo to some music stolen from the legitimate Act 1 and there is an intimate, not to say daring, *pas de deux*, and José dries his hands on the curtains. Finally we are brought to the entrance of a bull-ring. A famous Toreador displays his enormous conceit in an hilarious dance, while the ladies swoon all round him. Then José and Carmen are left alone in a tremendous contrast of silence and stillness. Gradually persistent drum-beats mount into a violent rhythm and José commits his second murder. Carmen hangs head down, leg quivering, from the now despairing figure of her lover. To a repetition of the fragment of melody which accompanied her bedroom solo, the curtain comes down just as loud 'Olés' issues from the arena and hats are thrown in the air as the Toreador despatches his bull.

Choreographically this is the Petit style as before. Each

situation, each emotion and each human relationship is expressed through a remarkable mixture of classicism, naturalism, expressionistic movement, mime and gesture, and stylized, some might say distorted, Spanish dance. A few dissident writers claimed that the décor overwhelmed the dance content; and others that Petit had no respect for the music. In fact his treatment had more respect for both these elements than the work of most of his contemporaries. It is not enough merely to use décor merely as a decorative and atmospheric background; nor is it enough to permit the music only to provide a rhythmic basis and perhaps a little atmospheric contribution of its own. In a real marriage of the various elements which go to make a ballet—a marriage which has been so frequently and so glibly demanded by critics as a necessary condition of the perfect ballet—each element must in turn play a vital and not a subsidiary part. Petit seeks, and usually finds, a scenic artist and costume designer who will make a powerful personal contribution to the essence of the ballet itself. Sometimes the décor rightly subjugates the actual dancing to its own expressive ends; and sometimes, admittedly less often but at times most effectively, Petit uses music in the same way, so that sound is for a moment perhaps the major element. Here surely he ranks with Massine, except that he permits the other elements to take control more frequently than Massine. It is interesting that both choreographers have worked with leading scenic artists, although Petit has the benefit of collaborators in the scenic field who have specialized in the theatre, whereas Massine was aided by great easel painters. As to the music, Massine was content as a rule to impose his work on an existing score, often indeed finding his inspiration and impulse from that score. Petit, on the other hand, frequently commissions new music or, as in *Carmen*, has it arranged to such an extent that some accuse him of mutilation. Despite these differences in their treatment, however, the two are alike in the manner in which they shift the stress and focus from one element to the other.

In 1950 Petit became one of the few choreographers to be invited to make a ballet for our national company at Covent Garden. To what extent he was permitted freedom in choice of theme and music I do not know; although in all probability he would not have accepted the commission had he not been accorded complete freedom as to choreography and a fair say in the other elements. Be that as it may, this all-French offering to British ballet, *Ballabile*, to music by Chabrier arranged by Lambert, with décor and costumes by Antoni Clavé, is quite different from any of Petit's other works, whether created before or since. Its style is characteristic of English humour rather than French *spiritualité*.

The ballet consists of five unrelated scenes, each ending with a blackout. The first represents a ballet classroom, the next a riverside scene in which some young people indulge in pursuits appropriate to summer nights and a romantic atmosphere. For contrast, next comes a funeral party in the rain, followed by a circus, with clowns and acrobats, all ending in a lively pseudo-Spanish romp.

Most of the critics were agreed that this effort by Petit was more suitable for a 'musical' than for Sadler's Wells at Covent Garden. On the other hand, most of them were also agreed that the work contained many subtleties of wit and humour. Once again Petit demonstrated his remarkable ability to discern hidden possibilities in a particular dancer; none who saw the ballet during its early performances will forget the delicious burlesquery of Anne Negus in the opening scene. For the rest the work reveals another Petit tendency to mix brief but excellent passages of pure choreography with unashamed show-manship, amounting at times to no more than stylizations of circus tricks. He has achieved a telling contrast here and there by first demanding such distortion of the classroom technique that the potential beauty of line of the human form is quite blotted out, only to be revealed to its greater glory a few seconds later in the perfection of a classical pose. But almost before we have had time to take it in, Petit is laughing at himself and us again in a chaos of hybrid dance, drollery, circus tricks and sheer high spirits. Throughout he has been admirably, at times ecstatically, aided and abetted by Clavé with some of the most brilliantly evocative sets ever to be seen at the Royal Opera House.

Every time he has brought a company to our shores Petit has dazzled us and bamboozled many of us with a mass of brilliant ephemera. On the other hand, each time he has also produced one outstanding and significant work which bears his own unmistakable signature but is at the same time in the main stream of the balletic tradition. In 1953 he twice brought his Ballets de Paris to the Stoll Theatre, providing an extraordinary repertory, all but one of the works presented being entirely new to London (the exception was *Carmen*), and all but one with choreography by himself. In several of these works the décor seemed to play an even more vital part than ever, with the result that a number of critics came to the conclusion that the ballets themselves—if they could strictly be termed ballets—were well-nigh obliterated in a mass of sensationally original scenic art work.

Perhaps the most ingenious of these trifles was *Deuil en 24 Heures*. A fair lady sees a chic black dress in a shop window and persuades her husband to buy it for her. Later in a café a young man whose eyes have wandered exchanges blows with the husband and a duel is the inevitable result. Inevitably too the husband is killed; otherwise there would be no need for the black dress. The widow for a short time appears to be inconsolable, but as grief must come to an end, the sooner the better. With our fair lady it is very soon, although in fairness one must add that she is helped considerably to forget her grief by the provoking tune of a maxixe. She fights for a short while against its irresistible rhythm, but then completely surrenders. Her arrival at Maxim's in a horse-drawn carriage—a magnificent prop if ever there was one—is hailed with great delight and the last traces of her sorrow disappear as she dances in a somewhat modernized but quite abandoned version of the Can-Can. She and the assembled company also provide the most hilarious burlesque of a ballroom tango that I have seen since *Ring Round the Moon*.

Call it ballet, call it music hall, call it nonsense, call it what you will, *Deuil en 24 Heures* is delightful entertainment. Long passages, particularly the duel, in its crazy setting of telegraph wires and broken-down fences, cannot be remotely connected with ballet; on the other hand there are several passages which create their humour purely by means of dance. The tango is I suppose a sitting target to a choreographer of Petit's stature, but there are many other choreographic chuckles. That in which the widow tries to resist the lure of the maxixe is for me an ineradicable memory.

During the season various little sensations were provided for the national press with such works as *The Lady in the Ice* and *La Belle au Bois Dormant*, which is not for a moment to be confused with the Petipa-Tchaikovsky version of La Belle and others. But if for nothing else the two seasons, which followed closely one after the other, were more than justified for the presentation of one outstanding ballet: *Le Loup*.

On the very day of his marriage a young man runs off with a gipsy girl. An animal trainer, by exercising one of his circus tricks, however, makes the bride believe that her husband has been transformed temporarily into a wolf. Happily she runs off with the creature and is, of course, terrified when she discovers the truth. But after a while she becomes attracted to the wolf, for, as the programme says, unlike humans he is incapable either of weakness or deceit. In fact she becomes so attached to him that when her husband appears and wants to take her into his arms, after one ecstatic moment she denies him and turns to the wolf. Together they run off into the forest. The villagers, headed by the animal trainer, hunt them down and the girl, seeking to protect her strange lover, is accidentally smitten by one of the unlikely-looking spiked instruments with which the villagers are armed.

The choreographic content of *Le Loup* is chiefly in the form of a *pas de deux*, with Petit himself quite remarkable as the wolf. Yet again he found the ideal girl for the important role, so that Violette Verdy was able, during the first performance, to display her innocent emotion, happiness and terror by means of an extraordinarily imaginative blend of dance and mime. Once again, through Petit's ability to create for a specific dancer, the choreography enhanced the quality of the dancer and the dancer enhanced the significance of the choreography.

The theme by Jean Anouilh is, of course, an extraordinary one; treated clumsily the work could have stressed the horrible and sordid aspects of such a strange affair. Petit, however, although investing the part of the wolf with a style of dance and gesture which abstracted the creature from physical humanity, yet made it alive with the qualities of honesty, gentleness and love so often missing from the human character. Even the scenes of passion were enacted by means of an extended use of the classical idiom, employing complicated lifts and dual pas-

avid Lichine and Tamara Grigorieva in *L'Après Midi d'un Faune*.

VASLAV NIJINSKY

he Mazurka from *Les Sylphides*.

MICHEL FOKINE

The choreographer in his own ballet, *Icare*. SERGE LIFAR

sages to communicate an affinity beyond the realms of physical love.

Petit has frequently been accused, especially by certain distinguished music critics, of being unmusical and of an inability to compose his dance images in keeping with the score. From Lifar he understandably inherited the attitude which denies the subservience of dance to music. Sometimes he feels the need to diverge in the pulse of his dance patterns from that laid down by the music. And why not? It is after all only a convention in which steps must coincide with beats: a convention, moreover, which has led to endless and pointless banality. I am not suggesting for a moment that correspondence between the visual and aural beat shall henceforth and for ever be abandoned. Petit has in various works produced passages which float on the rhythmic and melodic stream of the music rather than suffer distortion for purely temporal ends. In such cases the rhythm of the one stresses and even reinforces the rhythm of the other. *Le Jeune Homme et la Mort* provides the best example, although a similar quality is also to be found in *Carmen* and other works, so that instead of coincidence we have a perfect marriage, in which each element is permitted to make its own unique contribution to the whole, supported rather than trammelled and dictated to by its partner.

Those who claim that Petit uses the music merely as a necessary temporal background have failed to penetrate beneath the surface. Always he is concerned not with one particular element of the score, but the total effect of the whole.

In *Les Forains*, for example, he found no need to cut across the simple dance rhythms of Sauget's piquant melodies; whereas in Dutilleux's equally appropriate and sympathetic music for *Le Loup* he has sought correspondence with the overall pattern as distinct from any marked obedience to the rhythmic pulse. In *Les Forains* his actual dances are of a nature to demand such temporal obedience; in *Le Loup*, on the other hand, the dance element does not consist of clear-cut rhythms on a set pattern but a gradual development of a dramatic climax and indication of character together with a mood of realism within a framework of fantasy.

By avoiding a continuous and obvious correspondence between the accents and even the pulse of the music and the dance, he has stressed the expressive power of both elements in unison by minimizing the convention and artificiality of his medium.

Doubtless Petit will continue to create his amusing, his witty and his elegant ephemera. While we think of such work in terms of Entertainment rather than as Ballet, we shall continue to find ample pleasure in his original creations and marvel at his invention and fertility. Provided he occasionally gives us ballets such as *Les Forains, Le Jeune Homme et la Mort, Les Demoiselles de la Nuit, Carmen,* and *Le Loup,* most of us will not cavil at the uncertainty with which we wait for the curtain to go up on each new Petit work—an uncertainty as to whether we are to enjoy a 'musical', be amused at something from the Moulin Rouge or to undergo an emotional transformation under the influence of a truly great ballet. Few choreographers in this century have in so short a space of time produced as much work of real merit. Yet fewer have succeeded in creating, no matter what their theme, in strictly contemporary terms. Perhaps posterity will remember Petit more for his ability to associate ballet with the life of his time than for the excellence of any particular example of his creative genius.

CHAPTER SIXTEEN

John Cranko

THE OBSTACLES ARRAIGNED against anyone who attempts to find fame in the choreographic field are far greater than those encountered by writers, painters and composers. Nevertheless several new names have been added since the war to the still comparatively short list of ballet creators. But very few of them have achieved more than slight notice, their output rarely exceeding one or two ballets. A notable exception is John Cranko, a South African who in 1946 left easy success in Cape Town to battle for the highest possible stakes in London. Here, after gaining favourable attention as a dancer in various roles with the Sadler's Wells Theatre Ballet, he was given choreographic opportunity. In 1947 he did a delightful trifle, the *Tritsch-Tratsch Polka*, and *Morceaux Enfantins* for the Royal Academy of Dancing Production Club, this work later being taken into the repertory of the 'Theatre Ballet' under the title of *Children's Corner*. With this ballet Cranko was hailed by many as a choreographer of infinite promise. *Children's Corner* has in my opinion many blemishes but it certainly does afford some evidence of rhythmic invention and originality (notwithstanding that it is founded on a hackneyed theme).

In 1949 Cranko produced *Sea Change*, a very different kind of ballet from the two efforts which had already won him approbation. In this work he sought to express himself in terms of dance-drama, succeeding in his first essay in this *genre* in the maintenance of a nice balance between stylization and naturalistic mime and gesture. What is more important, this work evokes a series of strong moods, alternating from filial devotion, parental love, love between the sexes and tragedy.

Before the fishermen set out to make their catch the scene is well set and a number of characters neatly adumbrated, although the choreographer never succeeds in winning more than perfunctory interest in them. Certainly we do not become deeply concerned in their lives, nor are we anxious to understand them in any profundity.

Cranko's first intention was to base this ballet on Sibelius' 'Tapiola', using a simple story of a lonely girl in a village community who one day finds a fisherman washed ashore. This theme, with the girl lavishing her love on her discovery and her ultimate loss when he returns to his own world, would I think have made a more suitable plot for a first attempt at this kind of work. Unfortunately, however, the score was rejected, another Sibelius work, 'En Saga', being chosen. The plot now took quite a different form from that of Cranko's original intention, growing more complex and less clear-cut in all but the main climaxes.

According to his own statement ('Dance and Dancers', March 1951), Cranko first caught the germ of the idea for *Sea Change* while on holiday in the South of France. Here he was fascinated by all the activity of a beach:

> the nets hanging out to dry, people mending them, various types standing round watching, all the usual incidents that happen in a fishing village. Certain movements, such as boys kicking a football, gave me ideas for a choreography.

Doubtless Cranko devoted himself to a close observation of all the phenomena and activity which held so much fascination for him. But observation is not enough. The more ballet deals in naturalistic terms the greater is the danger of its becoming no more than an emaciated mimeo-melodrama. In order to create a significant ballet out of some aspect of contemporary life it is necessary to study that aspect in minute detail, to find some emotional stimulus from it, so that the movement patterns by means of which the ballet eventually comes to life are charged with the inner as well as the apparent rhythm; so that the physical expression evokes an emotional response. De Mille in *Rodeo* has expressed the life and character of the cowboys and Helpmann in *Miracle in the Gorbals* the existence of a Glasgow slum not merely by naturalistic imitations of certain instinctive and characteristic movements and gesture, but by a complete stylization of such movements. Such stylization cannot be successfully accomplished if the original source has not first been thoroughly observed and understood.

Nevertheless, although Cranko has not suceeded in creating a great and exciting ballet, he has demonstrated his ability to organize his movement, to think in terms of choreographic contrasts and to invent in theatrically acceptable terms. Throughout the ballet there are no boring passages when either the theme or the music, or both, stifle his own imaginative invention. Neither does the ballet—a blemish that would have been understandable in a first effort in dance-drama—tend at any point to seek expression by means of mime at the expense of dance. Always the two elements are skilfully blended so that the impact of the movement is allowed to take full effect.

Cranko's next ballet was *Beauty and the Beast*. To what extent he was influenced to experiment with this particular theme through the Cocteau film which had already been shown in London, I do not know. Certainly the décor, or rather the action of the highly stylized tree in preventing the escape of the terrified girl, owed something to Cocteau effects. And why not? Cocteau had treated the fairy story in a new and entirely contemporary French style. If the film made a powerful impact on Cranko there was no reason at all why he should not seek inspiration from it for the purpose of his ballet.

As the work was produced near Christmas it seemed to me that it might have been offered as children's entertainment. If so it was singularly inappropriate. But neither does it offer more sophisticated or subtle entertainment. There is none of the nuance of feeling and atmospheric background developed in the extended *pas de deux*, which makes up the ballet, that is suggested in the music, which is tense and exciting. The triumph of beauty over ugliness is shown by a simple trick with a mask rather than by any true choreographic imagination. Nevertheless there are several passages which are choreographically interesting without at any time rising to great heights of expressiveness.

Cranko again tried to come to grips with Ravel's music when he composed *The Witch* for the New York City Ballet. Here he succeeded only in producing a hackneyed work on a hackneyed theme, enlivening it with some acrobatic tricks which the dancers in this company could perform with surpassing skill, and an erotic *pas de deux* of no great artistic value.

Pastorelle, his next work, composed for the Sadler's Wells Theatre Ballet, has been the cause of a certain amount of controversy in which I find myself ranged on the side of a small minority. This work is in my view a much sterner test of Cranko's ability, except of course that the music, a Mozart Divertimento, provides much more obvious potential affinities with dance patterns than did Ravel. Apart from that, the choreographer is thrown almost entirely on to his own resources, since the ballet is of an 'abstract' nature and depends chiefly for its appeal on classical dance. It is perhaps a trifle too long—although they who pass this censure perhaps overlook the fact that the score would be extremely difficult to cut without mutilation. I have found the work rich in composition, delicate humour, and quite brilliant in the way that contrasts in dance impulse are expressed in the various *enchaînements*. There are, it is true, several rather obvious plagiarisms from the work of his contemporaries, especially Balanchine; there are also certain elements of repetition which ought to have been eliminated even if, as is often claimed, the work was produced in something of a hurry. But no matter! I think that in this work Cranko first demonstrated his major status.

Wisely he has avoided complete abstraction by inserting a faint wisp of a theme in which some minor gods and their paramours indulge in charming and amusing amorous hide and seek and entertain one another with dance and play in an appropriately pastoral setting.

Still experimenting, still seeking his *métier* in theme and treatment, Cranko next presented *Pineapple Poll*. Based on one of W. S. Gilbert's ballads, 'The Bumboat Woman's Daughter', the plot is concerned with the swooning infatuation of the maidenhood of Pompey for a bold, debonair and bewhiskered sea captain. Jealousy having caused the men to go absent, the resourceful young women, suitably trousered and bearded, seek to impersonate them in manning the ship. But at cannon practice they betray a timidity supposed fallaciously to be typical of their sex, and Poll, the most enravished of them all, drops in a dead faint when the ancient weapon does actually go off. All is of course discovered. And as the gallant captain is engaged to a very feminine young lady who would surely never descend to such ruses to get her man, Poll is for a while humiliated and sick at heart. But soon, her potboy simpleton of a sweetheart having been made more attractive in her eyes by the donning of nautical garb, she warms to him, and all—as must be in a work of high spirits such as this—ends in happiness and hilarity, with a nice touch of patriotism to bring down the curtain.

Although *Pineapple Poll* depends very largely upon comedy of situation rather than comedy expressed through movement, there are several passages rich in more penetrating choreographic humour. The swooning of the young women at the proximity of the captain is brilliantly worked out and not insisted upon too long; the antics with the cannon of the same young women aboard ship remain amusing after several viewings of the ballet. There are also touches of more subtle humour, perhaps an outstanding example being that wherein Poll, in her nautical disguise, crosses the gangplank, with excitement and trepidation, *sur les pointes*. In the first act too there is a delightfully amusing dance between Blanche, the captain's fiancée, and her aunt. While the captain, as Beaumont says, 'never departing from the authority and good manners expected of an officer in the Senior Service', has been blessed with deft phrases of humorous dance always in keeping with his character.

Further than this the ballet is well served by Osbert Lancaster's settings, which in themselves have wit and humour; as well as the rich and lively arrangement of Sullivan music by Charles MacKerras. But despite his skilful handling of such a self-sufficient theme Cranko has been compelled for long passages to fall back on the burlesque of situations rather than the wit and invention of his own choreography. In fairness, however, anyone who passes even the mildest of strictures must add that the ballet has been tremendously successful with all kinds of audiences; probably it ranks as the most popular item in the 'Theatre Ballet' repertory.

Harlequin in April, which was given its first performance some weeks later, is based on a very different theme, and is worked out choreographically in a style quite new to Cranko, with liberal use of symbols and an attempt to search beneath the surface of natural appearances. The programme note quotes the opening lines of T. S. Eliot's 'The Waste Land':

> April is the cruellest month, breeding
> Lilacs out of the dead land, mixing
> Memory and desire, stirring
> Dull roots with spring rain.

and more lines from a little further on in the poem:

> What are the roots that clutch, what branches grow
> Out of the stony rubbish? Son of man,
> You cannot say, or guess, for you know only
> A heap of broken images, where the sun beats,
> And the dead trees give no shelter, the cricket no relief
> And the dry stone no sound of water.

Both the words and the rhythm suggest to me the slow writhing of the tendrils of a plant struggling to break through to the surface of the earth in order to reach light and air. A film showing some weeks in the growth of such a plant, compressed into a few minutes, expresses very clearly the image evoked by the opening lines. Although I find that such words produce in me imaginings far more vivid than those which any choreographer can conjure up by means of his human instruments, in this particular ballet Cranko certainly has worked out a series of movements which suggest the 'stirring of dull roots', at the same time relating those stirrings to the human struggle. But wisely the choreographer has not sought—at least according to my interpretation—any further affinity with the Eliot poem; instead he has gone to Eliot's sources and employed conventional characters more amenable to choreographic expression. Pierrot, Harlequin and Columbine are given some dance passages of a strikingly original nature, and a sequence dominated by a group of Unicorns—traditional guardians of chastity—is full of invention. Serious and at times slightly pretentious symbolism is varied by a certain number of lighter episodes, almost in the manner of asides, for Pierrot.

Not unnaturally there are many interpretations of all this choreographic symbolism. My own, for which I did not unduly stretch my imagination, is that Columbine represents the true and beautiful ideal, which now recedes and now approaches; Harlequin is the struggling and futile spirit of man; and Pierrot is ridiculous, material humanity.

But what matter? Although parts of the ballet seem a trifle pointless, and others a mere striving after some nebulous effect, a series of most striking dances have been welded into some interesting and even exciting groups in an effort to express an adult theme. For that one should be truly thankful, for very few of the ballets in this youthful company's repertory are based on anything but juvenile scenarios.

A year later, in 1952, Cranko's name was included among the established and the exalted when he did his first work for the national company at Covent Garden. To mark this signal honour he produced *Bonne Bouche*. Already in *Pineapple Poll* he had shown himself to be a young man abundant in theatrical ideas, but ideas of a kind that would sometimes impede his choreographic development. This tendency he had apparently overcome in *Harlequin in April*, but now he swamped his work with every trick and every device to eliminate choreography. In addition to this *Bonne Bouche* was made the subject of especially lavish production—another feature which frequently spells the ruin of dance, together with a detailed plot which Cranko apparently never visualized in choreographic terms.

A simpering young woman, living with her scheming mother in a London square of Edwardian days, as evoked by Osbert Lancaster, jilts a penniless young man for a rich old one who dies just before she gets him to the altar. Next she is about to wed a Guards officer, when this project is ruined by the material-ization of a wife and family. Finally she becomes the wife of an African chief, who arrives in the square amid great excitement, but needs her only for his gastronomical gratification. The jilted young man, who had gone to Africa with the Salvation Army, now returns, to find that nothing remains of his beloved but a necklace beneath an enormous dish cover and a satisfied gleam in the eye of the chief.

There are undoubtedly some delightfully hilarious passages in *Bonne Bouche*. Perhaps the funniest are the parades of the Salvation Army, first in the Edwardian square and later in the jungle. The negro aspect is also well exploited. But apart from that, there is very little dance. All is a very amusing hotch-potch of burlesque Edwardian costume, amusing situations and ingenious tricks, such as that in which the young man, digging for gold, is slowly let down through the floor by means of a trap. For that very large part of the Covent Garden audience which is made up of those who perhaps pay one or two visits a year, and who want to be amused when they do go, *Bonne Bouche* is undeniably an asset to the repertory. But it will certainly not go down to posterity as a great or even an import-ant ballet.

Once again alternating between his light and serious moods, Cranko now succumbed to the temptation which no young choreographer seems to be able to resist for long, to do a 'psychological' ballet: *Reflection*. Hopelessly confused in his working out of the plot, which is itself badly expressed in the programme note, Cranko achieved little more in his ballet than to expose his rudimentary and sometimes inaccurate knowledge of psychology. Employing a method which Tudor has found so successful in endowing his characters with legendary names, in this case Echo and Narcissus, Cranko endeavours to develop a sort of choreographic psycho-analysis by means of crude symbols. In any case none of the subtleties of the characters are expressed, and a Tender Child and an Aggressive Child do no more than afford Cranko scope for a certain amount of well-contrasted dance. Indeed, for each of the characters, particularly those of the lovers and Echo, he has devised some outstanding movements. But isolated dances cannot save a work, if its author is dealing in matters beyond his comprehension.

Now called upon to create a second ballet for the national company, Cranko gave us *The Shadow*. From a nebulous theme he developed some charming and romantic dance based on the classical technique. For dramatic emphasis he gave the figure of The Shadow an enormous black cloak by means of which the girl was startlingly revealed at a given moment. In spite of its inventiveness and originality, however, *The Shadow* does not add up to a great ballet; not only does it lack any real choreographic impetus and climactic development, but its images have not the power to evoke any powerful audience response.

The scenario for *The Lady and the Fool* has been devised by Cranko himself with such skill that the plot, in all its simplicity, can completely dispense with a programme note and yet remain abundantly clear to the dimmest wit. Undoubtedly it is the best constructed of all Cranko's ballets to this time, for ample scope has been allowed for the dancing to integrate both with plot and character development. As in a modern musical, into which category in fact it almost fits, the dances never retard the action, and sometimes advance it. But unfortunately this excellent scaffolding has been used to erect an edifice of inferior material which lacks both originality and excitement.

The dances consist of the *pas de quatre* of La Capricciosa and her suitors, the *pas de deux* of the clowns at the ball, the *pas de trois* of Signora Scintillarda and her lovers, with some interpolations from the two wives, and the background dances. Every one of them is well composed, although none of them reaches any great height of brilliance; and certainly none of them possesses any marked emotional appeal. The humour of the clowns is forced and lacking in punch, and the Scintillarda episode is hackneyed in dance content and dependent far too much upon mime and gesture.

The ballet ends on a note of sickly sentiment, the gush of the music being well matched by the activity on the stage, in which Bootface places his insufficient scarf over La Capricciosa's feet as she reclines exhausted on the bench in the street, her head on Moondog's lap.

Like all young creative artists, Cranko now lies in danger of living too much and too closely within the bounds of the theatre. If he is to create original works by means of powerful dance images he must seek inspiration outside the theatre. The detachment of ballet from contemporary life is today a disturbing factor; it can be rectified only by choreographers, in common with creative artists in other fields, going out into the world to observe closely and then to recreate what they have seen beneath the surface by means of their own original expressive forms.

CHAPTER SEVENTEEN

The Moderns

FOR A PARTICULAR STYLE of dancing which first manifested itself through the American, Isadora Duncan, at the beginning of the twentieth century, developed in central Europe and then returned to the U.S.A.—now its natural domicile—between the wars, there are many titles: Modern, Central European, Free, Expressionistic. Each of these titles is incomplete and misleading, but each provides a partial definition. Obviously it is referred to as 'modern' for the simple reason that it represents a twentieth-century attempt to break with the classical tradition; Central European refers to the area in which it made its physical advances and incidentally acquired a philosophy which in the opinion of many is far in advance of its practice; the attractive adjective 'free' is applied to the attempted revolution as a token that the new form was not bogged down by technique but left the body completely free to move in whichever way it liked without any proscriptions but those imposed by its own anatomy. The 'expressionistic' aspect cannot adequately be put down in a few words, especially as a wide diversity of views prevails as to what exactly the word means in connection with pictorial and other art. My own view, for what it is worth, can however be fairly simply expressed. I regard as the father of expressionistic painting the Russian Kandinsky, who interestingly enough painted his first work in this style in the first few years of the century. Avoiding all obvious reference to material objects, Kandinsky set out to express something about himself by means of completely abstract patches of colour and sweeping lines. There is in these works something of a glowing vitality and vivid combinations of *fauve* colour, two qualities which provide undoubted excitement, never mind to what extent they express any intellectual or emotional state of mind in their creator. Similarly much 'expressionistic' dance seeks to do away with subject-matter and express various states of mind. In this way, whether we are concerned with painting or dancing, it is upheld that the creator can make direct communication with his audience without the confusing interference of subject-matter.

Although Duncan was the first of the great 'modern' dancers this intellectual approach can be put down to Darwin, who set out a number of rules governing gesture and discovered that various involuntary movements betrayed a certain state of mind. Delsarte took this theory further and formulated his nine laws of gesture, basing them on his theory that various attributes of the human personality are located in different parts of the anatomy: the intellect in the head and the emotions in the torso, with a number of sub-divisions. Doubtless Delsarte's theories have encouraged the mass of abstruse theories with which 'modern' dance has become enshrouded.

Anyone wishing to make a detailed study of what I shall hereinafter refer to as modern dance should try to obtain a copy of 'Borzoi Book of Modern Dance', by Margaret Lloyd. [1] Miss Lloyd discusses Duncan, Mary Wigman and other pioneers in great detail before dealing biographically with contemporary moderns and analytically with their work.

In the opening paragraph of her introduction Miss Lloyd says:

> Modern dance is what modern painting and modern music are—a new development of an old art—a creative manifestation of our time. It is an outgrowth of all that has gone before, and is subject to constant new growth and change. It is, specifically, the continuous opening of new paths of the expression of the human spirit through the human body.

One's immediate reaction to this statement is that modern dance is claiming a development for itself which is common to all living forms of expression. Since Arbeau the technique of classical ballet has made tremendous strides in many directions. Even since Fokine, Balanchine has extended the vocabulary if not the expressive power of the classical technique. But a little later in her introduction Miss Lloyd throws more light on that opening statement:

> Primitive man expressed himself in the most direct way possible, that is, through rhythmic bodily movement, his reverential awe at the world of mystery and wonder

[1] Knopf, 1949.

around him. The modern dancer, with less awe, perhaps, and a more intelligent sense of wonder, expresses, as directly, his reaction to the more complex modern world. . . . modern dance is not alone in expressivity. The departure is in the why and what and how of its expression. Where other forms are content to imitate nature, modern dance discloses nature, particularly human nature—the inner nature of man. Where primitive forms are semi-conscious expressions of the conscious and the unconscious through the body, modern dance consciously uses the body to express states of consciousness, and more recently, of the unconscious. Modern dance is fantasy, a palimpsest of unreality, through which the underlying realities are brought to life more sharply than in every-day life.

That is as clear an exposition of the aims of modern dance as I have ever seen, although lovers of ballet, at least in Britain, will still wonder as to where modern dance makes any real definable break with ballet. Two main differences are that much modern dance is a solo effort, the choreographer and the dancer being one and the same. The dance is therefore conceived as a solo, with perhaps background figures, not as a ballet in the way that Opera House audiences think of that term. Further, the modern dancer is seeking to express 'a state of consciousness' or even of unconsciousness, whereas most ballet, but not all, seeks to express human relationships—except of course in that kind of ballet, fortunately plentiful, which expresses nothing but the rhythmic and plastic beauty of its own self.

Apart from these differences in principle there is also a difference in practical technique. Notwithstanding that freedom was one of the tenets of the pioneers, even Duncan found the necessity to codify for her own benefit certain practical fundamentals. Freedom is perhaps the most widely misunderstood word in the English language, and it is not generally recognized that too much freedom can easily lead to slavery. Although sometimes not amenable to textbook description, technique of a kind enters into the freest of all the free dancers, no matter to what extent they endeavour to employ spontaneous and involuntary movement for the expression of their innermost feelings.

From a purely practical point of view the chief differences between the vocabulary of classical ballet and that of modern dance lies in the fact that the one is developed largely on the turn-out from the hips and a general outflowering of movement; or, as some moderns would put it, a centrifugal impulse; whereas the other makes no such preliminary demands. The use of the *pointes* has also been confined to ballet, although as we shall see, certain moderns have now modified their original ideas as to the 'distortion' caused by this practice.

Continually the moderns seek to relate their organized rhythmic movements to life—an admirable ideal—in such a way as to gain audience response through a sympathetic muscular reaction to a common experience. That is undoubtedly why theoretically the movements of modern dance in most cases depart so radically from those of classical ballet.

The muscular control for most kinds of dancing lies in the back. Modern dance is no exception, although it also calls upon more than usual flexibility and control of the whole torso, especially round the pelvic girdle. Apart from that, however, several of the actual steps bear an easily recognizable resemblance to those of the classical form. Kurt Jooss has for many years employed a modified form of turn-out as well as *glissades* and *cabrioles*—while most of the Americans, it appears, call frequently upon modifications of a large range of *pas* tabulated in Cecchetti and Vaganova textbooks. Martha Graham, undoubtedly the most original of all moderns, employs a kind of *developpé* which is either derived from classical ballet or else represents an extraordinary coincidence. Many steps of elevation bear a certain resemblance to the older form; also, but very rarely, the foot is pointed or the leg turned out while the dancer is in the air.

Another aspect in which the modern technique differs from the classical is that concerned with *épaulement*. The classical choreographer uses the turn-out and outflowering movement to display the dancer as a being of little weight; the modern, on the other hand, frequently seeks monumentality as a deliberate aid to expression. Similarly the classical form does not lend itself with any facility to broken rhythm and disjointed movement despite successful fragments of such movement by Ashton, Robbins and Balanchine; whereas the modern form makes extensive use of off-balance movements and gestures which come to an end unexpectedly, long before the power of their initial impetus has been expended.

But just as surely as classical ballet has undeniably exerted . a strong influence upon the very form which came into being as the result of a heavy revulsion against classical sterility, in the same way modern dance has influenced ballet. Massine, Tudor, Helpmann, and even Fokine before them, despite his denials, have come under its power. Today in various ballets it is hardly possible to discern how much they depend upon the classical and how much on the modern vocabulary. Like any strong, growing language, ballet is constantly taking new words into itself, so that the two forms are gradually becoming one. Long before the end of the twentieth century I think that the modern form will have been absorbed completely into ballet, to enrich it beyond measure and to bring it back into contact with the life of its time.

In Great Britain concert dance, particularly of the modern school, has failed to attract a large public. Even when in the early years after the second world war three ballet companies could attract ample audiences simultaneously in London, and when there were about five applications for every seat at every performance of the Sadler's Wells Ballet, the occasional exponent of modern dance found no small difficulty in gaining an adequate audience for a few performances at one of the small private theatres. Unfortunately Martha Graham, due to visit the metropolis in 1952, was compelled owing to an accident to postpone her visit until 1954. Thus the vast post-war ballet and dance-conscious public in England was unable for some years to see the modern dance in its highest form of manifestation as it has developed in the U.S.A.

A modern disciple of a different kind did however have a certain following in Great Britain, and was able to make extensive tours of the country. I refer of course to Kurt Jooss. But Jooss possesses not only a different vocabulary; he also tackles his subject with a philosophy almost directly opposed to that of his 'modern' contemporaries. While they seem mostly to be concerned with the expression of conscious and unconscious states of mind, he has attempted to subjugate the ego into an expression of various problems and aspects of the outward physical world.

Further, Jooss, by the time he gained international fame as the choreographer of a prize-winning ballet *The Green Table*, was no longer creating purely in 'modern' terms. No doubt because his extrovert tendencies inclined him towards objective ballet rather than subjective dance, he became deeply interested in several works from the Diaghilev repertory; after Diaghilev's death he composed his own version of works such as *Petrouchka*, *Prince Igor* and *La Boutique Fantasque*. These works he mounted on his own group at Essen. At the same time, recognizing that the self-imposed limitations of the modern school were leading him up a blind alley, he sought to enrich his vocabulary with certain elements of the classical technique. These elements are clearly evident in most of his ballets, but for some untypical and illogical reason he refused the ultimate stylization of the complete turn-out and the use of *pointes*. Presumably his reason was that the Central European style was based on natural movement, and that these two elements represented an unacceptable distortion. Following his return to Essen in 1953, however, after an unsuccessful season in London, he is said to be experimenting with these two fundamentals of classic ballet. Whether by means of the enlargement of his vocabulary he will be able to find something new to say, remains to be seen. It seems likely that his work will now join the general stream of ballet and that he will compose more and more in terms of dance-drama in the same style as a number of choreographers who have throughout their creative careers shunned no type of movement which seems to them appropriate for a particular communication; folk dance, natural movement, social dance or classical technique. After all, modern dance is but one of many streams which all flow into the ever swelling river of expressive human movement.

In *The Green Table* Jooss employed a theme which is at once age-old and contemporaneous: the failure throughout history of words, of argument, of limitless hot air, to prevent war; and the horrifying effect of war. Skilfully, in a way that has since been copied with great success, Jooss completed the cycle by a return to the 'green table' of talk at the end. Inevitably more talk must end in more war.

It was a cynical outlook, but for the intellectual fringe of ballet-goers of the 'thirties it was an outlook in which they found boundless sympathy.

The complexity with which the pattern of *The Green Table* was

worked out, the power to arouse emotion in some of its characters, each of which was endowed with its own strongly individualistic movement patterns, the cohesion of the whole work in spite
of its episodic nature, together with brilliant stagecraft and
lighting, which was something new to those who had not seen
the Diaghilev productions, suggested that Jooss had much to
offer the ballet theatre. As he had. But his offering has now been
thoroughly assimilated, and I find difficulty in believing that
he can once again become an innovator by accepting a little
more of the classical technique in order to enlarge his vocabulary.
Much of his originality was produced through the very limitations of his vocabulary, but obviously he could not continue to
create in the same terms without constant repetition and loss of
his own impetus. What I should like to see now is *The Green
Table* (perhaps in a slightly revised form, in order to modify its
episodic nature) brought into the repertory of a firmly established company. It would be a great asset to several companies
and would be the means of saving a ballet which otherwise looks
likely to pass into oblivion.

When Martha Graham did eventually appear in England her
work naturally aroused much controversy. For many years she
has been accepted in America not only as one of the greatest of
all the modern dancers, but as a vitally important creative
force in American culture, even though there are many there
who dislike her work with an intensity almost equal to the
fanaticism of her admirers. In 'Dance to the Piper' Agnes de
Mille has devoted a chapter to her which develops a vivid
picture of the woman, the dancer and her work. Margaret
Lloyd in 'The Borzoi Book of Modern Dance' naturally discusses
her work in some detail, with a perceptive analysis of several of
the Graham productions. Lincoln Kirstein can perhaps be
forgiven for making but one short reference to her (and that
only in connection with her appearance in Massine's version of
The Rite of Spring) in his opus 'Dance', for this volume was published in 1935, although she received her Guggenheim Fellow-
ship in 1932, and was the first dancer ever to be thus honoured.
Balanchine had less excuse in his 'Complete Stories of the Great
Ballets' published in 1954. Not one of her works is discussed in
this 600-page book, although she is treated to a short but
glowing reference in its Chronology:

... Like Isadora Duncan before her, Martha Graham has greatly influenced the theatrical dancing of her time, but more than Duncan—whose art was personal and inimitable—Martha Graham has developed in addition to a stage personality a new non-balletic dance vocabulary expressive of inner tension. This new system of dance can be imparted to others, can be taught with the same rigor as the classic ballet, and has become, under Martha Graham's tutelage not only a contemporary contribution, but a lasting discipline.

After this compliment such an omission seems strange. Perhaps Balanchine's reference to her 'non-balletic dance vocabulary' provides the explanation, but this seems a quibble, quite apart from the fact that a more apt choice of words would surely have been 'non-classical ballet dance vocabulary'.

During her London season she produced several works in which it became abundantly clear that the movement vocabulary of her particular style is considerable, although audiences accustomed to much classical ballet sometimes felt uneasily that the natural climax of certain figures was a pose *sur le pointe*. The subject-matter for which this great choreographer seeks expression, however, is vastly different from that of those who create in the balletic as distinct from the 'modern' idiom. Graham is concerned with the physical world only in so far as she must recognize its existence for the expression of the subconscious and the strictly private emotions of a variety of characters in special circumstances. Many London dance-lovers were puzzled; others were bored, and a few were enthusiastic. Perhaps the works were too long, their plots too slender, their movement insufficiently spectacular, for many to enjoy purely as theatrical entertainment. But the effort necessary for the audience to make in order to grasp as a whole if not in detail her intimately personal communication yielded a rich reward in moments of exciting revelation.

. . . and Others

A<small>T THIS STAGE</small> I am painfully aware of certain omissions, the most important perhaps being a lack of reference to some of the younger choreographers; although older enthusiasts will also berate me for not devoting a chapter to the work of Frank Staff and Celia Franca. Both of these highly talented and creative artists have enriched the repertory of British Ballet, but Miss Franca is now successfully building up the National Ballet of Canada, while Staff seems to have dropped out of the ballet scene. Very little of their work remains in production.

Staff was perhaps at his best with the humour of parody and even burlesque. *Czernyana* is notable for delightful laughs at the expense of romantic ballet of the nineteenth century and at certain aspects of 'abstract' ballet. Among well initiated audiences this ballet was so successful that a second edition came into existence two years later. But what the esoteric audiences of the Duchess and Arts theatres appreciated immediately, the less balletically enlightened audiences in the commercial theatres of provincial tours have naturally failed to apprehend.

One of Staff's works has however appealed strongly to every kind of audience, novitiate or balletomane, juvenile or septuagenarian. I refer to *Peter and the Wolf*, which in 1940 seemed to indicate that in Staff we had found that rarest of all phenomena, a choreographer who could create humour in movement. Ashton had shown his comic invention in such works as *Façade* and *Les Patineurs*, but in most English works up to this time humour had been obtained more by means of situation than by choreography. Now Staff produced a ballet consisting of sustained humour expressed largely in dance terms. In the composition of this ballet Staff imposed upon himself some extremely severe limitations, for in choosing to make a ballet upon Prokofiev's musical fairy-tale he had necessarily to follow the actual spoken story as well as the charming score. But instead of struggling under these limitations Staff immersed himself thoroughly in the piquant comedy of the delightful fairy-tale to produce a master work. The décor is a great help in the suggestion of children's make-believe, for the tree is made up of a tall step-ladder, a mop and a plank. Peter and his grandfather are immediately established as Russian fairy-story characters, for they are familiar through many a picture-book.

The simplicity with which the ballet is worked out adds to its charm, for the actions of the animals—and the birds—are not too slavishly copied from nature. The duck in her 'pond' provides a kind of humour which all can enjoy, while the stalking of the hunters is one of the most brilliantly developed passages of dance burlesque I have ever seen. Matching the rhythm of the music in its mock relentlessness, the hunters observe the conventions of the hunt in a sort of 'follow-my-leader' chain.

I have taken many family parties to see this ballet, always with unbounded success. There is pleasure in it for every age and almost every outlook. The capacity of a work to appeal to such a diversity of ages and interests does not, of course, necessarily testify as to its greatness, but in the case of *Peter and the Wolf*, I think, it does show conclusively that the simple tale has been unfolded by means of effective dance images which are simple and clear-cut, with subtle undertones of parody and comedy to make the work far more than a mere children's game.

For the Metropolitan Ballet, Staff made *Lovers' Gallery* and *Fanciulla delle Rose*. The first of these two works had certain scenic ambitions, being set in a picture gallery. Some of the pictures, not unexpectedly, came to life, the fabulous and mythological characters indulging in some high jinks which never added up to anything more than an inferior romp.

Fanciulla delle Rose, on the other hand, was a simply constructed work. A Young Girl in front of an enormous but hazy Mother Image in a skilfully established ecclesiastical atmosphere, is tempted by the seven deadly sins, successfully resisting them all. The Girl, danced magnificently by Svetlana Beriosova, who even at that early age was obviously set fair to become one of the few really great dancers of this epoch, did a *pas de deux* with each of the Sins, her movements consisting of a variety of *bourrées* and *arabesques*, her wonderful emotional control being expressed through an equally remarkable physical control in which her arms remained for long passages at her sides, the strength of the temptation being exposed through the intensity of her movements. Each of the sins was symbolized by contrasting movements, although some of them were undeniably more notable for their melodrama than their choreographic expression.

Even in his failures Staff has consistently shown a potentiality to greatness, but he has not since the war had an opportunity to do his *afflatus* full justice. Had the Metropolitan Ballet not run out of money he would I think have benefited from the security of a permanent company upon which to work, and would have gradually asserted himself as a major creative artist in the field of ballet.

Celia Franca also needed that same facility of a company upon which to mount her works. She too was associated with the Metropolitan Ballet as ballet mistress, but her duties in that capacity were far too arduous for her to create important ballets. Her two works for the Sadler's Wells Theatre Ballet, particularly *Khadra*, both had atmospheric charm and some original composition, but this young company was hardly the appropriate milieu for a choreographer of her kind. She lays stress on the romantic element—an element which can only suffer if it is put over boisterously or without sympathy. The young company certainly devoted themselves to making a success of such a charming work as *Khadra*, but somehow never quite succeeded in performing this work with the delicacy vital to the complete expression of its exotic and fragile charm.

After making one other small but quite effective ballet for Ballet Workshop Miss Franca left for Canada. Perhaps when the National Ballet there is completely established she will be able to produce a series of ballets without having to worry unduly about all the administrative details of the company at the same time.

One has a right to expect new companies to discover new choreographers. Whatever other success it is gaining in its extensive tours over large parts of the globe, the Grand Ballet du Marquis de Cuevas is certainly giving opportunity to several dancers to try themselves in the choreographic field. Most successful up to the present is undoubtedly the work of George

Skibine. During the company's visit to London in 1954 he produced in *Idylle* a really outstanding work. Employing only three dancers and the simplest possible décor, he developed his images entirely by choreographic means. Two ponies in a field are in love with each other, but as is so often the way the filly is overcome by infatuation for another pony whose habiliment is so much finer than that of her true lover. Off she goes with him to enjoy a most charming *pas de deux*. But when, playfully, she bites at the finery and it comes off, so that she sees the charmer in all his nakedness, back she goes to her lover. That is all.

To very appropriate music by François Serrette, Skibine has made a ballet rich in dance content, at times exciting and at times charged with sentiment. He has made other works for the same company, but none before nor since, so far, half as successful as this.

Of all the other works by overseas choreographers to come to England, the most outstanding in my opinion have been those of Janine Charrat. Two of her productions during a very badly attended season at the Stoll in the Spring of 1954, in particular, come vividly to mind: *Concerto* (a *pas de deux* set to the first two movements, both cut, of Grieg's Piano Concerto) and *Les Algues*.

The *pas de deux*, danced with extreme delicacy and sensitivity by Charrat herself and a brilliant young man, Peter van Dijk, showed the influence of Lifar in its neo-classical choreography, but Charrat in places finds a more remarkable correspondence with the music than I have discovered in any other choreography of this kind.

Les Algues is of an entirely different character, being a complicated work dealing in a most original and fantastic style with insanity. By staying away in large numbers London balletgoers once again betrayed their lack of discrimination, their inability to get to grips with anything which trades in terms which search beneath the surface of general appearances.

In England today the potential choreographer certainly cannot complain of lack of opportunity. In 1951 Ballet Workshop was founded by David Ellis and Angela Dukes (a daughter of Marie Rambert) to give Sunday evening performances at the Mercury Theatre, which is virtually the birthplace of modern British ballet. The avowed aim of Ballet Workshop is to give opportunities to young dancers, designers, composers and choreographers. This it has certainly done, having now presented about sixty entirely new ballets, and given a number of young choreographers their first opportunity. Most of the work produced is naturally of a not very high standard. Choreographers of genius will never multiply like tadpoles simply because of the provision of suitable conditions. Every enlightened critic has praised the function of Ballet Workshop, although some adverse criticism has been directed against its administration on the grounds that far too much obviously inferior work has been exhibited. But the administrators felt it desirable to present a reasonable number of performances during each year, and have had to overcome the enormous casting difficulties attendant upon any organization which is offering work only for three Sundays about every three months; added to which the thousand-odd members from which their audience is made up at every performance comprises the most enthusiastic but also the most critical collection of ballet-goers in the western world. It is an audience, too, that has the highest quality ballet right at its very doorstep. The adjustment necessary for such an audience to make when watching ballet on the tiny Mercury stage is sometimes beyond its powers of adaptability.

When this project was first mooted I remarked that if one choreographer of real talent were discovered in every hundred ballets produced, then the scheme would prove of great value. But this has been more than accomplished; one certainly and others possibly are well on the way to establishing themselves as choreographers with important companies.

Yet without the stage, instruments and shop window provided by Ballet Workshop they would probably never have gained an opportunity to discover, much less to demonstrate, their talent. The first to receive a commission to produce a ballet for an established company was Michael Charnley. Having seen some of his work at Ballet Workshop performances, Anton Dolin commissioned him to add to the repertory of Festival Ballet. Charnley's maiden effort for this company was *Symphony for Fun* in 1952. Set to Don Gillie's rhythmic score, 'Symphony No. $5\frac{1}{2}$', this work was immediately successful and showed that Charnley, transferred from the tiny stage of the

Mercury to the very wide but shallow one at Festival Hall, had acclimatized himself without apparent difficulty. *Symphony for Fun* is an admirable title, for the music and choreography, as well as the simple play-suits for the dancers, all express admirably the fun and high spirits of the proceedings. It was not surprising that Charnley showed great skill in his composition of solo dances, but I had hardly expected him to provide felicitous work for groups. Yet in fact he succeeded in composing some highly effective group movements. *Symphony for Fun* seeks nothing more than to match infectious modern musical rhythms with infectious modern dance rhythms; to provide some delicious fragments of humour and a little sentiment. These modest aims are so brilliantly achieved that what might have been a moderately successful little ballet became a really outstanding addition to the repertory of an important company.

Another organization of a similar nature to Ballet Workshop to start two years later, was the Sadler's Wells Choreographic Group. The first few performances of this group were untidy and ill-rehearsed, but fully justified themselves in demonstrating the outstanding promise of Kenneth MacMillan. One work by him, *Laiderette*, proved so interesting, abounding as it was in an original talent, that it was taken into the repertory of the Sadler's Wells Theatre Ballet. There is not much risk, I think, in the prophecy that within the next few years MacMillan will become a really important choreographer.

The future, then, from a choreographic point of view, seems fairly well assured. But if ballet is to make a worthwhile and substantial contribution to the culture of our time, choreographers, and everyone else concerned with the production of ballet, must maintain firm contact with life and not live in an intellectual vacuum. Dancers work harder than any other theatrical performers; a life in which such an arduous physical technique, the constant perfection of their human instrument, remains the unceasingly predominant anxiety, is hardly conducive to orient dancers to the outer world. And it is only from today's dancers that we can reap tomorrow's choreographers. From Noverre onwards the great ones have exhorted ballet-makers to study intensively a variety of subjects outside their own immediate sphere of activity. How many really ambitious potential choreographers at the present time can read a musical score with any facility? How many of them I wonder have enriched their minds with any real study of English literature? How many of them are to be found with any frequency in the great art galleries? More important still, how many of them try with earnestness to understand humanity—to discover the motivation behind the act, the complexities of personal and mass relationships?

Clearly, until the feet of the creative artist are planted firmly on the ground he will be quite unable to make the leap into that most exciting of all worlds, the creative world of imagination founded in reality. There are some, of course, who believe that ballet should never aspire above fairy-tales and light entertainment; just as there are many who want all pictures to be 'pretty' and all books 'nice'. But those who have experienced what the disciplined movement of ballet can achieve in the expression of human emotion will never be satisfied while it does no more than dally with make-believe and trumpery spectacle. Much ballet must naturally continue to trade in these detachments from life, but if out of all the ballets produced every year one, just one, makes its own distinctive contribution to the culture of our time, then ballet itself lies in no danger of artistic extinction.

INDEX